I0800451

IMAGES
of America

THE JEWISH COMMUNITY OF BALTIMORE

ON THE COVER: The boys' choir of the Aisquith Street Shul (Ohel Yakov Congregation) stands on the *bimah* (raised platform) with Cantor Aaron Bell around 1938. Identified boys include Harvey Basik, Harold Brager, Sol Brager, Henry Dickman, Donald Horowitz, Chaim Levy, Isaac Litt, Harold Rosen, Heyman Shapiro, Morton Tucker, and Sheldon Tucker. (Courtesy of the Jewish Museum of Maryland, 1988.199.1a.)

IMAGES
of America

THE JEWISH COMMUNITY OF BALTIMORE

Lauren R. Silberman
Foreword by Avi Y. Decter

ARCADIA
PUBLISHING

ISBN 978-0-7385-5397-9

Published by Arcadia Publishing
Charleston, South Carolina

Printed in the United States of America

Library of Congress Catalog Card Number: 2007943601

For all general information contact Arcadia Publishing at:
Telephone 843-853-2070
Fax 843-853-0044
E-mail sales@arcadiapublishing.com
For customer service and orders:
Toll-Free 1-888-313-2665

Visit us on the Internet at www.arcadiapublishing.com

Dedicated to my grandparents

CONTENTS

ACKNOWLEDGMENTS

This book would never have been created without the assistance of many individuals and organizations. My deep gratitude begins and ends with my fiancé, Matthew, for his steadfast support and devotion. Thank you to all of my colleagues at the Jewish Museum of Maryland, particularly the editorial guidance of Karen Falk and Deb R. Weiner; direction from Avi Y. Decter; collections assistance from Rachel Kassman, Jonathan Roscoe, Jennifer Vess, and Jobi Zink; my colleagues in the West Wing: Ilene Cohen, Ilene Dackman-Alon, and Simone Ellin; and the support of my mentor, Deborah Cardin. Special thanks to Jeff Korman and the staff of the Maryland Department of the Enoch Pratt Free Library for their tireless assistance in helping me collect images. Thank you to Allan T. Hirsh for opening the Etting Cemetery. Thanks to the Baltimore Hebrew Congregation, particularly Irving Simon and Harry Macks, for sharing your archives. Many thanks to Herta Baitch, Eric Beser, Sen. Ben Cardin, Ross Kelbaugh, and John McGrain for sharing your personal collections; Inge Weinberger and Ellen Rosen for information about the Hebrew Immigrant Aid Society (HIAS); and Betsey Kahn for recommending sources. I would be remiss not to include my editor, Lauren Bobier, who has answered every single question I've had. And I could never have written a word without the love and support of my parents, David and Brenda, or my brother, Matt. Finally, thank you to the Jewish community of Baltimore. Without your stories and photographs, this book would never have come to be. Thank you for providing such an interesting tale to tell.

Images in this book are from the Jewish Museum of Maryland (JMM), Enoch Pratt Free Library (EPFL), Maryland Historical Society (MDHS), American Jewish Historical Society (AJHS), Baltimore Museum of Industry (BMI), Baltimore Hebrew Congregation (BHC), and private collections.

FOREWORD

The Jewish community of Baltimore is one of many outposts in a global Diaspora. Like other cities in North America, South America, and Europe, Baltimore became home to generations of immigrant Jews throughout the 19th and 20th centuries. In a succession of neighborhoods, the newcomers went to work, established businesses, started families, organized themselves in congregations, clubs, and social service agencies, and celebrated life.

In certain respects, the Baltimore Jewish community exemplifies important trends in American Jewish history. Jewish Baltimoreans experienced rapid rises—despite prejudice, discrimination, and occasional legal barriers. For hundreds of years, Jews in Europe had engaged in commerce, developing the skills required to succeed in business; also, Jewish culture had given high value to education and learning, so the immigrants' children were quick to take advantage of American educational opportunities offered to speed their advance. In Baltimore, as in other American cities, Jews were remarkable for their mobility—social, occupational, economic, and residential. In addition, the Jewish community in Baltimore is very visible: Jews are active in political life, in cultural organizations, and in community affairs.

However, many Jewish Baltimoreans see and characterize themselves as distinctive. Jewish families that are long-settled remark on how intimate the community is and how continuous is its history. Many of those who reside here now but were born and raised elsewhere—and who now comprise half of the Baltimore Jewish community—often share these views, noting how tight-knit the community appears to recent arrivals. Certainly, in the Associated: Jewish Community Federation of Greater Baltimore, the local Jewish community enjoys one of the most highly organized communal groups of any city in North America, one that touches myriad aspects of life in both the Jewish and non-Jewish communities.

Yet Baltimore Jewry is hardly monolithic—it is a veritable community of communities. Baltimore Jews hail from Central and Eastern Europe, from the Middle East, and from many locales in the United States. A substantial number of Baltimore Jews are first-generation immigrants who came over from Germany and Austria in the 1930s. Some are survivors of the Holocaust who came here from Europe in the 1940s. In recent decades, Jews have arrived from Iran, from the Soviet Union, and from Israel.

Baltimore Jewry is almost kaleidoscopic, quite aside from a multiplicity of languages and cultures. More than 20 percent of the Jewish population identify themselves as Orthodox, making the Baltimore Jewish community the most heavily Orthodox in the United States. A third of Baltimore's Jews identify as Reform and another third as Conservative—and about one in 10 members of the community identify as secular or cultural Jews. Jews also range across the political, social, and economic spectrum—and their residences now span a wide (and growing) area, from the old downtown to rural villages at the margins of the metropolis.

This volume provides telling glimpses into the history and culture of the Baltimore Jewish community. Here readers will find classic scenes of immigrant life and traditional observance juxtaposed with the unexpected and the contemporary. Lauren Silberman's judicious selection of historical photographs and her informative captions capture key aspects of the community, past and present. I encourage your close attention to the small details that give Baltimore Jewry its distinctive and its universal character—tales of enterprising immigrants who made good; of neighborhoods dotted with rich, engaging life; of congregations that moved and merged and morphed to meet the social and spiritual needs of their members. As they say, "life is with people," and in these miniature stories is a composite portrait of Jewish life as lived in the world we call Baltimore.

—Avi Y. Decter
Jewish Museum of Maryland

One

Paving the Way

Baltimore's Jewish Pioneers

Today Baltimore is home to a thriving Jewish community that is large, diverse, and well organized. However, this has not always been the case. Whereas other American cities from New York to Savannah had developed Jewish communities as early as the late 17th century, Baltimore, comparatively, was a late bloomer. The earliest known Jewish resident was Jacob Hart, who signed his name to a petition in 1768. By 1820, only approximately 120 Jews lived in the entire state, and it would be another decade before Maryland welcomed its first incorporated Jewish congregation.

The community's growth was slow for several reasons. Maryland's Toleration Act of 1649 gave freedom of religion only to Catholics and Protestants, and later Maryland's state constitution also restricted the rights of non-Christians. Economically, the city remained a minor port into the mid-18th century and only began to flourish after the Revolutionary War. Even with these obstacles, a handful of Jews trickled into Baltimore.

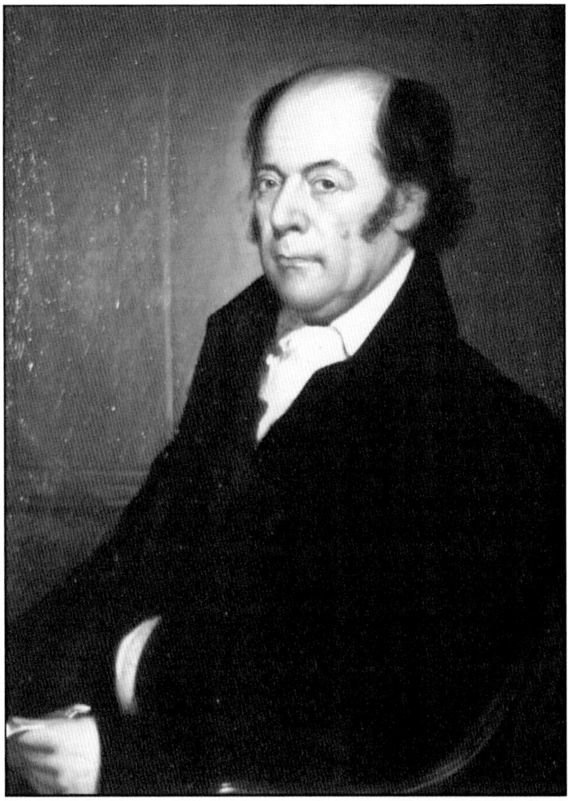

While Jewish merchants passed through Baltimore on business for decades, Jacob Hart (1745–1822) was the first permanent Jewish resident. Born in Furth, Hart moved to Baltimore in his 1920s. A prominent merchant, he supplied clothes and supplies to the Marquis de Lafayette during the Revolutionary War. (Courtesy of AJHS.)

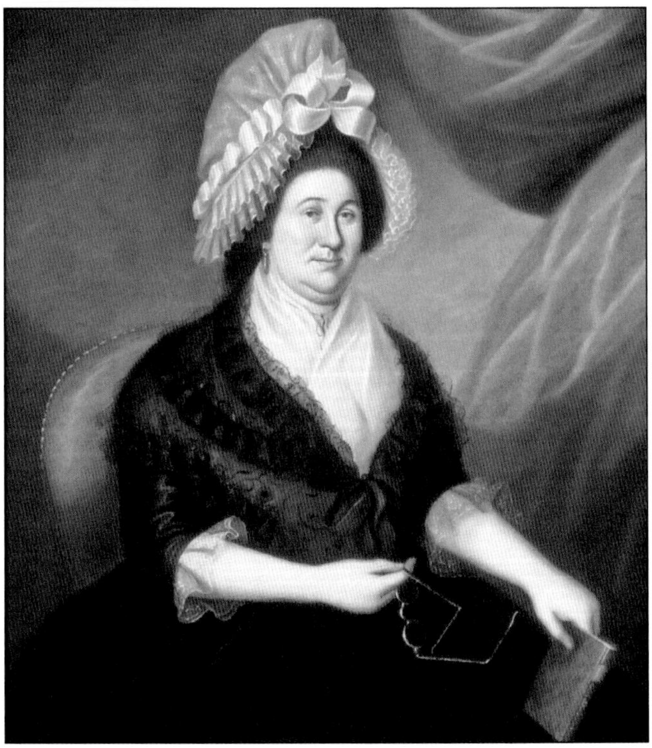

In 1780, Shinah Solomon Etting (1744–1822), a young widow with eight children, moved from York, Pennsylvania, to Baltimore, where she opened a boardinghouse for gentlemen. Etting became the matriarch of Baltimore's first prominent Jewish family. Capt. Alexander Grayson described her as "always in spirits, full of frolic and glee." In this 1792–1793 painting by Charles Peale Polk, Etting wears a *sheitel* (a wig worn by married Orthodox Jewish women). (Courtesy of the MDHS, 1957.90.1.)

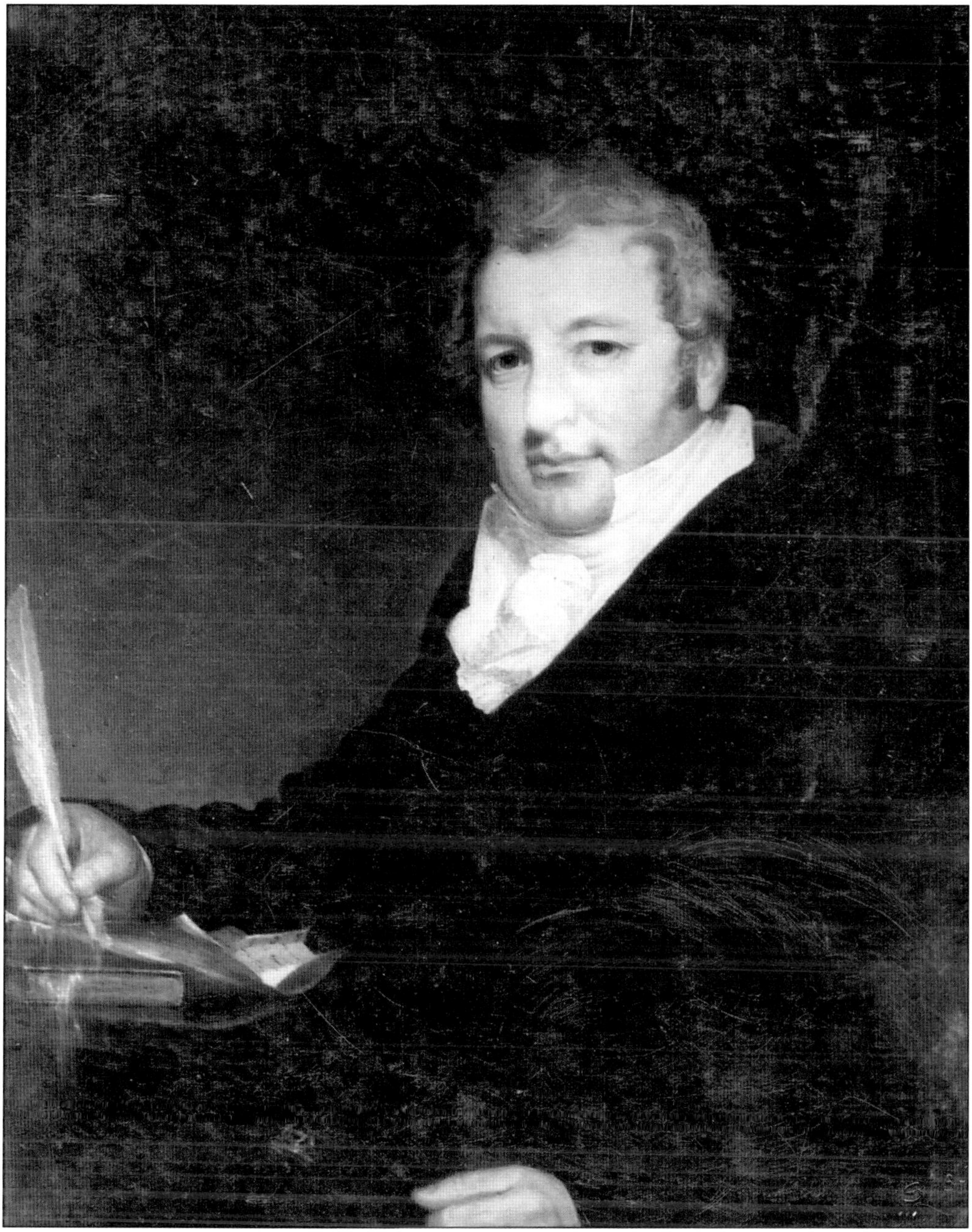

Solomon Etting (1764–1847), shown here in this portrait by Jacob Jarvis, was an important business figure and a key architect of Baltimore's Jewish community. Owner of a hardware store on Calvert Street, he was the city's first *shochet* (kosher slaughterer). For 20 years, he petitioned for the Jew Bill, which would grant Maryland Jews full rights as citizens. When the U.S. Constitution was ratified in 1776, a Jew could be elected president but not to the Baltimore city council because the Maryland state constitution stated that "a declaration of belief in Christian religion" was required for "admission to any office of trust or profit." Because of this requirement, Jewish citizens could not join the legislature, become commissioned officers, or serve as lawyers until the Jew Bill finally passed in 1826. (Courtesy of the EPFL.)

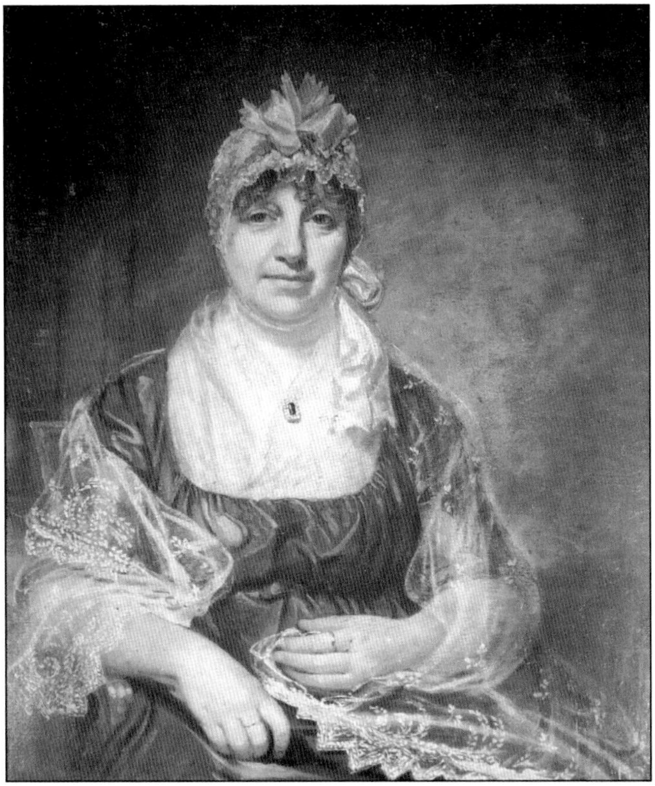

Depicted in a painting by Jacob Jarvis, Rachel Gratz (1764–1831) married Solomon Etting in 1791. The family prospered. Etting's brother, Reuben, fought in the Revolutionary War and received a commission for the first captain of the Baltimore Independent Blues. However, because of the Christian oath required by the state constitution, he was unable to accept. Instead, Pres. Thomas Jefferson appointed him to be the U.S. marshal for the District of Maryland. (Courtesy of the EPFL.)

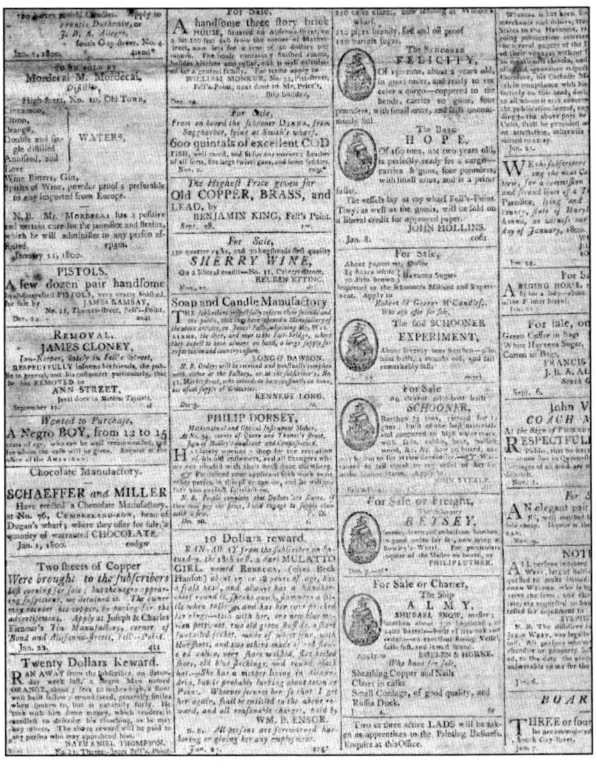

190 boxes mould Candles. Apply to
Francis Duchemin, or
J. B. A. Allegre,
south Gay-street, No. 4.
Jan. 1, 1800.

TO BE SOLD BY
Mordecai M. Mordecai,
Distiller,
High-Street, No. 10, Old Town,
Cinnamon, Citron, Orange, Double and single distilled Annifeed, and Love — WATERS,
Wine Bitters, Gin,
Spirits of Wine, powder proof; preferable to any imported from Europe.

N.B. Mr. Mordecai has a positive and certain cure for the jaundice and strains, which he will administer to any person afflicted.
January 11, 1800.

PISTOLS.
A few dozen pair handsome brass-barrelled PISTOLS, very neatly finished, for sale by JAMES RAMSAY,
No. 21, Thames-street, Fell's-Point.

REMOVAL.
JAMES CLONEY,

Wanted to Purchase,
A Negro BOY, from 12 to 15

Chocolate Manufactory.
SCHAEFFER and MILLER

Two sheets of Copper

Twenty Dollars Reward.

For Sale,
A handsome three story brick HOUSE, situated on Albemarle-street, on a lot 100 feet east from the corner of Market-street, now lets for a rent of 40 dollars per month. The house contains 7 finished rooms, besides kitchen and cellar, and is well calculated for a genteel family. For terms apply to
WILLIAM MONKUR, No. 31, Pitt-street,
Fell's-Point, next door to Mr. Price's,
ship builder.

For Sale,
From on board the schooner Diana, from Sagg-harbor, lying at Smith's wharf,
600 quintals of excellent COD FISH, well cured, and fit for any market; Leather of all sorts, five large twist guns, and some saddles.
Nov. 2.

The Highest Price given for
Old COPPER, BRASS, and LEAD, by
BENJAMIN KING, Fell's Point.
Sept. 28.

For Sale,
350 quarter casks, and 30 hogsheads first quality
SHERRY WINE,
On a liberal credit—No. 31, Calvert-street.
REUBEN ETTING.

Soap and Candle Manufactory

PHILIP DORSEY,

10 Dollars reward.

210 casks claret, now landing at Wilson's wharf.
120 pipes brandy, first and 4th proof
180 barrels sugar.

The Schooner
FELICITY,
Of 150 tons, about 2 years old, in good order, and ready to receive a cargo—coppered to the bends, carries 10 guns, four pounders, with small arms, and sails uncommonly fast.

The Barge
HOPE,
Of 160 tons, not two years old, is perfectly ready for a cargo—carries 8 guns, four pounders, with small arms, and is a prime sailer.
The vessels lay at my wharf Fell's-Point. They, as well as the goods, will be sold on a liberal credit for approved paper.
JOHN HOLLINS.
Jan. 8.

For Sale,
About 50,000 wt. Coffee
84 boxes white, 50 ditto brown — Havanna Sugars
Imported in the schooners Milford and Experiment. Apply to
Robert & George M'Candless.
Who also offer for sale,

The said SCHOONER
EXPERIMENT,

For Sale
SCHOONER,

For Sale or Freight,
BETSEY,

For Sale or Charter,
The Ship
ALMY,

Two or three active LADS will be taken as apprentices to the Printing Business. Enquire at this Office.

For Sale,
A RIDING HORSE,

For sale, on

John V
COACH

RESPECTFUL

A N elegant pair

NOTI

BOAR

THREE or four

In January 1800, the *American and Daily Advertiser* featured advertisements from two Jewish distillers, Mordecai M. Mordecai and Reuben Etting. The earliest known advertisement from a Jewish merchant in Baltimore was in 1773 when Benjamin Levy advertised the opening of his store in the *Maryland Journal and the Baltimore Advertiser*. It was the largest advertisement in the paper. (Courtesy of the JMM, 1992.57.1.)

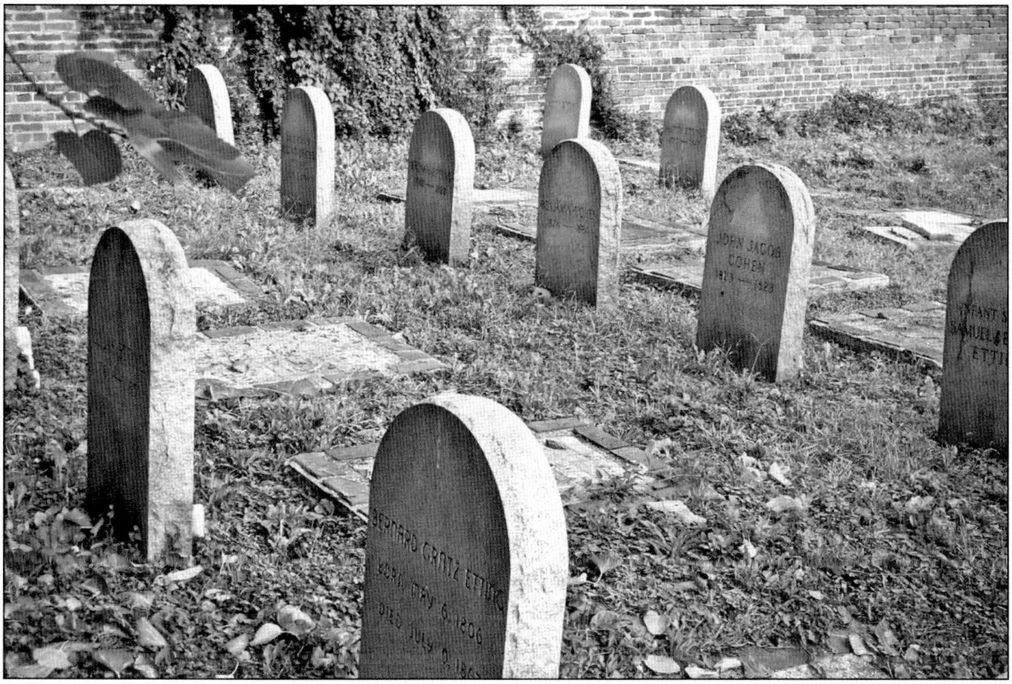

Solomon Etting purchased land for the first permanent Jewish burial site in Baltimore in 1801. It still exists today at the corner of North and Pennsylvania Avenues. (Courtesy of the JMM.)

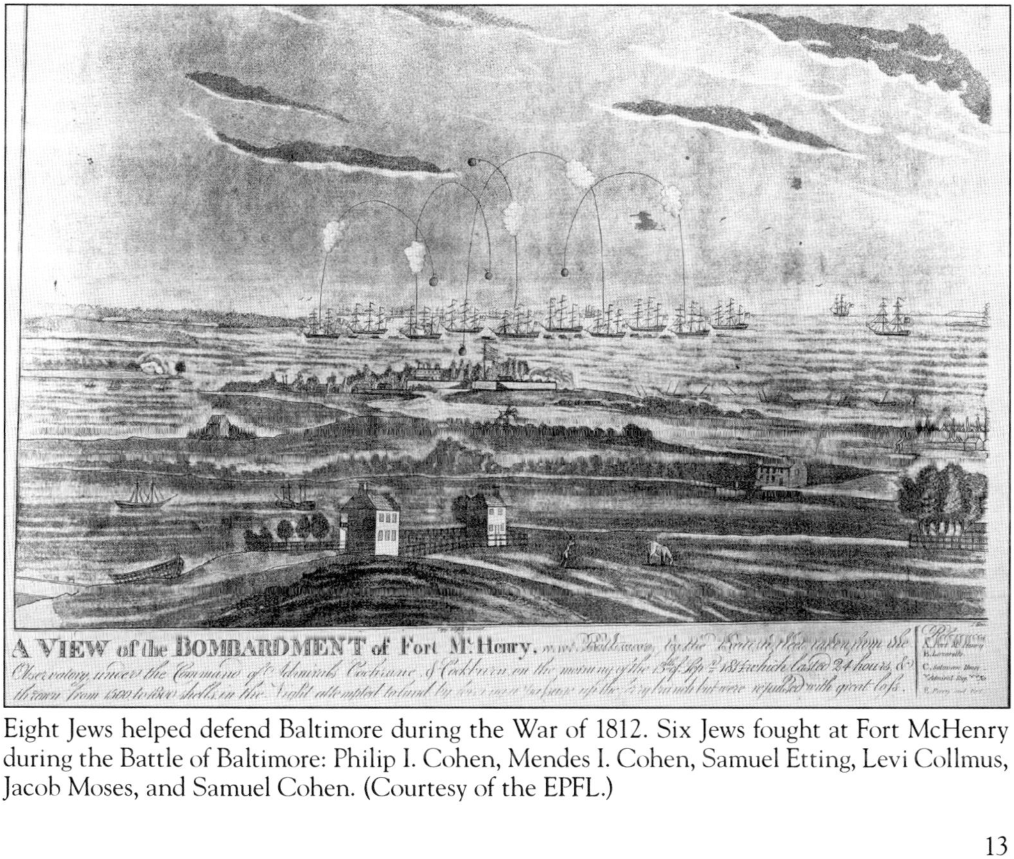

Eight Jews helped defend Baltimore during the War of 1812. Six Jews fought at Fort McHenry during the Battle of Baltimore: Philip I. Cohen, Mendes I. Cohen, Samuel Etting, Levi Collmus, Jacob Moses, and Samuel Cohen. (Courtesy of the EPFL.)

12

dance; it is therefore her interest to draw men of enterprise and of capital to her shores. The tide of emigration which is now flowing fast to the west, has already taken from Maryland many of her best and most industrious citizens, and although we need not hold out inducements to emigrants, we ought to let it be known that in Maryland, men enjoy civil and religious liberty, in as great a degree, as they do in any other state in the Union.

Your committee, therefore, are unanimously of opinion, that it is just, that it is expedient, that Jews and Christians should be placed on an equal footing in regard to their civil rights and privileges. That the adoption of this measure is recommended by reason as well as by scripture; stronger arguments are surely unnecessary. The mists of ignorance and of superstition are passing away at the approach of the sun of liberty; they are scarcely seen in the other states; let them no longer cast a gloom over our beloved Maryland, let their baneful influence be felt no more; let them vanish for ever.

Your committee therefore beg leave to report a bill, entitled, "An act to extend to the sect of people professing the Jewish religion, the same rights and privileges that are enjoyed by Christians." All which is respectfully submitted.

By order,

J. W. PRESTON, Clk.

AN ACT,

To extend to the sect of people professing the Jewish Religion, the same rights and privileges that are enjoyed by Christians.

WHEREAS, It is the acknowledged right of all men to worship God according to the dictates of their own consciences. And whereas, it is declared by the thirty-sixth section of the bill of rights of this state, "That the

13

manner of administering an oath to any person ought to be such as those of the religious persuasion, profession, or denomination of which such person is one, generally esteem the most effectual confirmation by the attestation of the divine Being. And whereas, religious tests for civil employment, though intended as a barrier against the depraved, frequently operate as a restraint upon the conscientious; and as the constitution of the United States requires no religious qualification for civil office, Therefore,

SEC. 1. *Be it enacted, By the General Assembly of Maryland,* That no religious test, declaration or subscription of opinion as to religion, shall be required from any person of the sect called Jews, as a qualification to hold or exercise any office or employment of profit or trust in this state.

SEC. 2. *And be it enacted,* That every oath to be administered to any person of the sect of people called Jews shall be administered on the five books of Moses, agreeably to the religious education of that people, and not otherwise.

SEC. 3. *And be it enacted,* That if this act shall be confirmed by the General Assembly, after the next election of delegates, in the first session after such new election, as the constitution and form of government direct that in such case, this act and the alterations and amendments of the constitution and form of government therein contained, shall be taken and considered, and shall constitute and be valid as part of the said constitution and form of government, to all intents and purposes, any thing in the declaration of rights, constitution and form of government contained, to the contrary notwithstanding.

SEC. 4. *And be it enacted,* That the several clauses and sections of the declaration of rights, constitution and form of government, and every part of any law of this state, contrary to the provisions of this act, so far as respects the sect of people aforesaid, shall be, and the same is hereby declared to be repealed and annulled on the confirmation hereof.

This copy of *An Act for the Relief of Jews in Maryland*, or, as it is more commonly known, the Jew Bill, dates to 1819. By the 1820s, only three states—Maryland, North Carolina, and New Hampshire—discriminated against non-Christians in their state constitutions. This bill passed the Maryland Legislature once in the 1822–1823 sessions but needed to pass in two consecutive sessions to be made into law. In a slightly revised form, the bill passed both the 1824–1825 and the 1825–1826 sessions. After its passage, both Solomon Etting and Jacob Cohen were elected to the Baltimore City Council. (Courtesy of the JMM, 1987.82.1.)

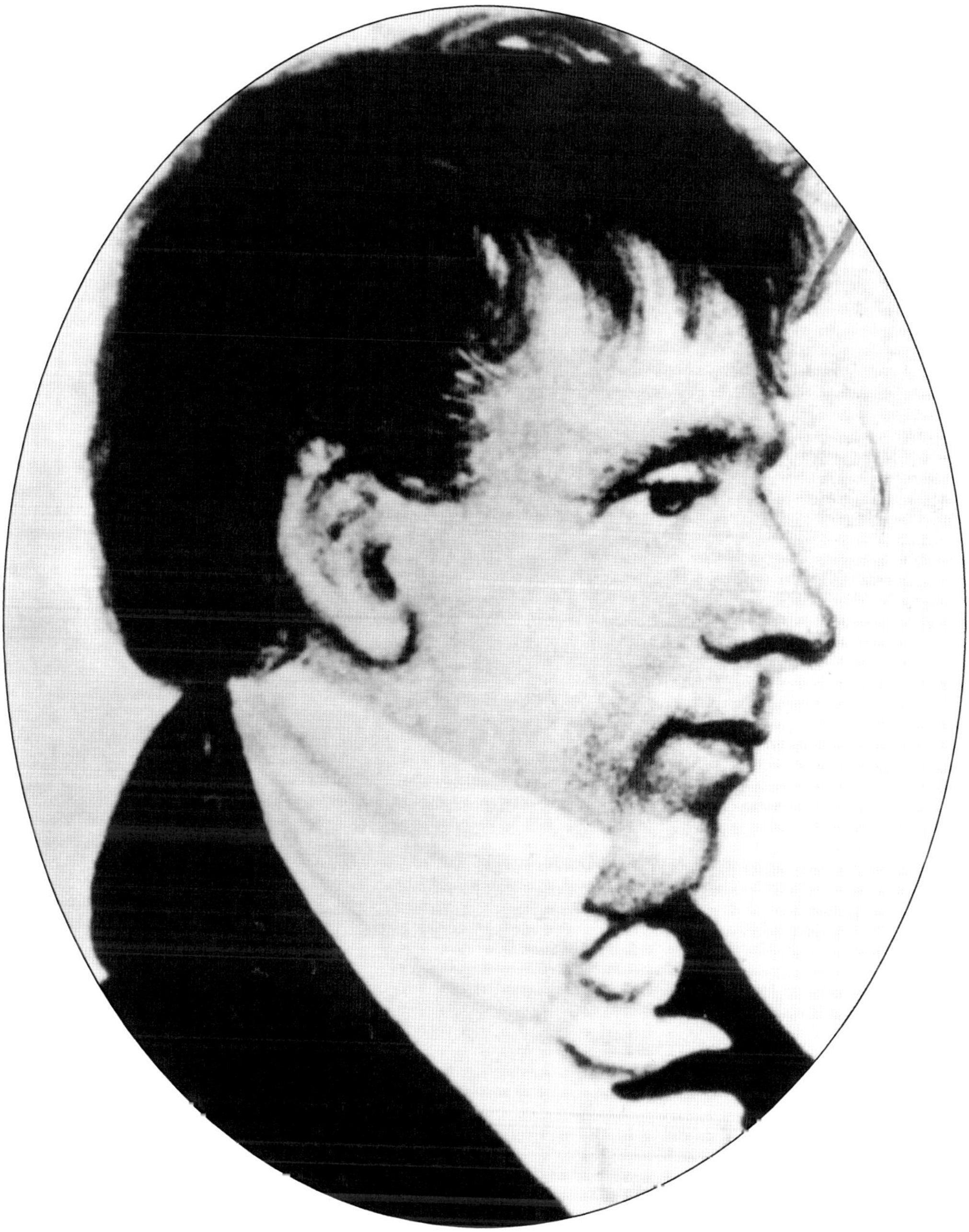

Originally from Hagerstown, Maryland, Thomas Kennedy (1776–1832) was elected a delegate to the Maryland Legislature in 1818. While he had never met a Jew, Kennedy was a devoted follower of the Jeffersonian belief in the equality of all men. For this reason, he spearheaded the cause of the Jew Bill with Henry Brackenridge. Initially proposed in 1818, the bill failed from lack of public support. In 1823, Benjamin Galloway defeated Kennedy by campaigning as the head of the "Christian" ticket. Kennedy was reelected as an Independent in 1825. (Courtesy of the JMM, 2003.47.24.)

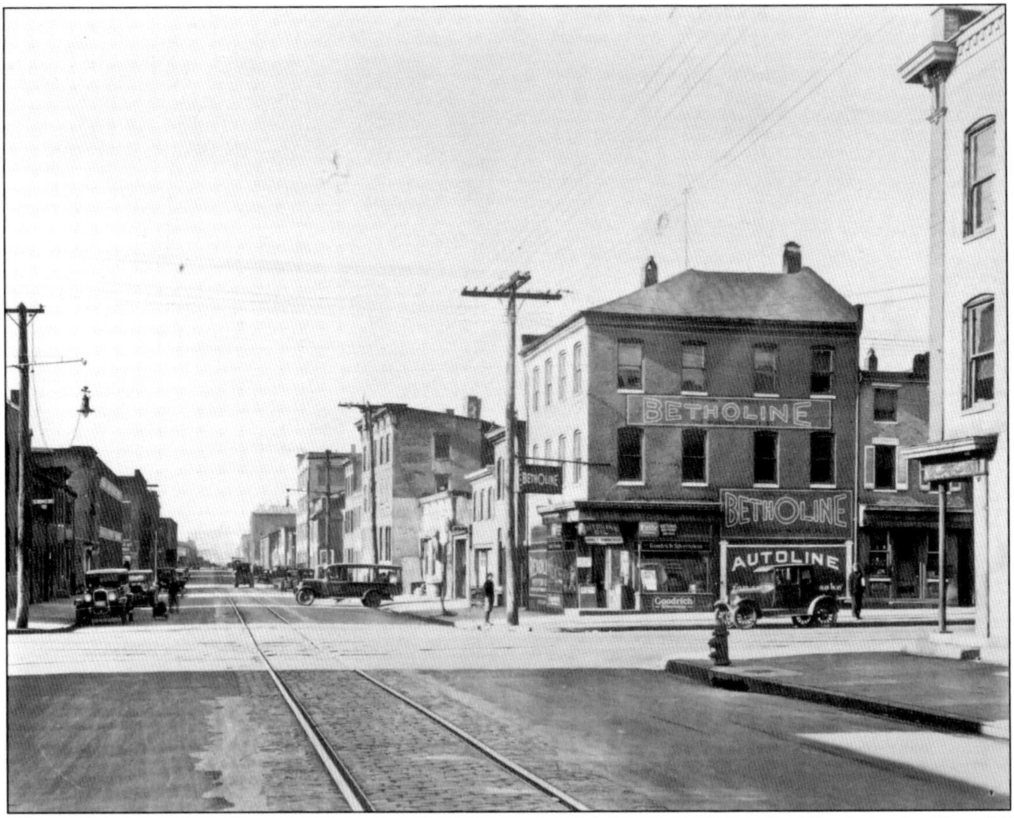

The Baltimore Hebrew Congregation, also known as Nidchei Yisroel, or the "Scattered of Israel," became the first chartered Jewish congregation in Maryland in 1830. Its members, mostly German Jewish immigrants, met in rented rooms above a grocery at Bond and Fleet Streets in Fells Point. This photograph was taken around 1930. (Courtesy of Baltimore Hebrew Congregation and the JMM, 1989.94.4a.)

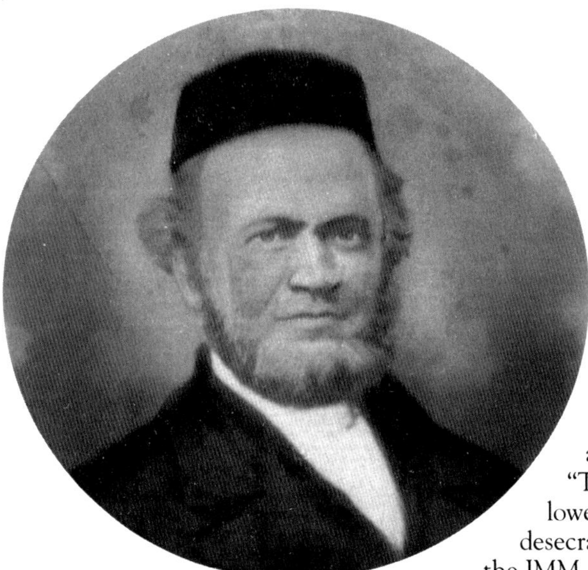

In 1840, the Baltimore Hebrew Congregation hired Rabbi Abraham Rice (1800–1862) of Bavaria, the first ordained rabbi in America. He remained with Baltimore Hebrew until 1849, having become disenchanted with the congregation's growing secularization and religious laxity. In a letter, Rice wrote, "The religious life in this land is on the lowest level. Most people eat foul food and desecrate the Sabbath in public." (Courtesy of the JMM, 1986.113.11.)

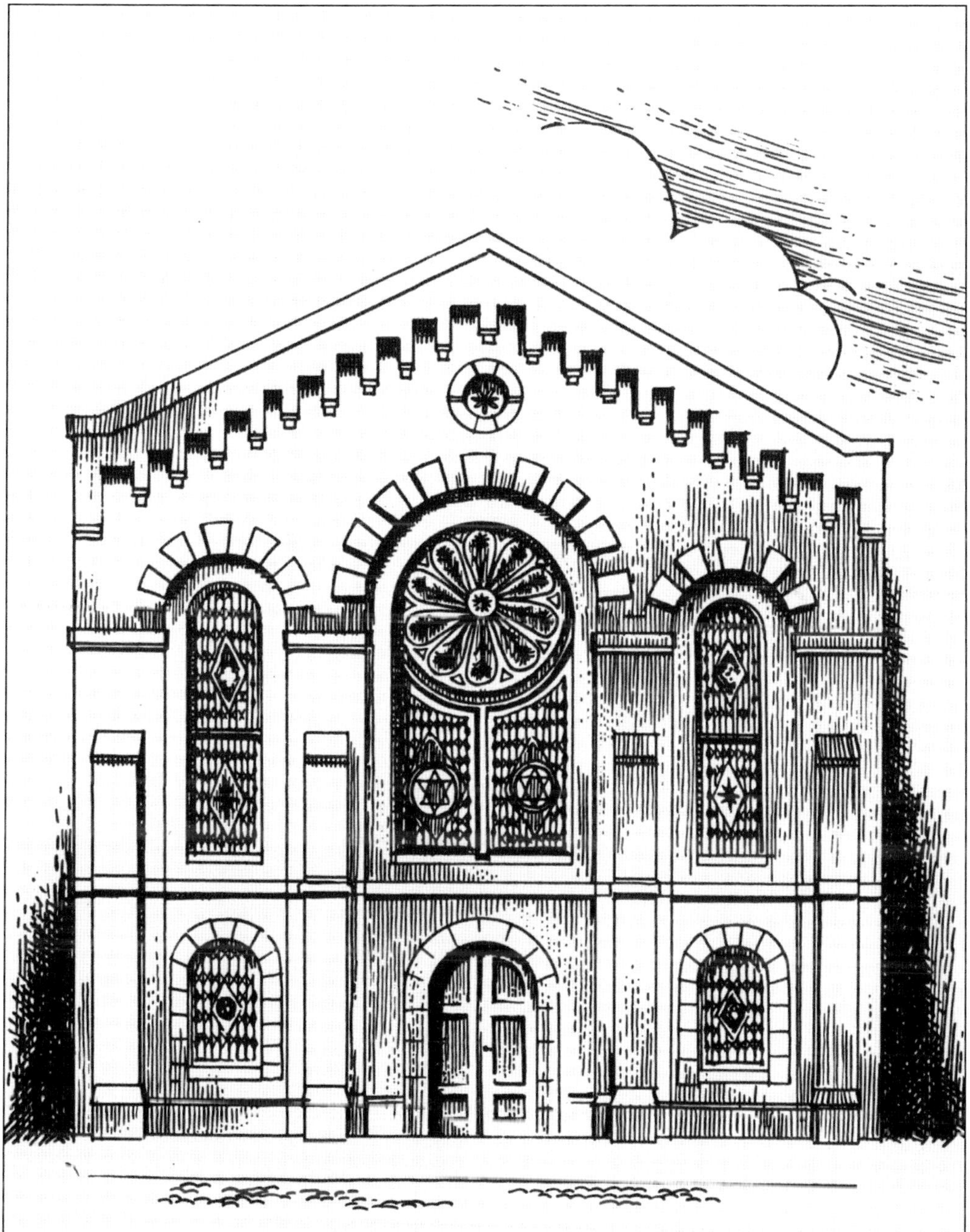

In 1842, Har Sinai Verein was established as a liberal alternative to Baltimore Hebrew's Orthodoxy. The group met in Moses Hutzler's home in Fells Point. Later renamed Har Sinai Congregation, it was the first in America founded as a Reform congregation. In 1850, Rabbi Isaac Mayer Wise visited Baltimore from Cincinnati, Ohio. Unimpressed, he wrote, "There seemed to be many Jews here [in Baltimore], although everything was very primitive. The community had three handsome synagogues and two schools that were conducted quite well, but the children sat with covered heads. In short, everything seemed to be orthodox and primitive, except in the Har Sinai Congregation." (Courtesy of the JMM, 1985.184.2.)

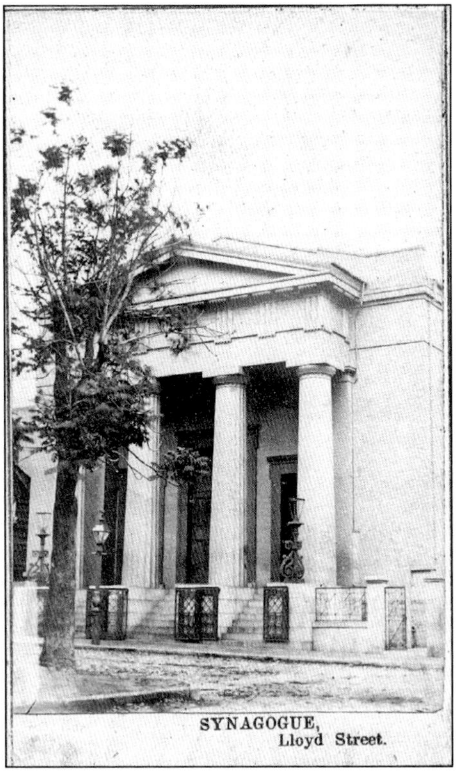

Baltimore Hebrew constructed the Lloyd Street Synagogue in 1845, the first synagogue built in Maryland and, today, the third oldest surviving synagogue building in the nation. Baltimore Hebrew remained there until 1891 when the congregation moved uptown to Madison Street. The building was sold to a Lithuanian Catholic congregation, St. John the Baptist. In 1905, it again became a synagogue for the Russian Jewish congregation Shomrei Mishmeres Hakodesh. (Courtesy of the JMM, 1997.071.1.)

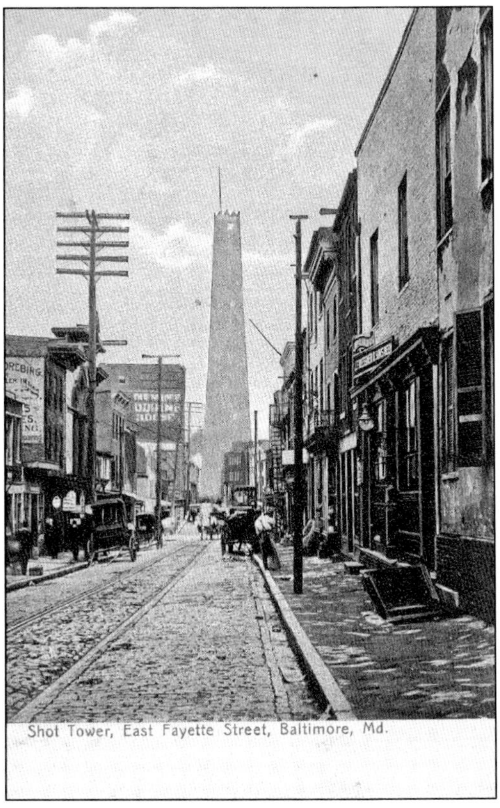

In the 1840s, approximately 10,000 German Jews entered Baltimore through Fells Point, though not all settled in the city. While these immigrants settled around the city, they centered their communal institutions in East Baltimore. One of East Baltimore's distinguishing landmarks is the Phoenix Shot Tower, which stands at the corner of Fayette Street and what used to be the Jones Falls (now President Street). (Courtesy of the JMM, 1988.117.1.)

In 1851, Rabbi Rice organized Shearith Israel Congregation, which remained traditional in practice. The congregation was small, and Rabbi Rice survived on the income of a grocery store he owned. He passed away in 1862. (Courtesy of the JMM, 1987.148.2.)

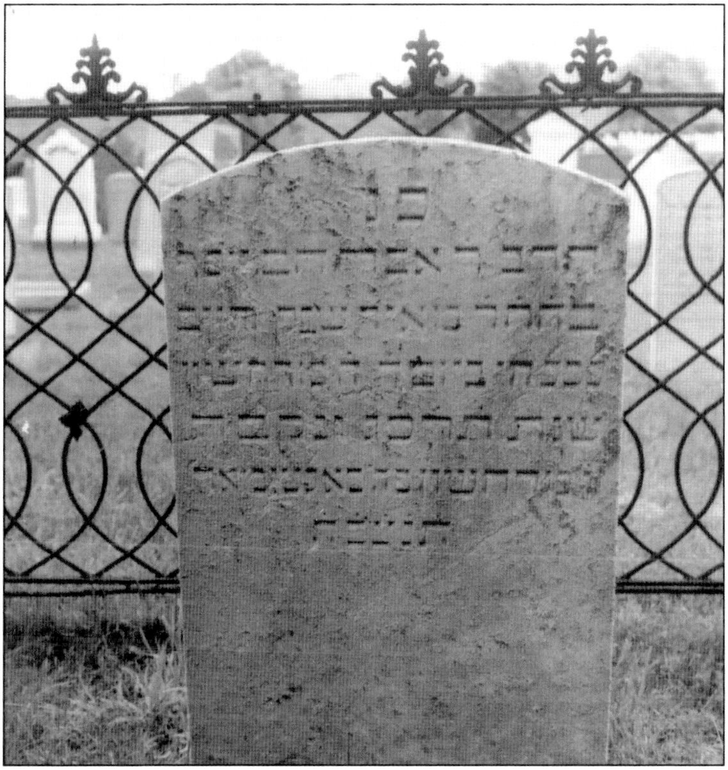

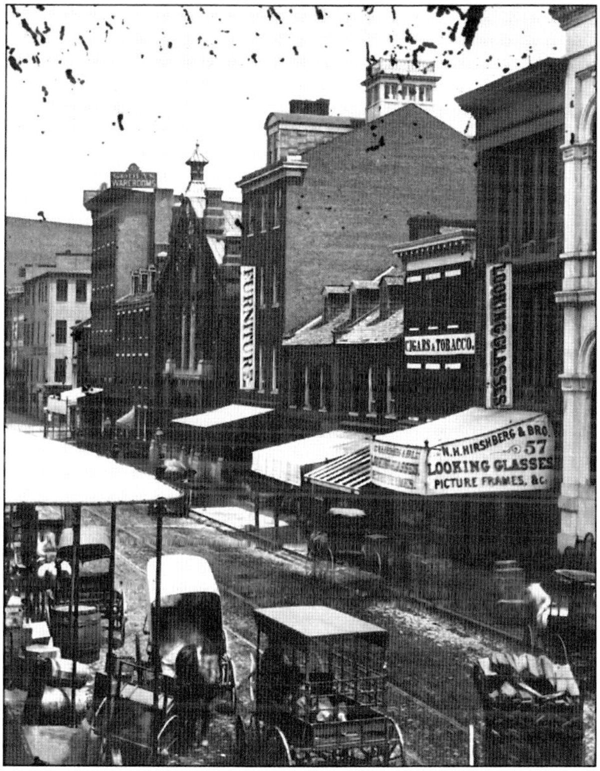

In 1853, Temple Oheb Shalom was founded as midway between orthodoxy and reform. Unlike the city's other German Jewish synagogues, its first home was in South Baltimore, on Hanover Street. (Courtesy of the JMM and the Ross J. Kelbaugh Collection, 1988.226.2a.)

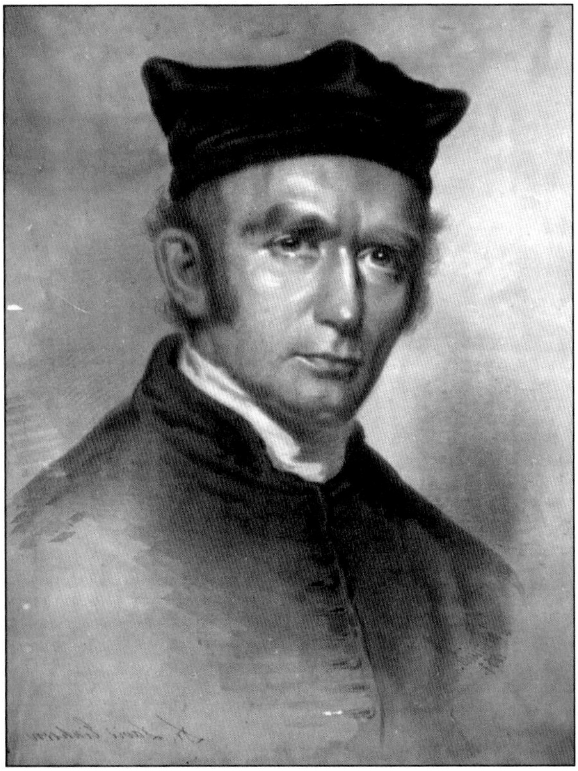

In 1855, Har Sinai Congregation hired radical Rabbi David Einhorn (1809–1879) of Bavaria. A political firebrand, Einhorn was strongly liberal, anti-slavery, and vehemently anti-traditional. He engaged in heated debates with Rabbi Rice and became a bitter enemy of Rabbi Benjamin Szold of Oheb Shalom. (Courtesy of the JMM, 1985.184.1.)

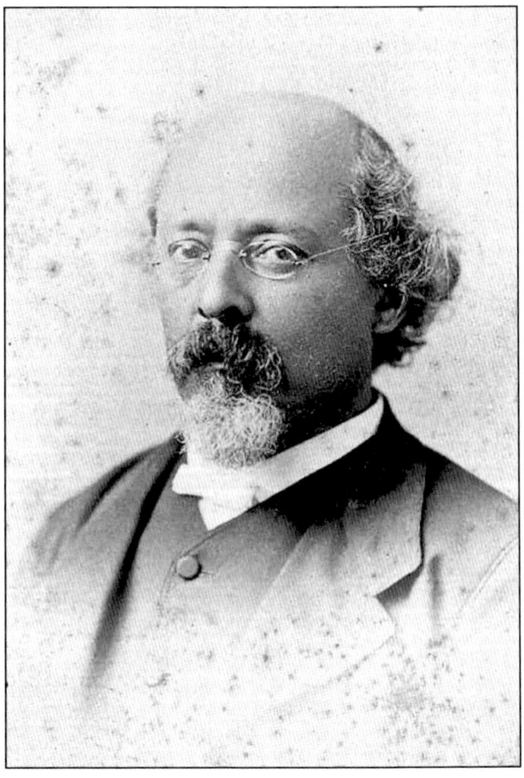

Temple Oheb Shalom hired Rabbi Benjamin Szold (1829–1902) of Hungary in 1859. In his inaugural sermon, Rabbi Szold expressed his moderate views, saying, "Many want to dress all religious demands in obsolete garb. . . . The others again yield everything to the authority of the times." (Courtesy of the JMM, 1992.242.006.031a.)

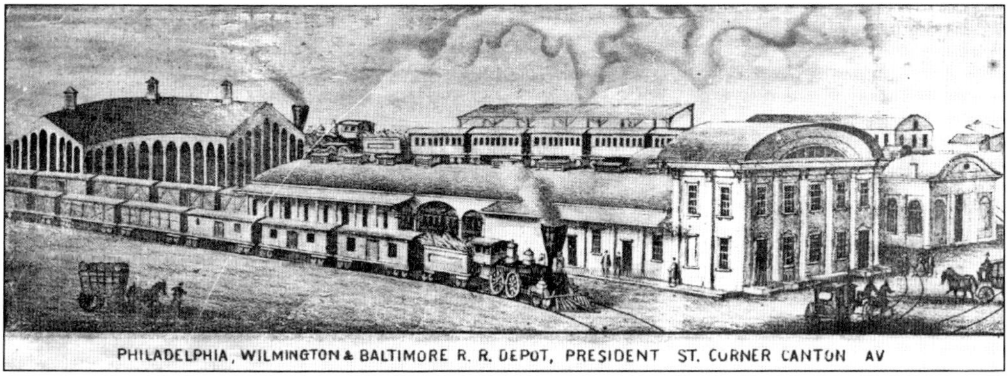

Riots broke out on April 19, 1861, at the President Street Station between Union soldiers and Southern sympathizers, signaling the beginning of the Civil War in Baltimore. The riot started only a few blocks from the heart of the Jewish community. The community was divided on the subject of slavery. Rabbi Bernard Illowy of the Baltimore Hebrew Congregation defended slavery, while Rabbi Einhorn preached abolitionism. (Courtesy of the EPFL.)

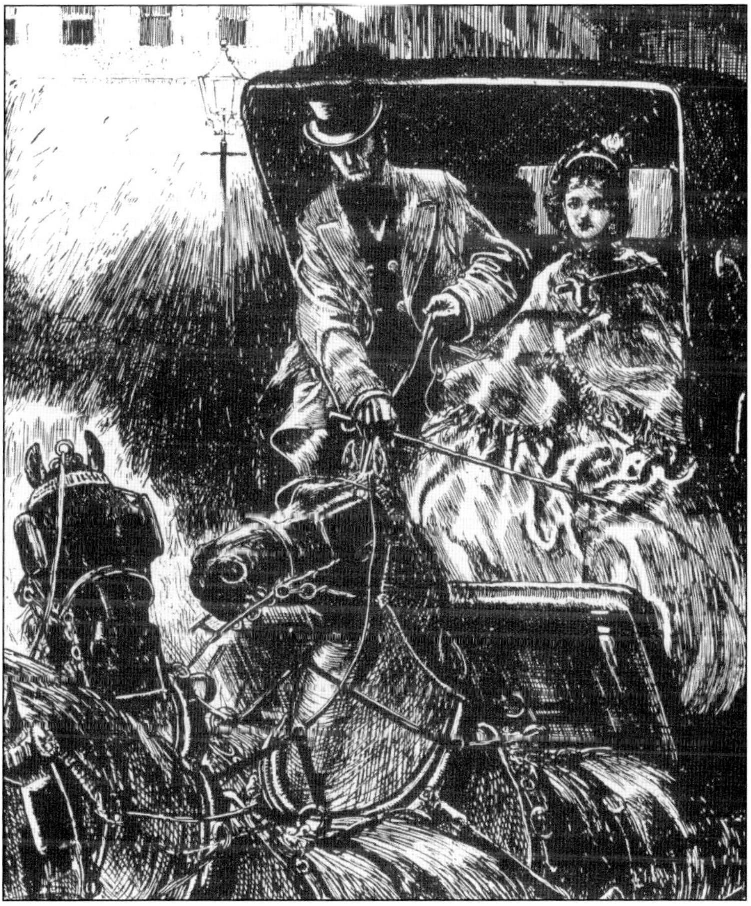

Rabbi Einhorn not only preached against slavery at the pulpit, but also published his views in his German language newspaper, *Sinai*. After the President Street riots, the offices of *Sinai* were destroyed by a pro-slavery mob, and Rabbi Einhorn was forced to flee with his family, seeking refuge in Philadelphia. On May 12, 1861, the president of Har Sinai Verein requested that he return but only if he was willing to tone down his rhetoric. Rabbi Einhorn refused and never returned to Baltimore. (Courtesy of the JMM library.)

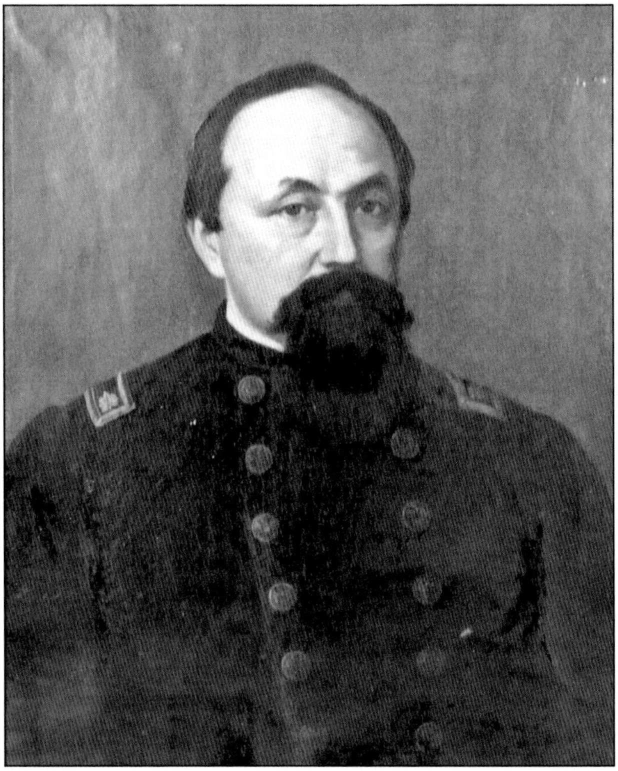

During the Civil War, Har Sinai congregant Gen. Leopold Blumenberg served on the Union side, one of only three Jewish military officers to become full generals in the Union army and the only one from Maryland. He was wounded at the Battle of Antietam. (Courtesy of the JMM, 1986.113.12.)

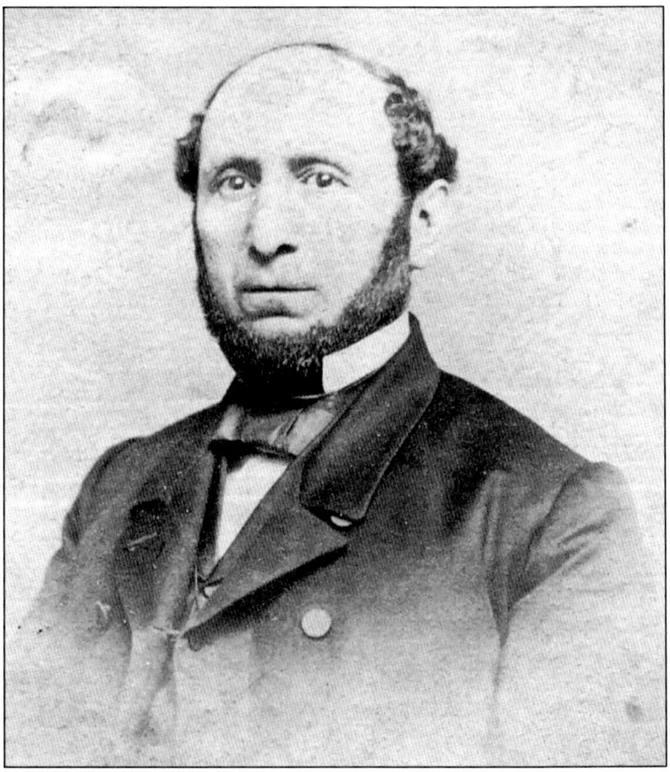

Born in the Duchy of Hesse Darmstadt, Moses Wiesenfeld (1819–1871) immigrated to Baltimore in 1838 and started Wiesenfeld and Company, which manufactured ready-made clothes. During the Civil War, he was arrested for making Confederate buttons and spent two years in jail in Albany. Wiesenfeld claimed innocence and was defended by several rabbis as well as General Blumenberg. After Wiesenfeld's release, Johns Hopkins, a noted Unionist, helped to reestablish him in business. (Courtesy of the JMM, 1990.2.12.)

Two

Baltimore or Bust!
Jewish Immigration to Charm City

Baltimore has always been an immigrant city. Before the Civil War, most immigrants entered through the wharves of Fells Point on the northern side of the Inner Harbor. During the 1840s, a large influx of Bavarian Jews surged into this port. They sought escape from anti-Semitic laws as well as the economic opportunities provided by the Baltimore-Bremen tobacco connection. By 1861, an estimated 7,000 Jews lived in Baltimore.

In 1868, the Baltimore and Ohio Railroad partnered with the North German Lloyd Steamship Line to construct two terminals at Locust Point on the southern side of the harbor. Immigrants poured into Locust Point, and by the 1880s, roughly one-third of Baltimore's residents were foreign-born. The number of immigrants surged from the 1880s to the 1910s, among them thousands of East European Jews who fled the pogroms, political turmoil, and poverty of their homeland to come to Baltimore.

Immigration slowed to a near halt when World War I began in 1914 and would not resume substantially after the war. When the U.S. Congress passed the Immigration Act of 1924, restrictive quotas limited the number of immigrants allowed into the country. After Adolph Hitler came to power in Germany, a wave of German and European Jews sought refuge in Baltimore in 1933. Even with the quotas in place, approximately 3,000 Jewish refugees managed to reach Baltimore and start new lives in the city. Restrictions were loosened after World War II, and many Holocaust survivors came to Baltimore.

Through the 20th century and into today, Jews have come to the city from countries across the globe, including the former Soviet Union, Iran, and Romania.

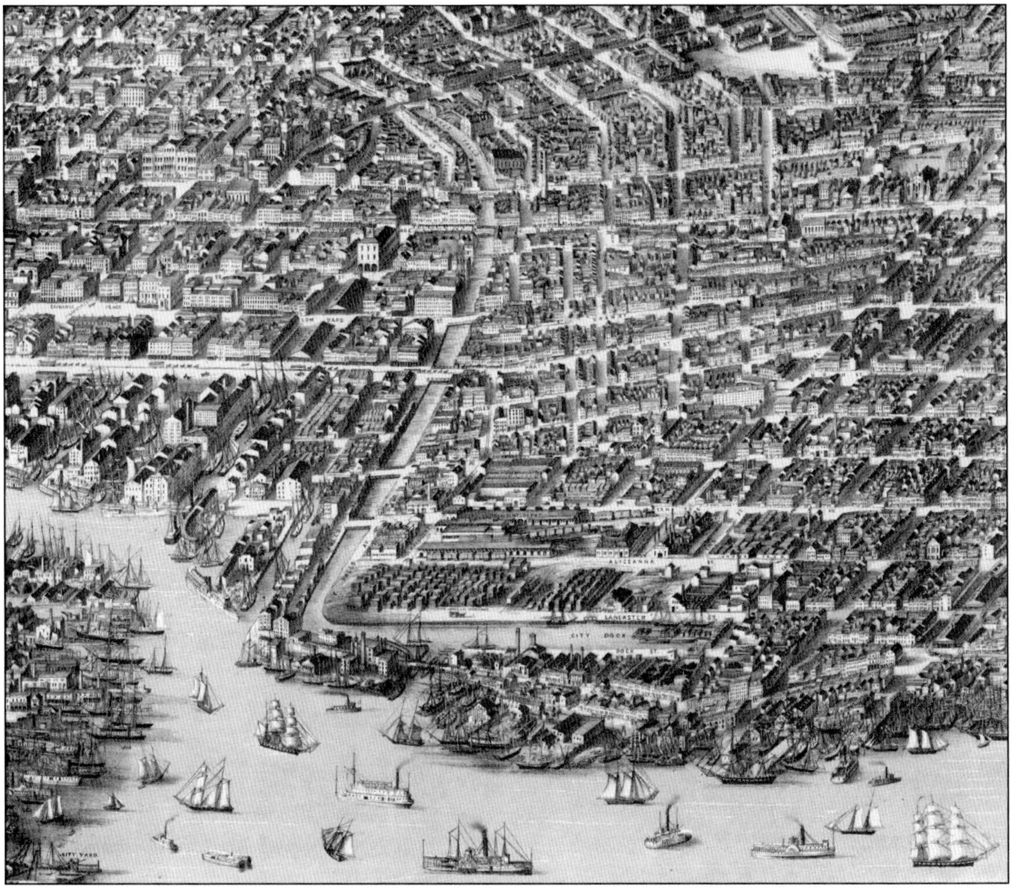

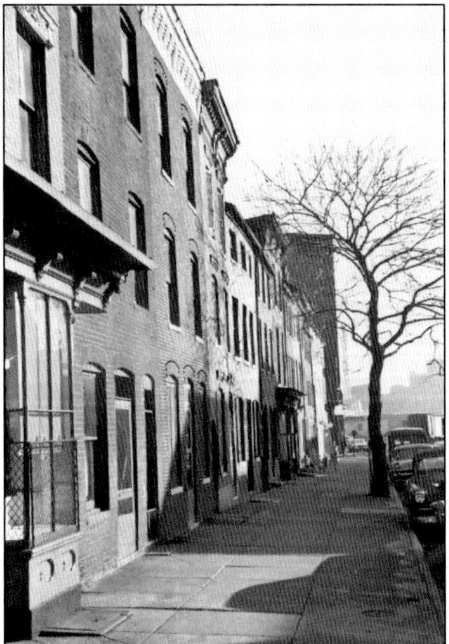

This map of Baltimore features some of the entry points for Jewish immigrants: docks at Fells Point and Locust Point. Modern-day immigrants generally arrive through the Baltimore–Washington International Airport. (Courtesy of the Library of Congress, Geography and Map Division.)

Fells Point was founded in 1730, just a year after Baltimore Town. William Fell turned the marshy swampland into a shipbuilding center and port used primarily for tobacco, flour, and coffee. Nearly 300,000 Bavarian, Austro-Hungarian, and Bohemian Jews came to America from 1820 until the Civil War. Approximately 10,000 passed through Fells Point, and many made their home in Baltimore. (Photograph by John McGrain; courtesy of the JMM, 1995.187.24.)

In 1867, the Baltimore and Ohio Railroad (B&O) formed a partnership with the North German Lloyd Steamship Line. Patrons could buy a single ticket, including passage to America, as well as a ticket west on the B&O. By 1868, ships teeming with immigrants docked at a new terminus at Locust Point. Besides passengers, these ships brought German manufactured goods and returned to Bremen, Germany, with Maryland tobacco and lumber. (Courtesy of the EPFL.)

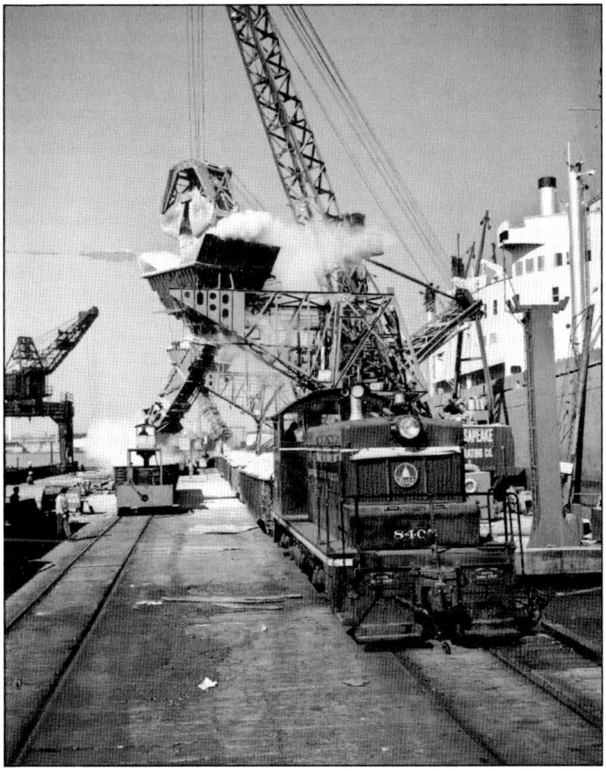

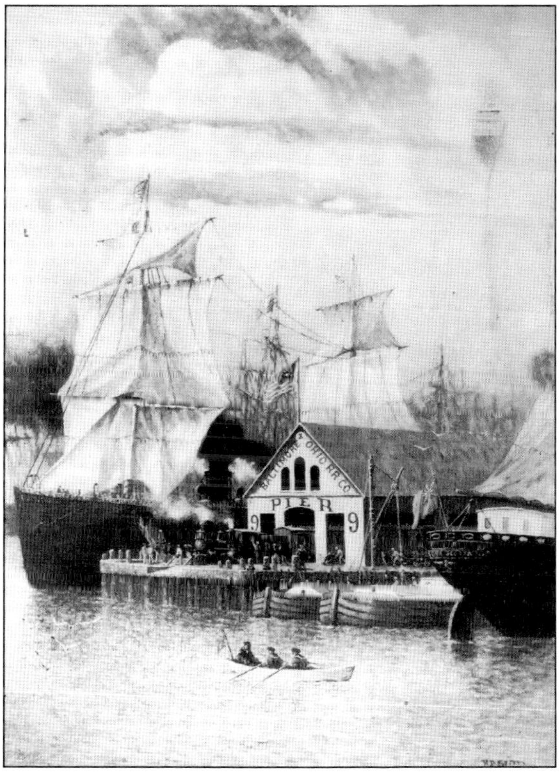

The new arrangement proved popular. More than 10,000 people docked at Locust Point in 1868, compared to fewer than 4,000 in 1867. In 1882, a total of 41,739 passengers disembarked there. Baltimore maintained the second largest number of immigrant arrivals in the country but was dwarfed by the 1,004,756 entering Ellis Island at its height. Most immigrants arriving after 1880 were from Eastern and Southern Europe. (Courtesy of the EPFL.)

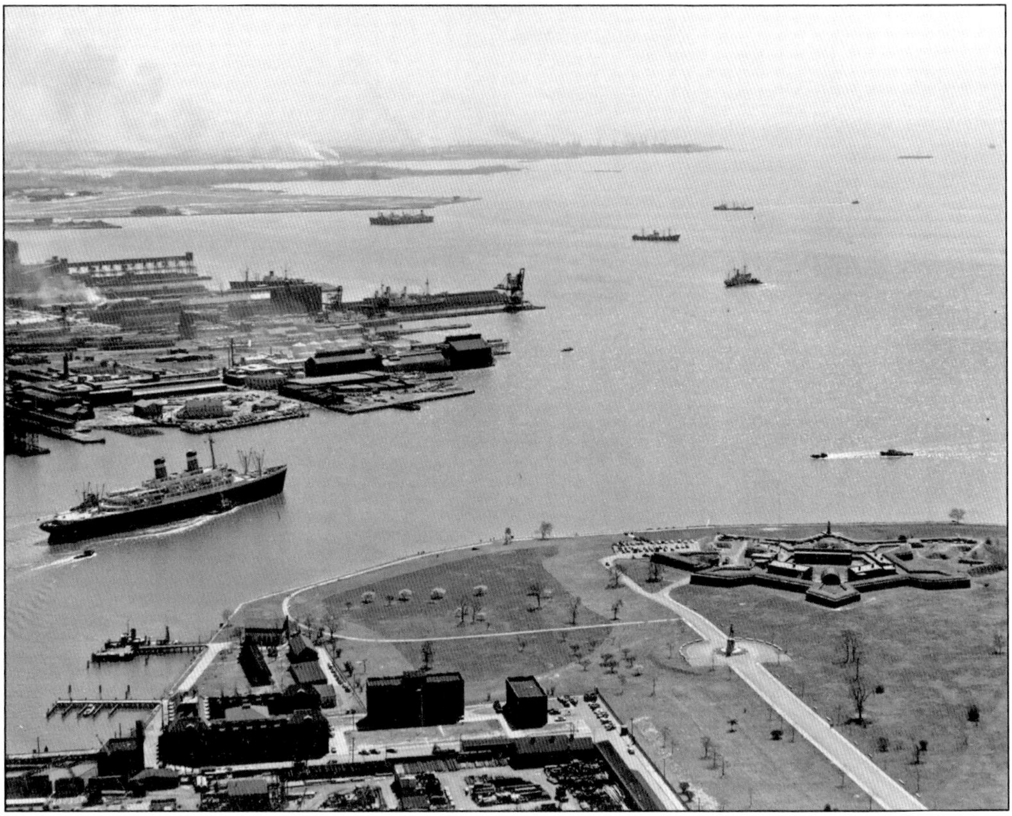

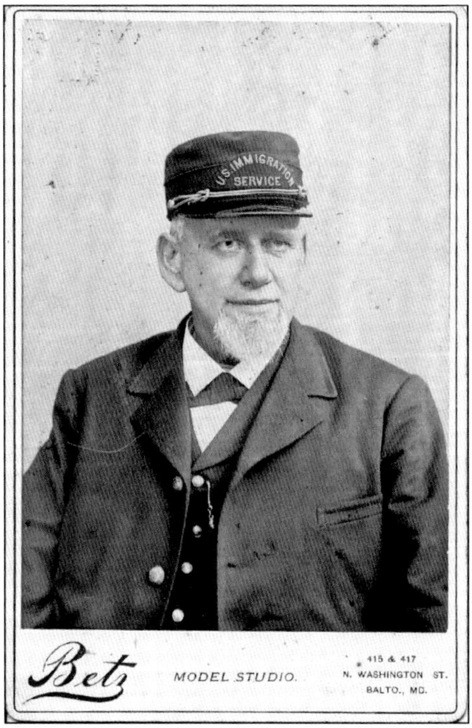

In 1904, the *Baltimore Sun* described the arrival of new immigrants at Locust Point near Fort McHenry: "While the gangways were being lowered, the mass of immigrants on board watched with stolid interest. Families were grouped together, holding tightly to each other and to the bags, bundles and boxes, little and big and medium-sized, that constituted their worldly goods, showing the dread of separation in the energy with which they all stuck together." (Courtesy of the EPFL.)

In the same article, the *Baltimore Sun* described how immigration officials performed "a careful examination of the eyes for the presence of trachoma—the contagious disease of the eyes most dreaded by every alien. . . . Quickly and skillfully the doctor lifted the eyelids of each one. . . . A quick glance was given to the head also for traces of favus, a disease of the scalp, before the alien was passed along." (Courtesy of the JMM, 1996.016.001.)

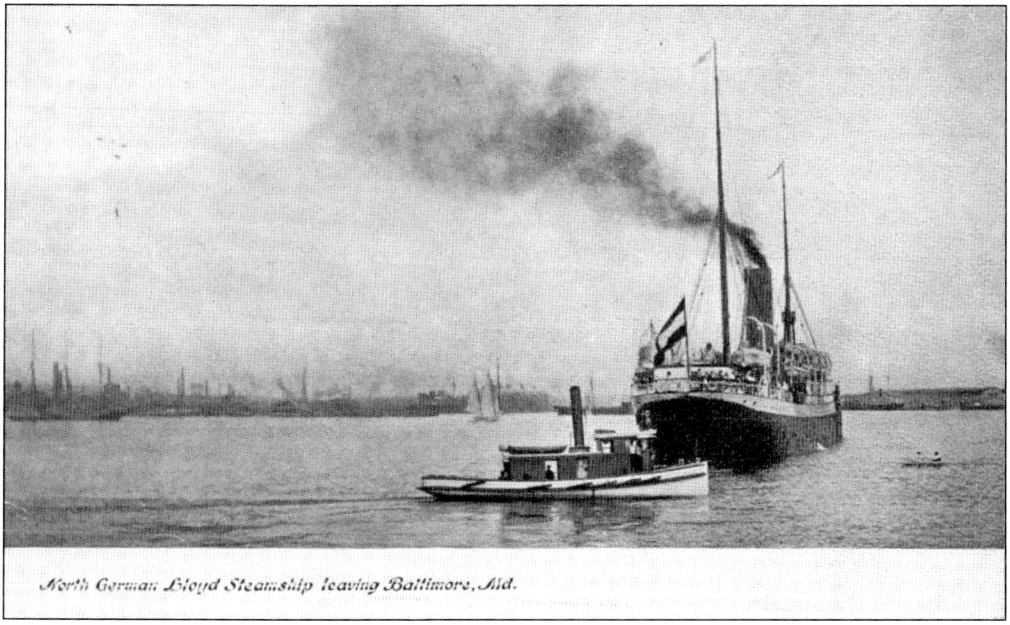

Some examinations took place on board the ships themselves, such as this North German Lloyd steamship. One steamship employee described how "the quarantine men boarded the boat on its way up the bay. Every immigrant went through a quick medical examination. Checking of the luggage by Customs was a quick and cursory affair." (Courtesy of the JMM, 1988.117.003.)

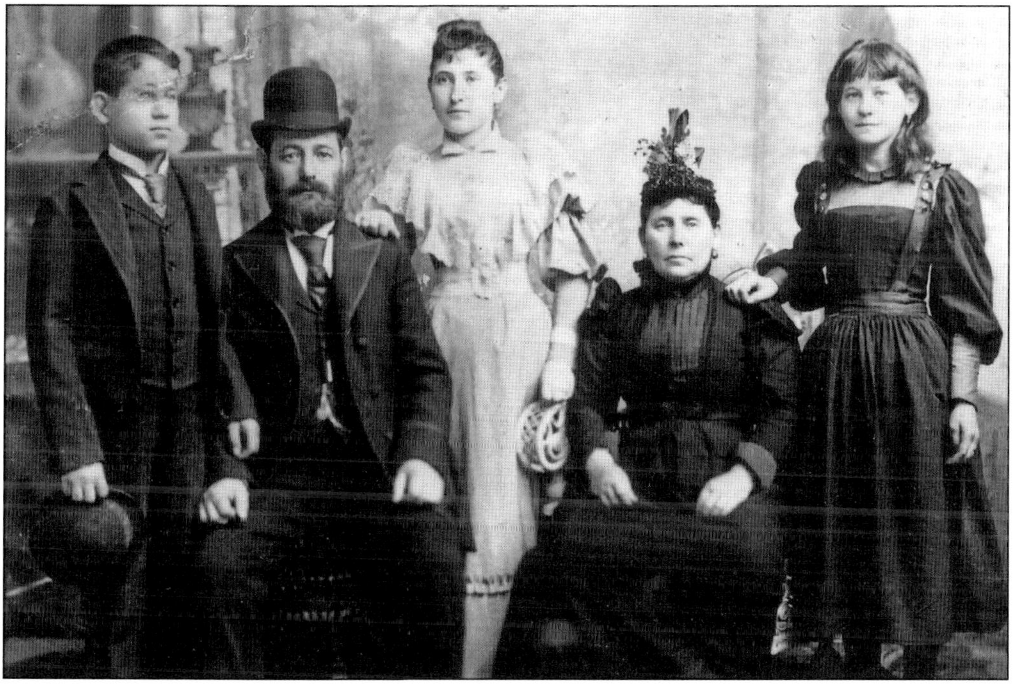

Yitzhak and Bessie Dubinsky and their family emigrated from Kiev, Ukraine, to Baltimore in 1891. From left to right are Moishe ("Morris") Dubinsky, Yitzhak Dubinsky, Chassa ("Anna") Dubinsky, Bessie Resnick Dubinsky, and Ruchel ("Rose") Dubinsky. Two additional sons, Ershlabe and Zusa, are not pictured. (Courtesy of the JMM, 1987.27.1.)

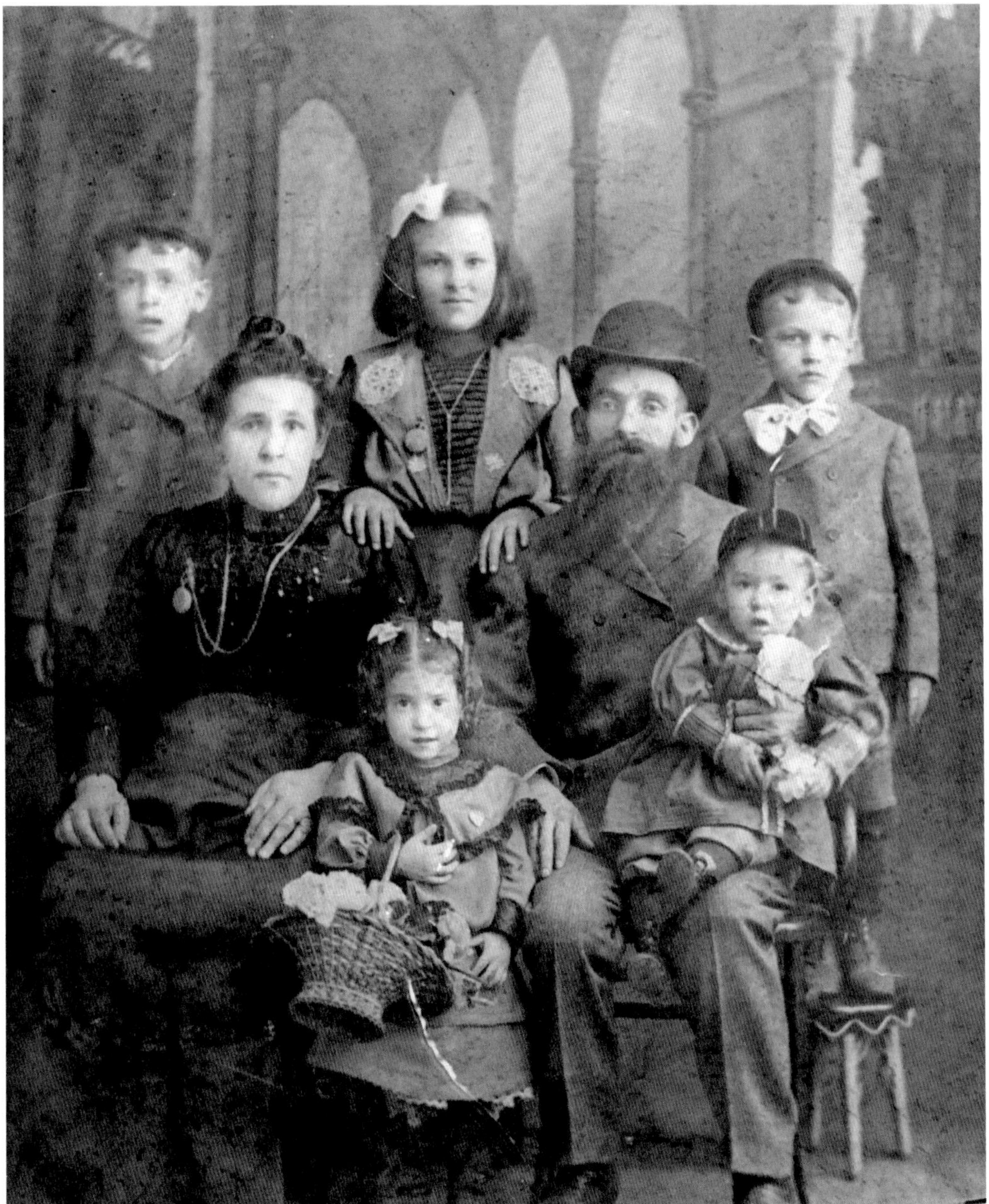

Solomon and Fannie Rodbell pose with their children, from left to right, (standing) David, Dora, Isidore, Kathyrn (with basket), and (sitting) Jacob, in 1905. Many immigrants endured additional trials before they could enter America. The *Baltimore Sun* described how one family "was gathered around a box near by, watching an official as he examined its contents. They had evidently brought all of the little belongings of the old home with them—little ornaments, a big clock swathed in folds of muslin, pictures and other little household treasures, scattered in among the garments and bedding. When the inspection was over, the mother folded up the little dresses that had been tossed out in confusion, and all of the family except the baby helped with the repacking." (Courtesy of the JMM, 1995.160.1.)

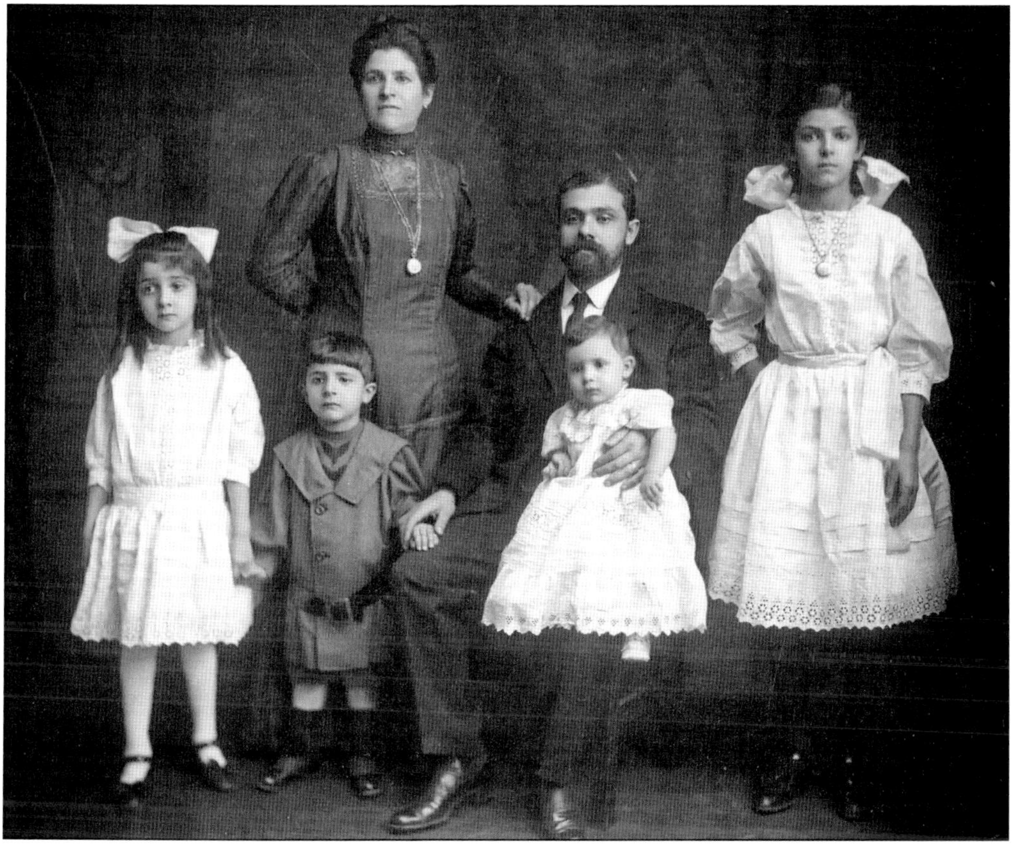

The Saye family included, from left to right, Fanny, Hymen, Ida, Louis holding Sara, and Bertha. They came to Baltimore from Russia around 1910. Louis Saye had served as a tailor in the Russian army before immigrating. In Baltimore, he was able to find work in a clothing factory. Hymen grew up to become an educator, teaching at Talmud Torah and serving as principal at Chizuk Amuno. (Courtesy of the JMM, 1991.7.5.)

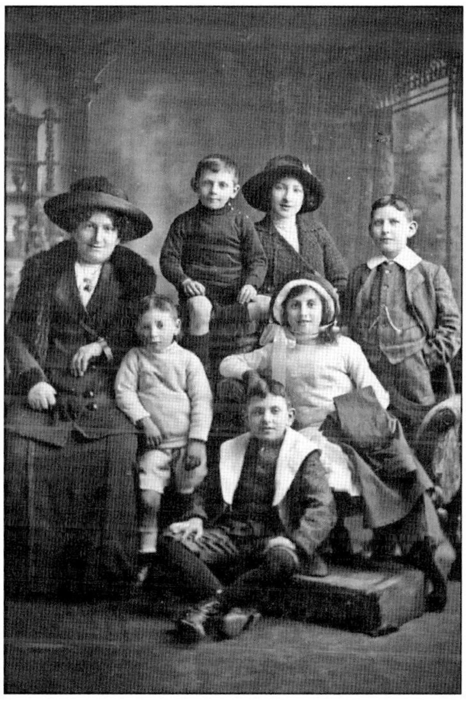

Ella Rudnick and her children—Jennie, Harry, Rose, Mannie, Lou, and Mike—traveled from Dublin, Ireland, to Baltimore around 1912. (Courtesy of the JMM, 1988.209.53.)

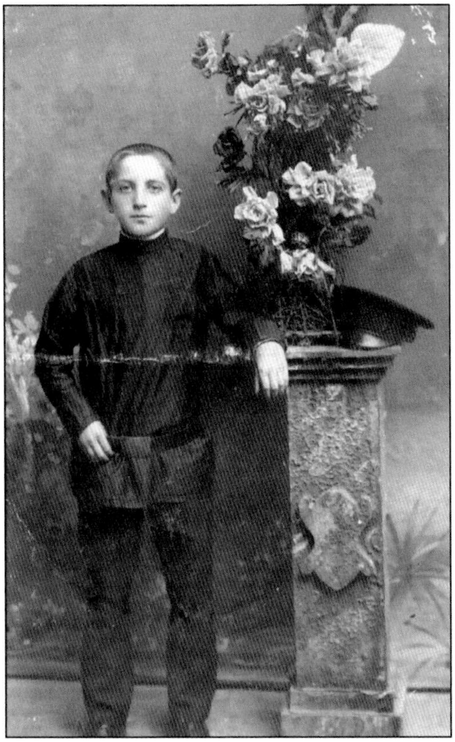

Israel Dvorine was 13 when he immigrated to Baltimore from Russia in 1913. Dvorine went on to become a Baltimore optometrist. He wrote a textbook for optometry schools and developed a set of "pseudoisochromatic plates," which were used to test for color blindness. (Courtesy of the JMM, 1987.214.9.)

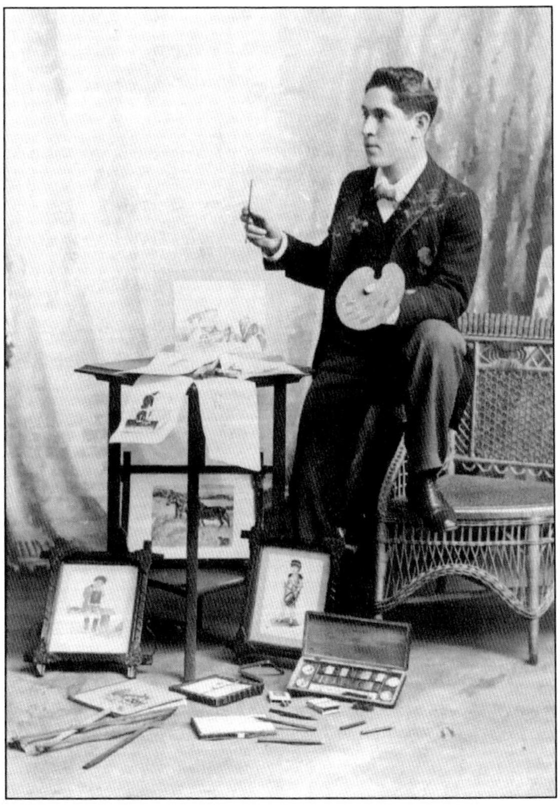

Saul Bernstein (1872–1905) came to Baltimore from Lithuania in 1889. He adorned his store with drawings of Czar Alexander II and George Washington, and sketches of Europe. He attended the Maryland Institute School of Art and Design (now the Maryland Institute College of Art). Some of his paintings hang in the Baltimore Museum of Art. This 1893 photograph was taken prior to his formal training. He is holding the palette incorrectly. (Courtesy of the JMM, 1986.10.5a.)

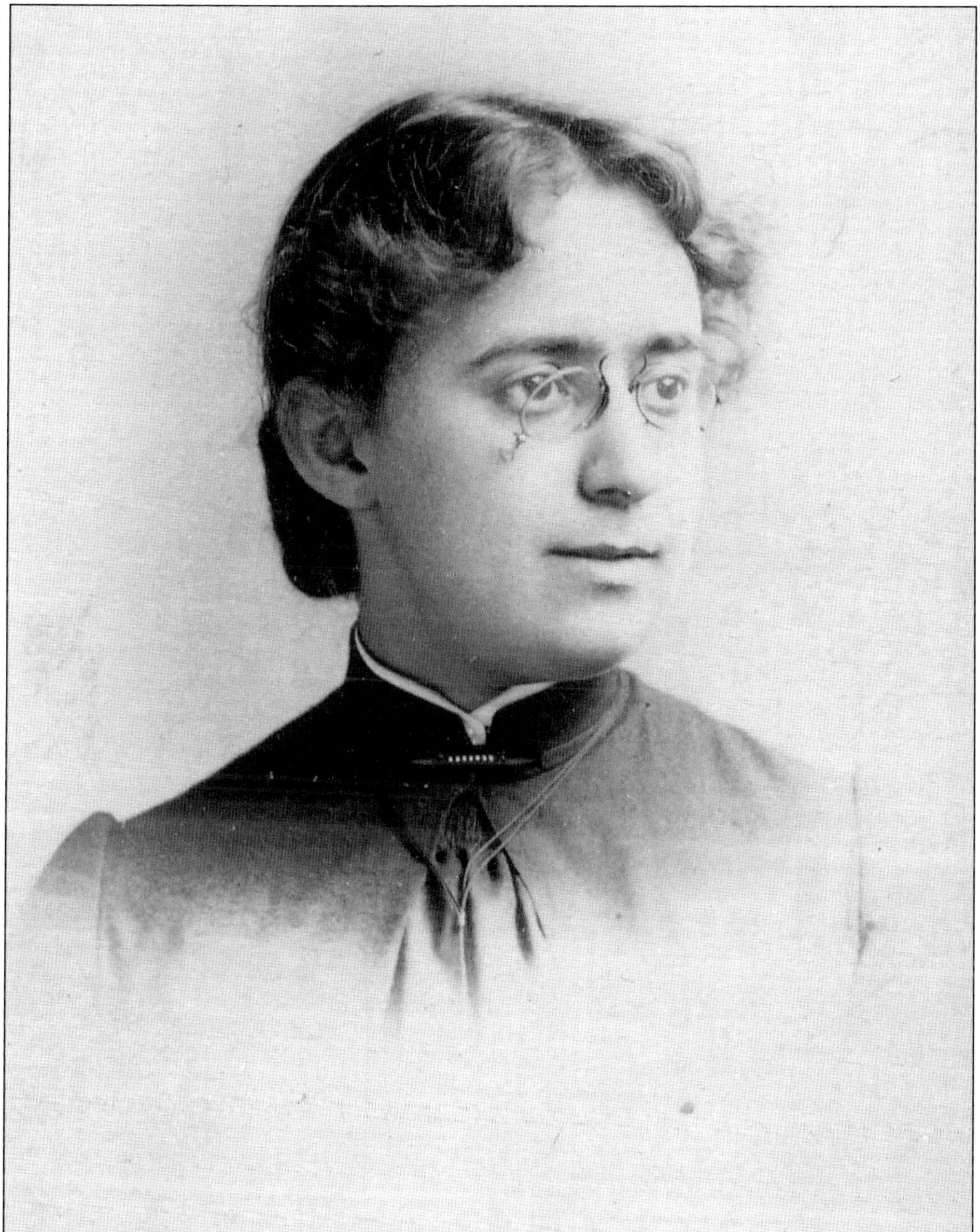

Henrietta Szold (1860–1945) was the oldest of Rabbi Benjamin Szold's eight daughters. Like her father, Szold was passionate about providing aid and assistance to new immigrants. She would often greet them personally at the docks. After becoming involved with the Isaac Baer Levinsohn Hebrew Literary Society, which promoted education, she decided to open a night school for immigrants in 1889. As she wrote in an 1891 letter, "I have no greater wish than to be able to give my whole strength, time, and ability to [the Russians]. . . . I eat, drink, and sleep Russians." She continued to manage and teach at the night school until 1893. (Courtesy of the JMM, 1989.079.006.)

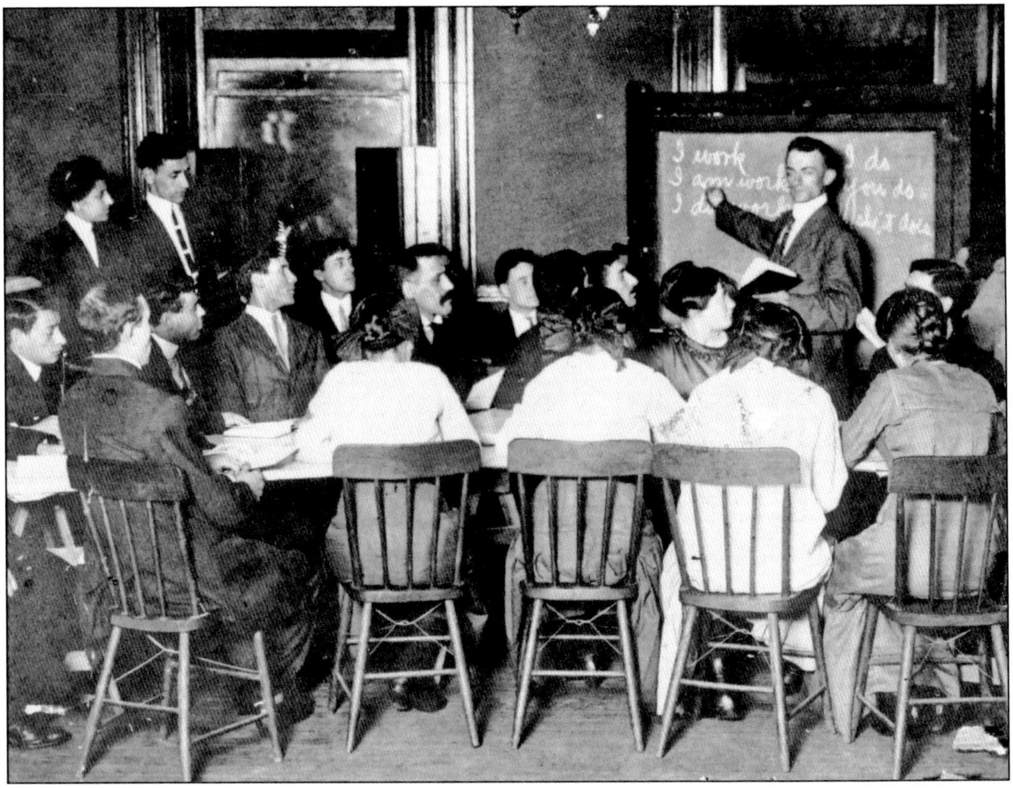

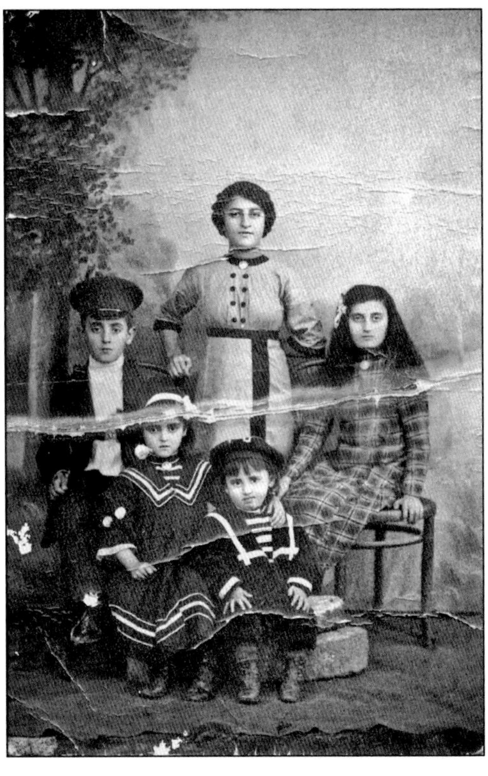

In 1889, Henrietta Szold opened a night school with 30 students. In 1890, they expanded to the entire building. From 1889 to 1897, thousands of students attended the night school. According to the *Baltimore Sun* in 1892, tuition cost 30¢ a month. The night school closed, but English classes continued at other institutions, including the Jewish Educational Alliance, as seen in this 1919 photograph. (Courtesy of the JMM, 1992.231.73.)

Ida (Rosen) Rehr (1896–1988), standing in the center, had this portrait taken with her siblings in Russia before immigrating to Baltimore. Rehr's experience was typical of many Jewish immigrants of the time. Originally named Chaya Bezoomna, she changed her name to Ida and adopted the Americanized last name of Rosen. She worked at Sonneborn's Clothing Factory. In 1923, Ida married another immigrant, Daniel Rehr. Together they opened a confectionary shop. (Courtesy of the JMM, 1988.217.2.)

In 1903, Russian Jews established the Hebrew Immigrant Protective Society to help immigrants adjust to American life, like the Ditlow family seen here. It was renamed the Hebrew Immigrant Aid Society (HIAS) in recognition of its close connection with a sister society in New York of the same name. Today HIAS is part of the Jewish Family Services, an agency of the Associated: Jewish Community Federation of Baltimore. (Courtesy of the JMM, 1991.223.7.)

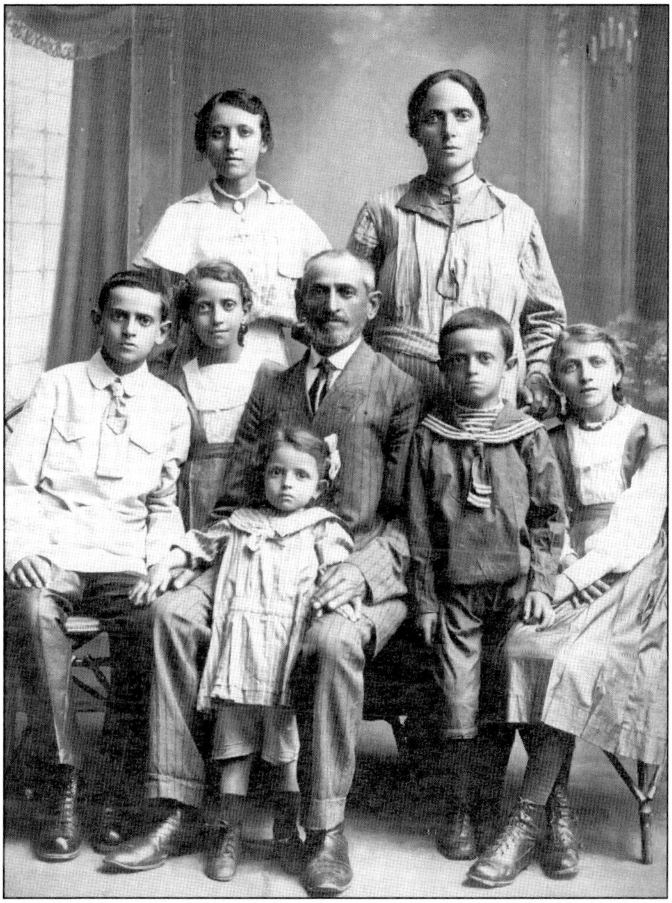

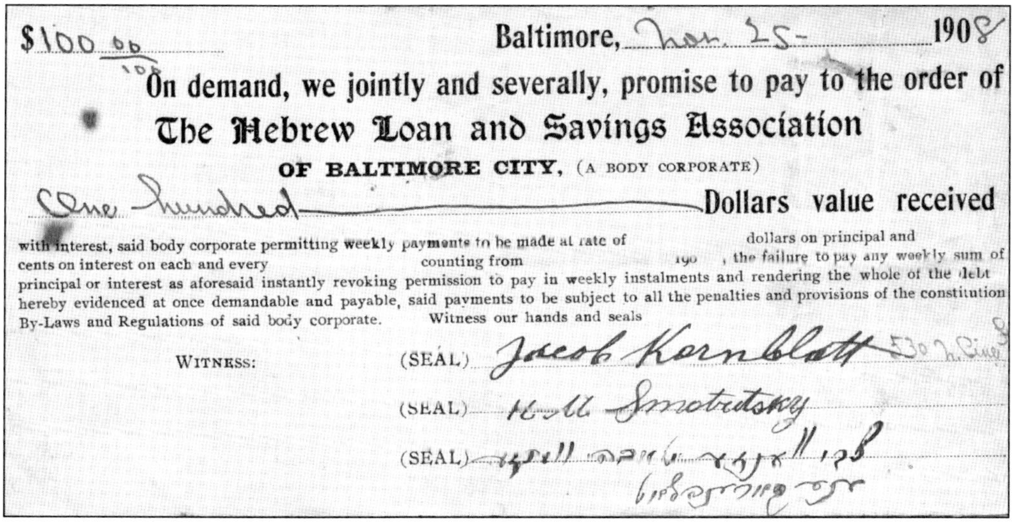

$100.00 Baltimore, Nov. 25- 1908

On demand, we jointly and severally, promise to pay to the order of

The Hebrew Loan and Savings Association

OF BALTIMORE CITY, (A BODY CORPORATE)

One hundred Dollars value received

with interest, said body corporate permitting weekly payments to be made at rate of dollars on principal and cents on interest on each and every counting from 190 , the failure to pay any weekly sum of principal or interest as aforesaid instantly revoking permission to pay in weekly instalments and rendering the whole of the debt hereby evidenced at once demandable and payable, said payments to be subject to all the penalties and provisions of the constitution By-Laws and Regulations of said body corporate. Witness our hands and seals

WITNESS: (SEAL) Jacob Kornblatt

(SEAL) H. M. Smotritsky

(SEAL)

The Hebrew Free Loan Association (HFLA) started in 1898 and played an important role in the economic development of the immigrant Jewish community. It offered interest-free loans to aspiring entrepreneurs, enabling many Jewish immigrants to start their own businesses. It continues to provide this service today. (Courtesy of the JMM, 1990.19.1.)

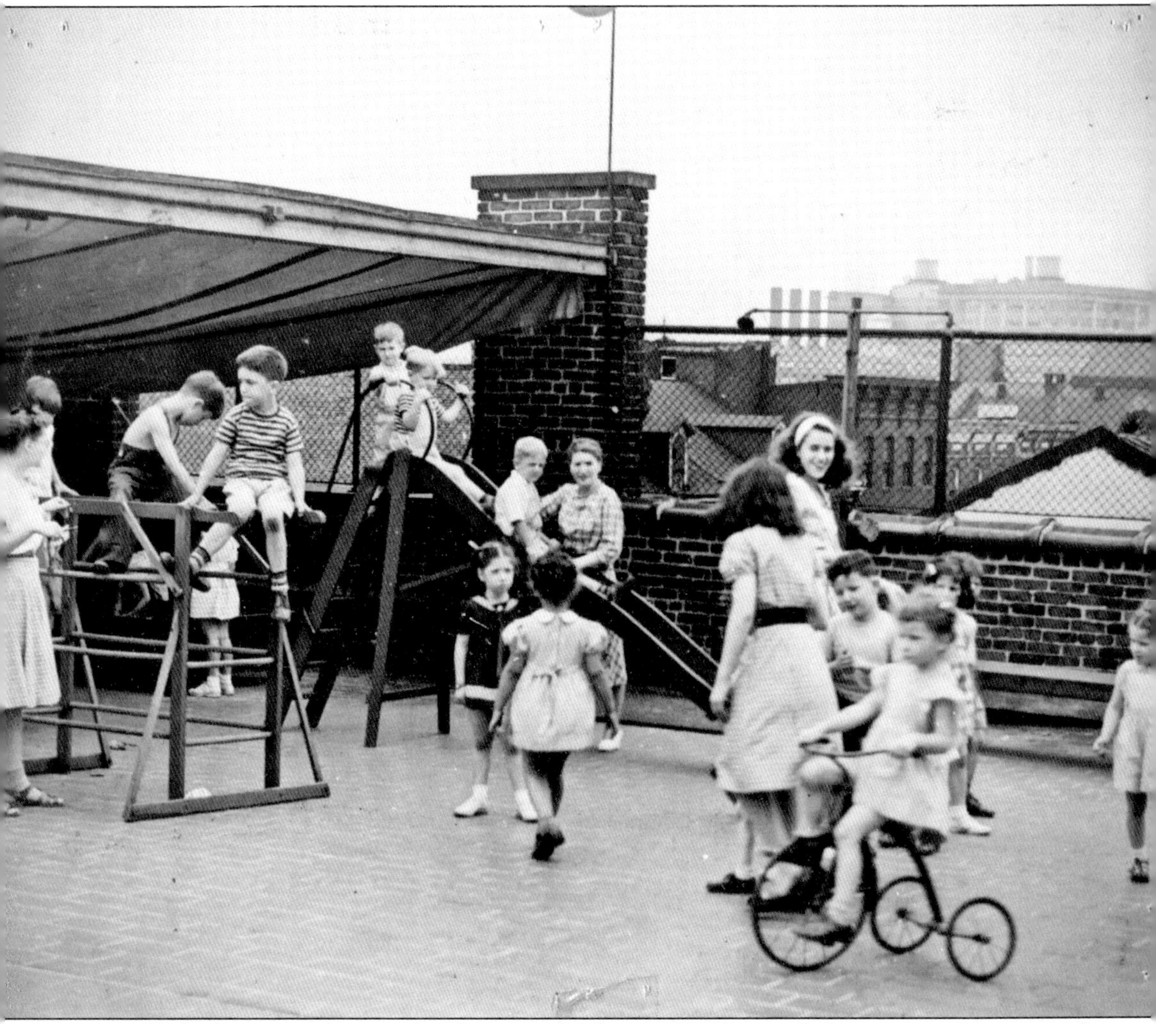

Established in 1909, the Jewish Educational Alliance (JEA) provided recreational activities for children and classes for immigrants. Al Olschansky described his memories of the nursery at the JEA, saying, "We were on the top floor where we played all kinds of children's games, and on nice days, we were taken to the roof where we played Cowboys and Indians, and Ring-Around-A-Rosie." (Courtesy of the JMM, 1992.231.29.)

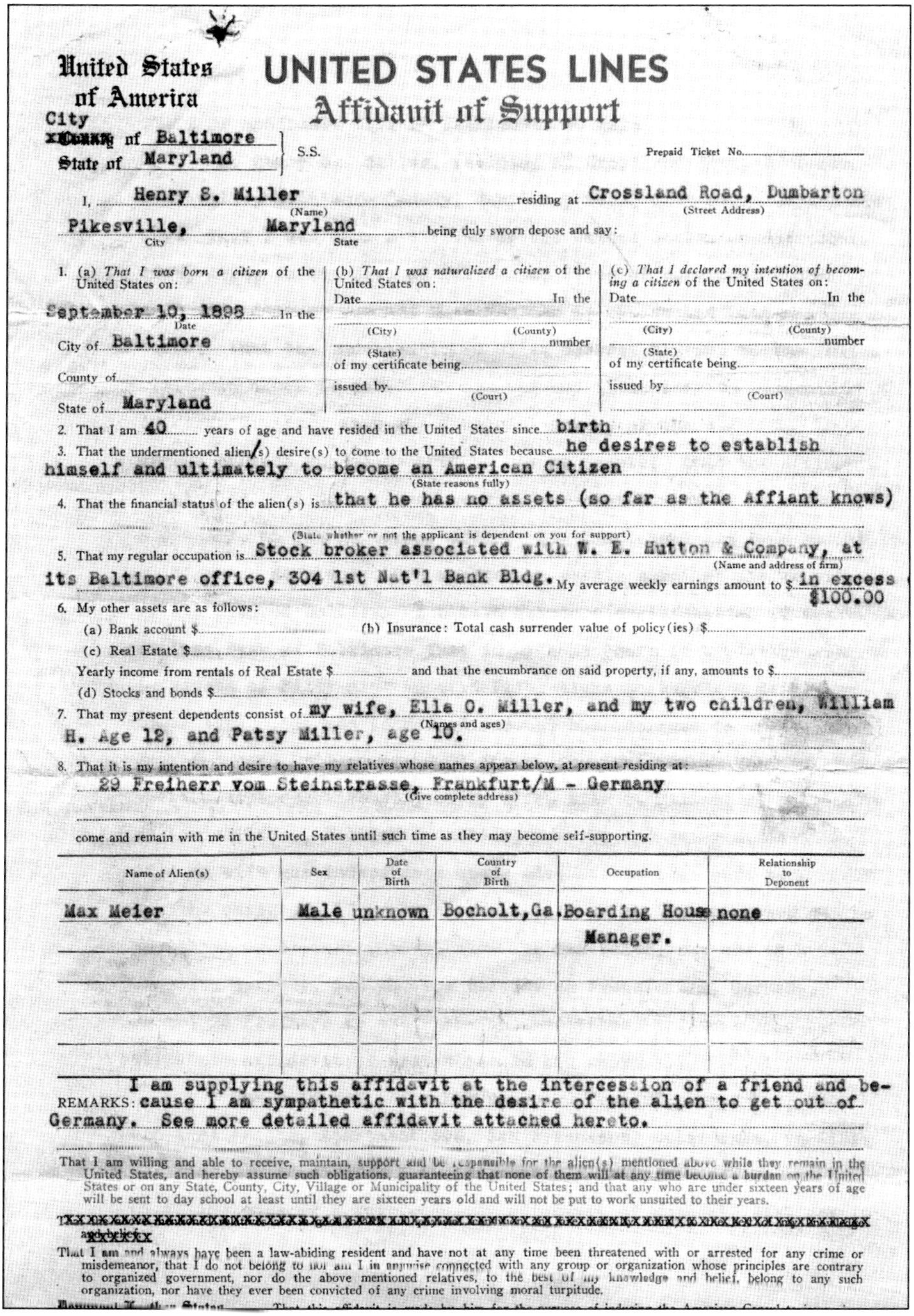
United States of America
City of Baltimore
State of Maryland } S.S.

UNITED STATES LINES
Affidavit of Support

Prepaid Ticket No.

I, Henry S. Miller (Name) residing at Crossland Road, Dumbarton (Street Address) Pikesville, (City) Maryland (State) being duly sworn depose and say:

1. (a) *That I was born a citizen* of the United States on: September 10, 1898 (Date) In the City of Baltimore County of State of Maryland

   (b) *That I was naturalized a citizen* of the United States on: Date In the (City) (County) number (State) of my certificate being issued by (Court)

   (c) *That I declared my intention of becoming a citizen* of the United States on: Date In the (City) (County) number (State) of my certificate being issued by (Court)

2. That I am 40 years of age and have resided in the United States since birth
3. That the undermentioned alien(s) desire(s) to come to the United States because he desires to establish himself and ultimately to become an American Citizen (State reasons fully)
4. That the financial status of the alien(s) is that he has no assets (so far as the affiant knows) (State whether or not the applicant is dependent on you for support)
5. That my regular occupation is Stock broker associated with W. E. Hutton & Company, at its Baltimore office, 304 1st Nat'l Bank Bldg. (Name and address of firm) My average weekly earnings amount to $ in excess $100.00
6. My other assets are as follows:
   (a) Bank account $ (b) Insurance: Total cash surrender value of policy(ies) $
   (c) Real Estate $
   Yearly income from rentals of Real Estate $ and that the encumbrance on said property, if any, amounts to $
   (d) Stocks and bonds $
7. That my present dependents consist of my wife, Ella O. Miller, and my two children, William H. Age 12, and Patsy Miller, age 10. (Names and ages)
8. That it is my intention and desire to have my relatives whose names appear below, at present residing at: 29 Freiherr vom Steinstrasse, Frankfurt/M - Germany (Give complete address)
   come and remain with me in the United States until such time as they may become self-supporting.

Name of Alien(s)	Sex	Date of Birth	Country of Birth	Occupation	Relationship to Deponent
Max Meier	Male	unknown	Bocholt, Ga.	Boarding House Manager.	none

REMARKS: I am supplying this affidavit at the intercession of a friend and because I am sympathetic with the desire of the alien to get out of Germany. See more detailed affidavit attached hereto.

That I am willing and able to receive, maintain, support and be responsible for the alien(s) mentioned above while they remain in the United States, and hereby assume such obligations, guaranteeing that none of them will at any time become a burden on the United States or on any State, County, City, Village or Municipality of the United States; and that any who are under sixteen years of age will be sent to day school at least until they are sixteen years old and will not be put to work unsuited to their years.

That I am and always have been a law-abiding resident and have not at any time been threatened with or arrested for any crime or misdemeanor, that I do not belong to nor am I in anywise connected with any group or organization whose principles are contrary to organized government, nor do the above mentioned relatives, to the best of my knowledge and belief, belong to any such organization, nor have they ever been convicted of any crime involving moral turpitude.

During the 1930s, only 38,000 people were allowed into the United States from Germany and Austria each year. Most years, this number was not even met because of the severity of the government's requirements. Refugees had to prove that they would not be a burden on the government—a difficult measure to meet. With the Great Depression raging, jobs were scarce. Most refugees did not speak English and were not allowed to bring more than 10 deutschmarks with them from Germany. Many resorted to seeking financial assistance from family members or even complete strangers abroad who would fill out affidavits of support on the refugees' behalf. (Courtesy of the JMM, 2001.74.)

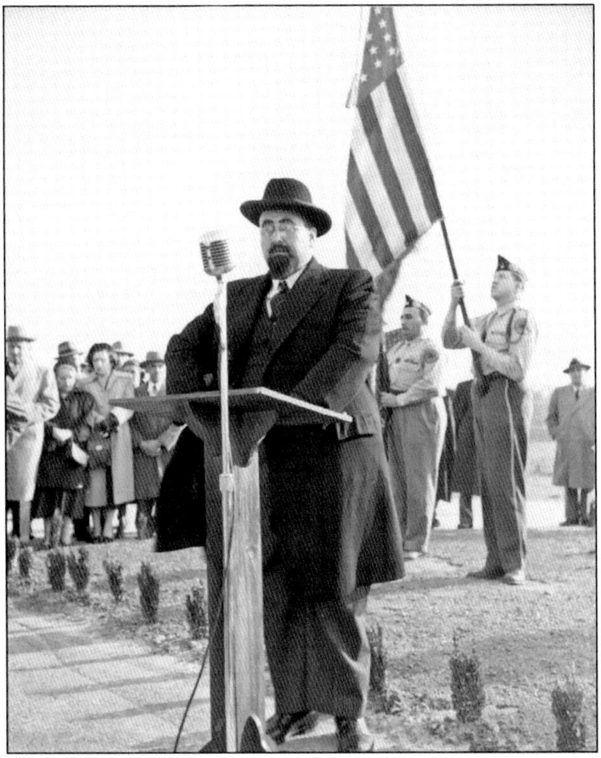

Rabbi Simon Schwab escaped Germany in 1936 and became the rabbi at Shearith Israel Congregation. He also served as the spiritual advisor to Chevra Ahavas Chesed, the mutual aid organization of Baltimore's German Jewish refugees, and taught at Ner Israel Rabbinical College. Here he speaks at the dedication of Chevra Ahavas Chesed's Holocaust Memorial in 1951. (Courtesy of the JMM, 1997.138.12.)

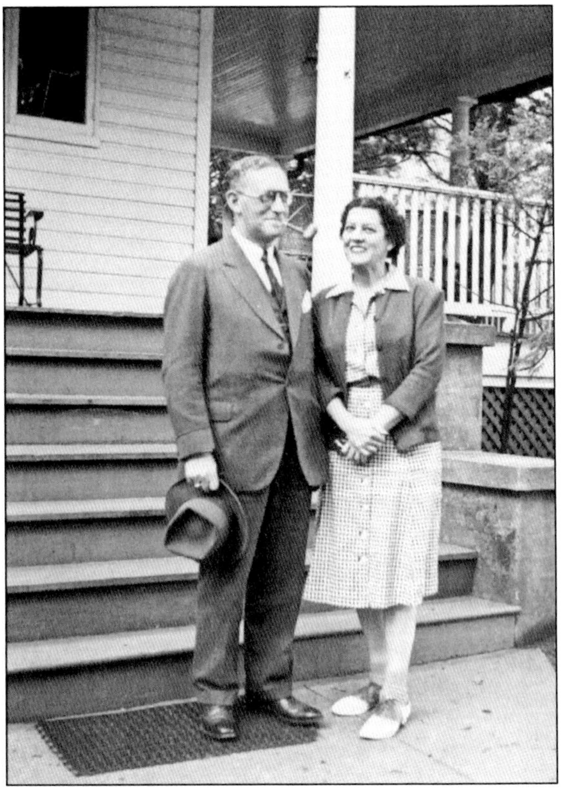

Myer and Julia Friedenwald Strauss signed more than 200 affidavits to enable Jewish refugees to immigrate to America. They assisted refugees in locating housing and jobs. Julia Strauss said, "There never were enough hours, day or night, to finish the duties and to attend to the needs of our clients." The couple adopted two refugee children after learning that their parents had perished in the Holocaust. (Courtesy of the JMM, 1984.23.)

In the 1930s, many families living under Nazism sent their children to the United States alone in a desperate attempt to save them. Herta Baitch was born in Austria. When she was seven, her mother said that she would move to a new country with a "new mother." Baitch arrived in Baltimore in 1940 and was placed with a foster family through the German Jewish Children's Aid Society. Her mother perished in the Holocaust. (Courtesy of Herta Baitch.)

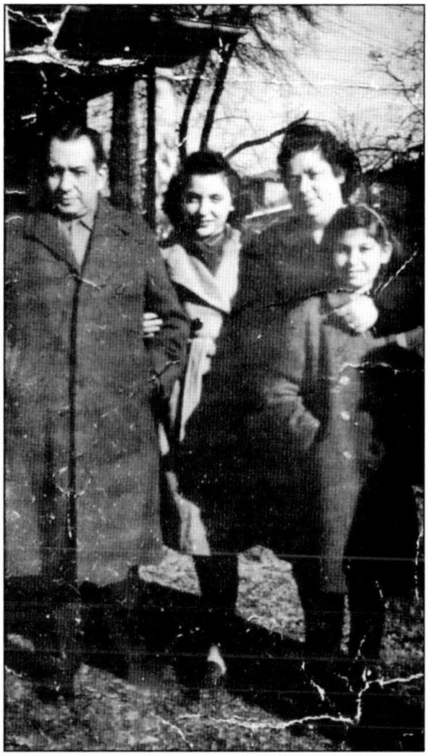

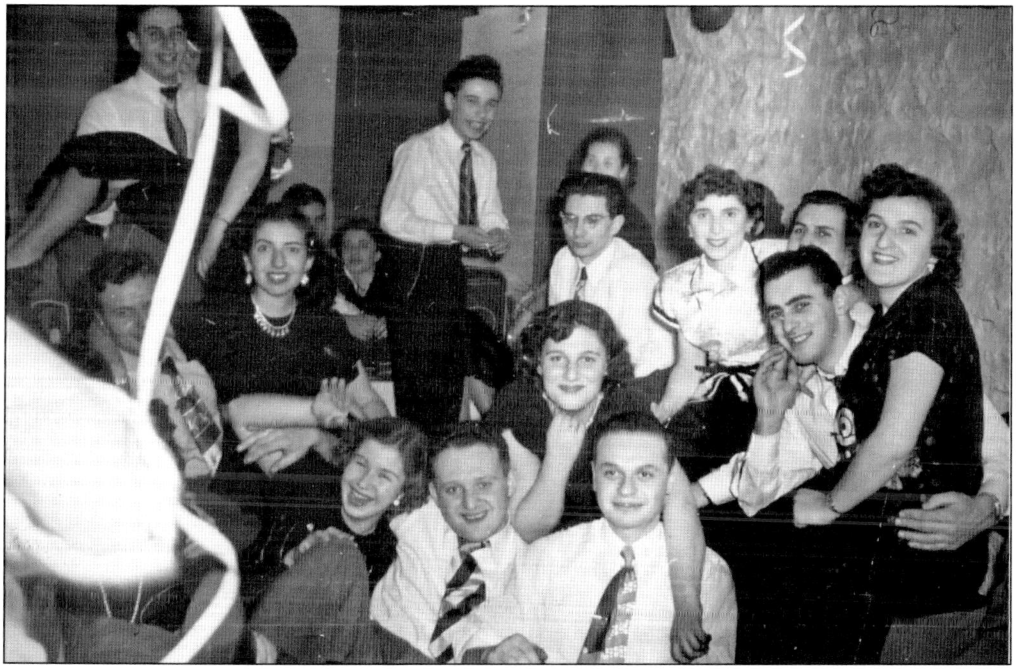

Young refugees started societies like the Tikvah Youth Group for ages 16 through 24. They rented halls and organized activities, such as swimming. Lotte Cassel, Margot (Ring) Stern, Ernest Braumann, Margie Lieberman, Marion Straus, and Gisela Miller are part of the group pictured here at a c. 1940s Tikvah Youth Group event. (Courtesy of the JMM, 2001.100.10.)

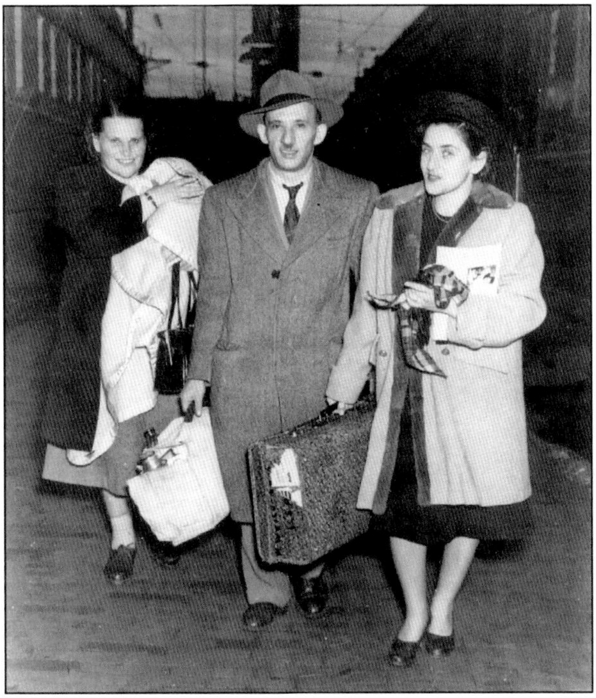

After World War II, HIAS continued to assist Jewish immigrants in Baltimore. Between 1945 and 1956, more than 1,000 Holocaust survivors and displaced persons arrived, about 20 percent of them sponsored by HIAS. In 1946, the Jewish Family and Children's Bureau Board of Directors joined with the Refugee Adjustment Committee to aid these survivors. (Courtesy of the JMM, 1995.114.7.)

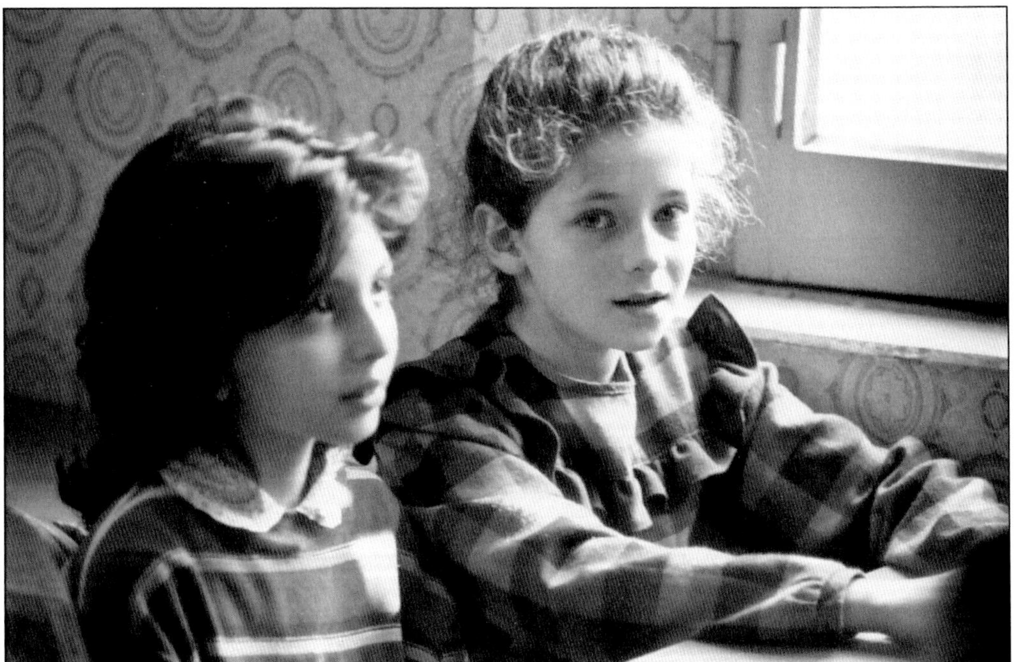

In the 1960s, HIAS assisted Czechoslovakian Jews, and during the 1970s, HIAS was instrumental in providing assistance to non-Jewish Ugandan and Vietnamese refugees, as well as Soviet Jewish émigrés. By 1980, more than 1,500 Soviet Jews had immigrated to Baltimore. During the 1970s and 1980s, HIAS supported immigrants from Iran, Romania, and Indo-China. In the 1990s, HIAS aided Jews from the former Soviet Union. (Courtesy of the JMM, 1995.189.605.)

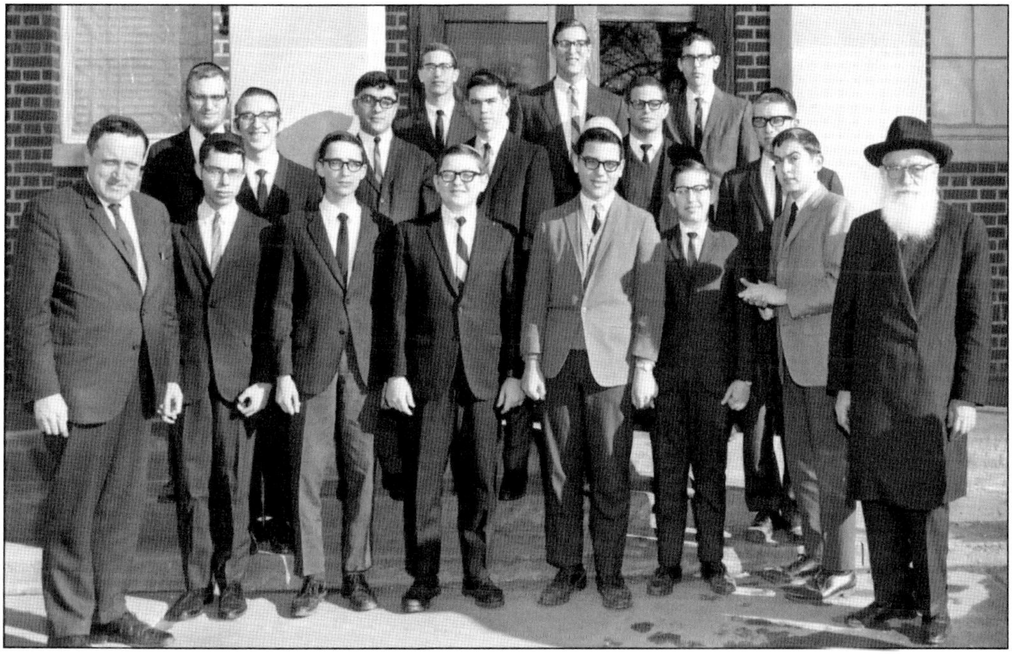

Rabbi Herman N. Neuberger (1918–2005) served as the president at Ner Israel Rabbinical College from 1940 until his death. In 1976, he began bringing young Iranian Jews to Ner Israel with the intent that they would return and share their knowledge. After the Islamic Revolution in 1979, he waived tuition for Iranian-Jewish refugees. Rabbi Neuberger was himself a refugee, having escaped Germany in 1938. Rabbi Neuberger stands on the far left. (Courtesy of the JMM, 1983.75.)

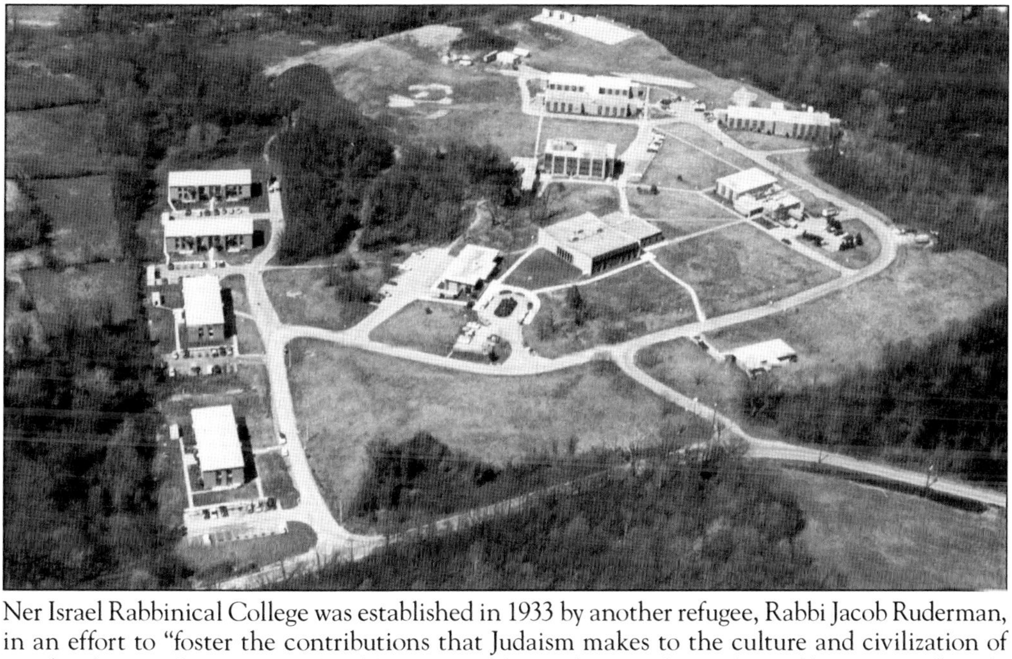

Ner Israel Rabbinical College was established in 1933 by another refugee, Rabbi Jacob Ruderman, in an effort to "foster the contributions that Judaism makes to the culture and civilization of mankind," as well as to "provide rabbis, principals, teachers, and an informed laity." Initially only 20 students attended. Today over 500 students study at the acclaimed school. (Courtesy of the JMM, 1983.75.3.)

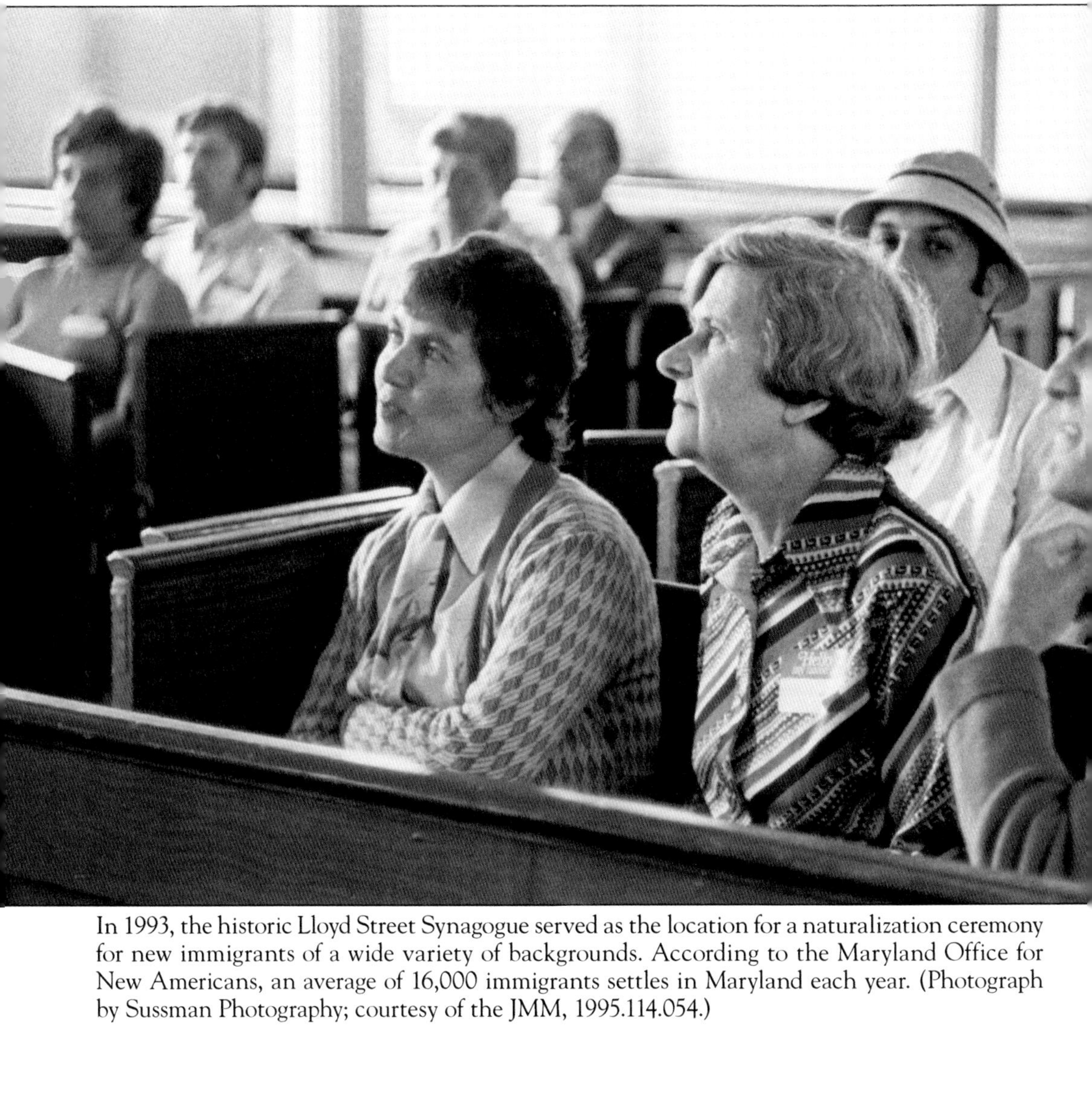

In 1993, the historic Lloyd Street Synagogue served as the location for a naturalization ceremony for new immigrants of a wide variety of backgrounds. According to the Maryland Office for New Americans, an average of 16,000 immigrants settles in Maryland each year. (Photograph by Sussman Photography; courtesy of the JMM, 1995.114.054.)

Three

From Little Jerusalem to Corned Beef Row

Jewish Communities in the City of Neighborhoods

The 1830 census reveals that approximately 30 Jewish families were spread out across 10 of the city's 12 wards. One small concentration of German Jewish immigrants lived around Fells Point, while some wealthier, native-born Jews lived along North Charles Street. As more Jews moved into the city, they tended to live close to their work. In addition to the port at Fells Point, many families also started to cluster around Centre Market downtown.

Early congregations moved several times in an attempt to find the best location to serve their dispersed flock. Eventually, many of them settled in East Baltimore between Fells Point and Centre Market. Once families had established themselves economically, they began to move nearer to their respective synagogues. When the surge of East European immigrants flooded into Baltimore at the dawn of the 20th century, many moved into this area. By the early 1900s, East Baltimore was the center of Jewish life in Baltimore.

Besides East Baltimore, Jews created additional communities in the "City of Neighborhoods." At the same time that Locust Point developed into an important terminal, so did the surrounding neighborhoods in South Baltimore. However, Jews had lived in the area for over a generation. Additionally, a contingent of families moved into Southwest Baltimore.

By the beginning of the 20th century, all of the German Jewish synagogues had followed their congregants to affluent Eutaw Place and surrounding neighborhoods. Within a few decades, the Eastern European families joined the trek to northwest Baltimore.

Today the majority of Baltimore's Jews live around Upper Park Heights Avenue. Many are moving farther into the suburbs, including Pikesville and Owings Mills.

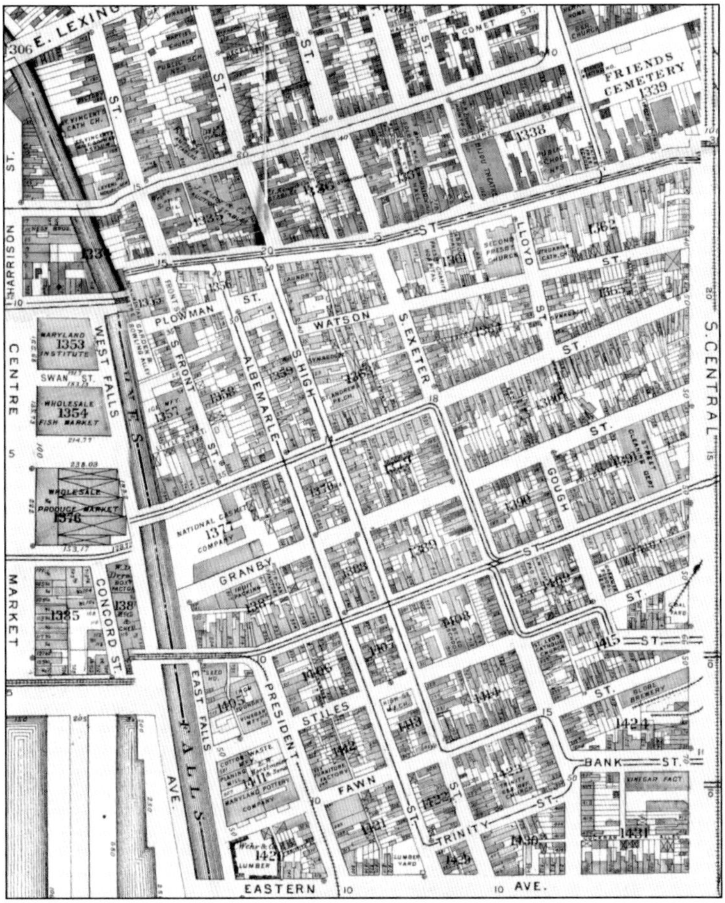

By the mid-19th century, small concentrations of German Jews had settled in Fells Point and Centre Market. In a move to cater to both crowds, Baltimore Hebrew Congregation erected the first synagogue in-between the two neighborhoods in 1845 in East Baltimore. As Baltimore's Jews became more economically established, some began to move closer to their synagogues, though they remained a minority in the neighborhood until the late 19th century. (Courtesy of the JMM Library.)

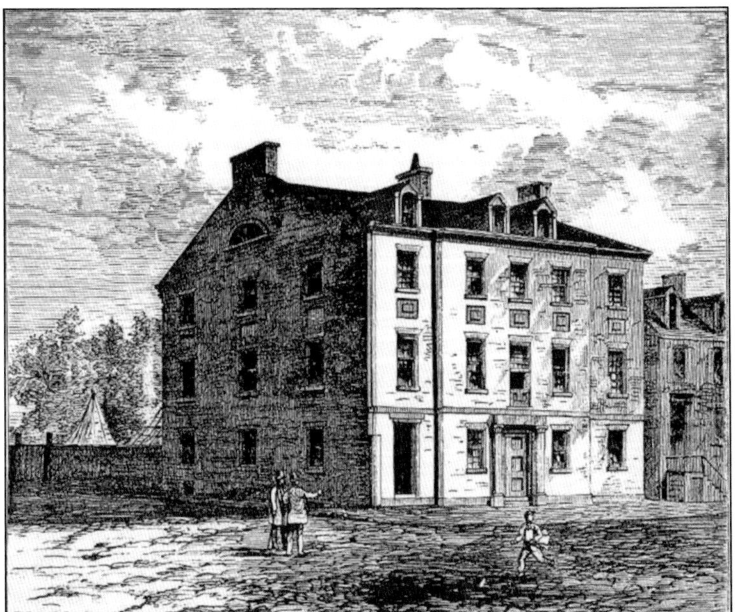

Named for Charles Carroll, a signer of the Declaration of Independence, the c. 1811 Carroll Mansion has stood through all the changes in East Baltimore. In 1855, the Sisters of Mercy purchased the house and rented it to Jewish immigrants. In 1914, the city turned the mansion into a vocational school and later a recreation center. Today it functions as a historic house. (Courtesy of Carroll Museums, Inc.)

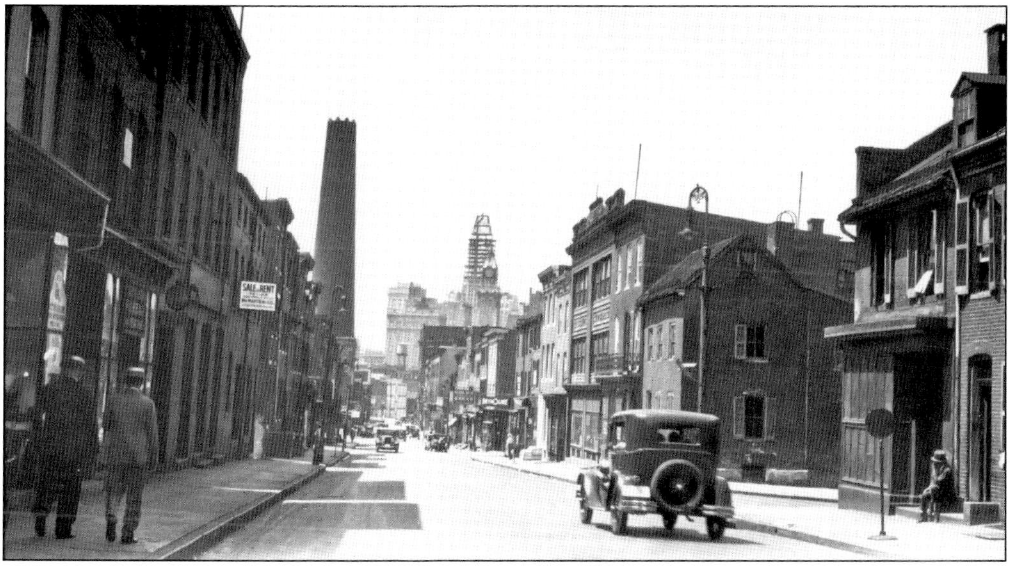

The Jewish neighborhood in East Baltimore was a vibrant mix of row houses, family-owned stores, organizations, bathhouses, and theaters. This microcosm of city life covered less than 3 square miles, bounded by Broadway on the east, the Fallsway on the west, Pratt Street on the south, and Orleans Street on the north. This photograph of Fayette Street in 1926 was taken by F. L. Bafford. (Courtesy of the JMM, 1990.112.1a-b.)

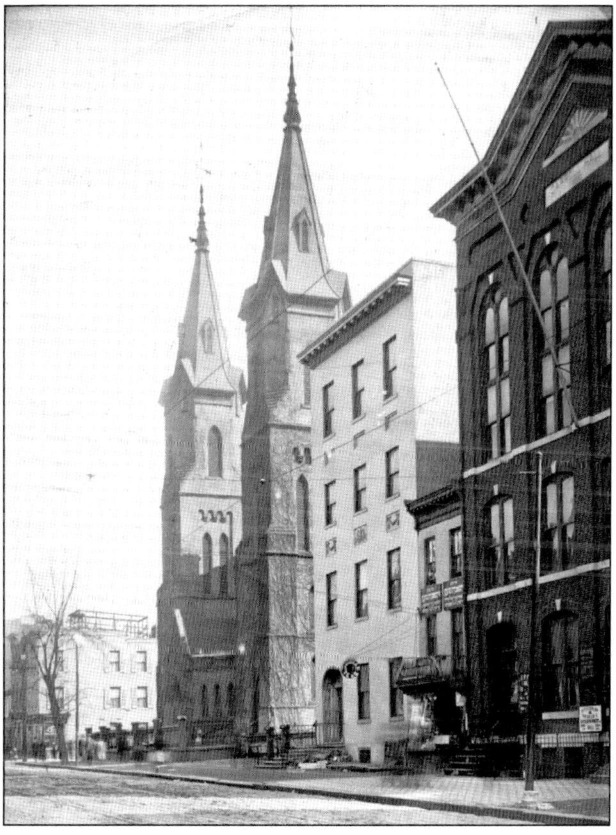

According to the *American Jewish Yearbook*, approximately 25,000 Jews lived in Baltimore in 1905, mainly concentrated in East Baltimore. This photograph of Baltimore Street was taken in 1909. (Courtesy of the JMM, 1985.90.14.)

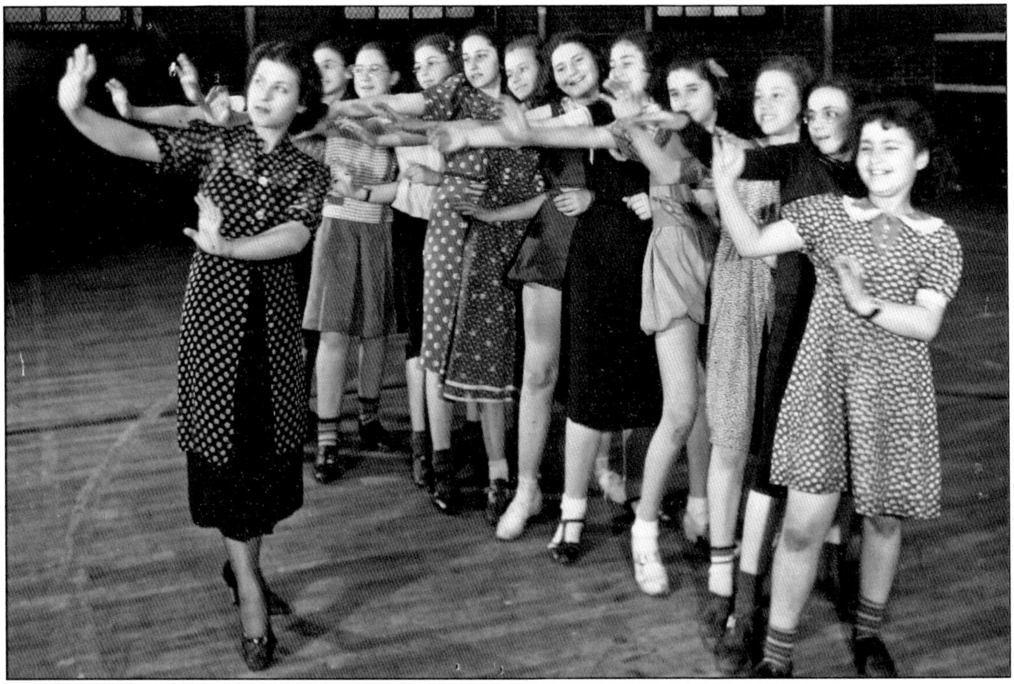

The Jewish Education Alliance (JEA) first stood at 1216 East Baltimore Street. Besides English classes, the JEA also offered a wealth of activities for neighborhood children, including basketball and dance classes. The JEA offered other amenities as well. "Practically all of my siblings went to the JEA," remembered Jacob Glushakow. "My brothers and I would go there to shower rather than go to the *shvitzbad* (public baths)." (Courtesy of the JMM, (above) 1992.231.79; (below) 1992.231.140.)

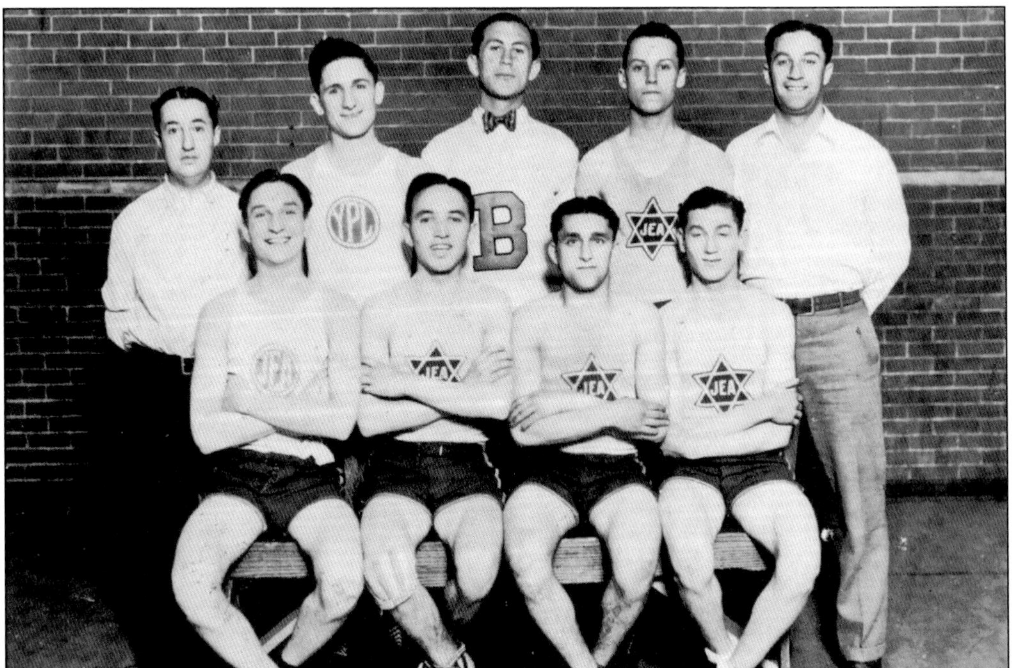

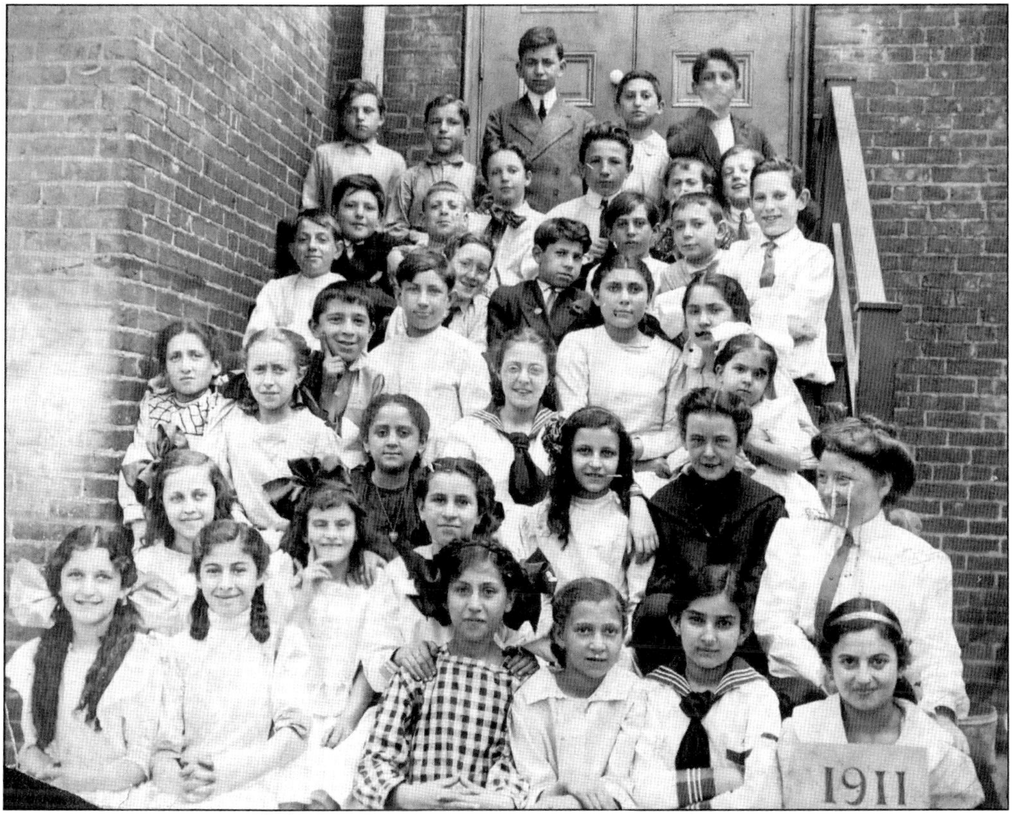

Public School No. 93 was located at Baltimore and Aisquith Streets. Also known as the German-English School, it is shown here in 1911. The German orphan asylum functioned only three blocks away. Isidor Terrell remembered, "Each day, you'd see about 100 children parading down Aisquith Street from the orphanage to the school. They'd walk two by two. Their faces were sparkling clean, their clothes neat." (Courtesy of the JMM, 1987.209.2.)

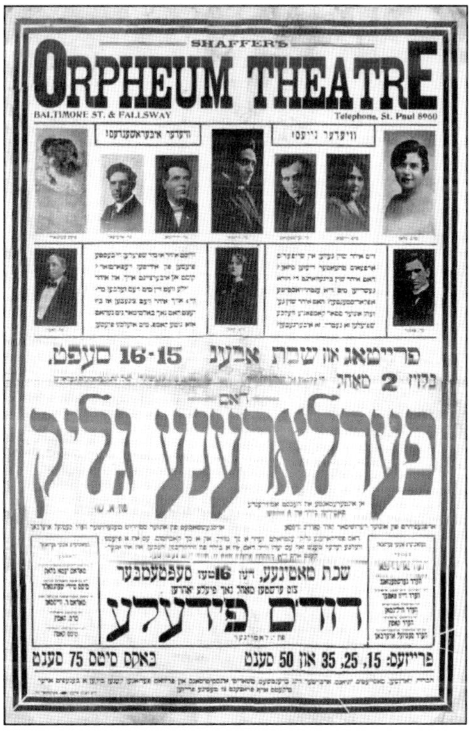

Yiddish theaters like the Orpheum were popular in East Baltimore in the early 20th century. Actress Bessie Baumfeld Thomashefsky (1873–1962) met her future husband, Boris Thomashefsky (1868–1939), when she went backstage after one of his shows, reportedly to meet the beautiful "actress" who had performed—only to discover that it was Boris! They performed across the country until divorcing in 1912. She then started a rival theater company. (Courtesy of the JMM, K2000.18.2.)

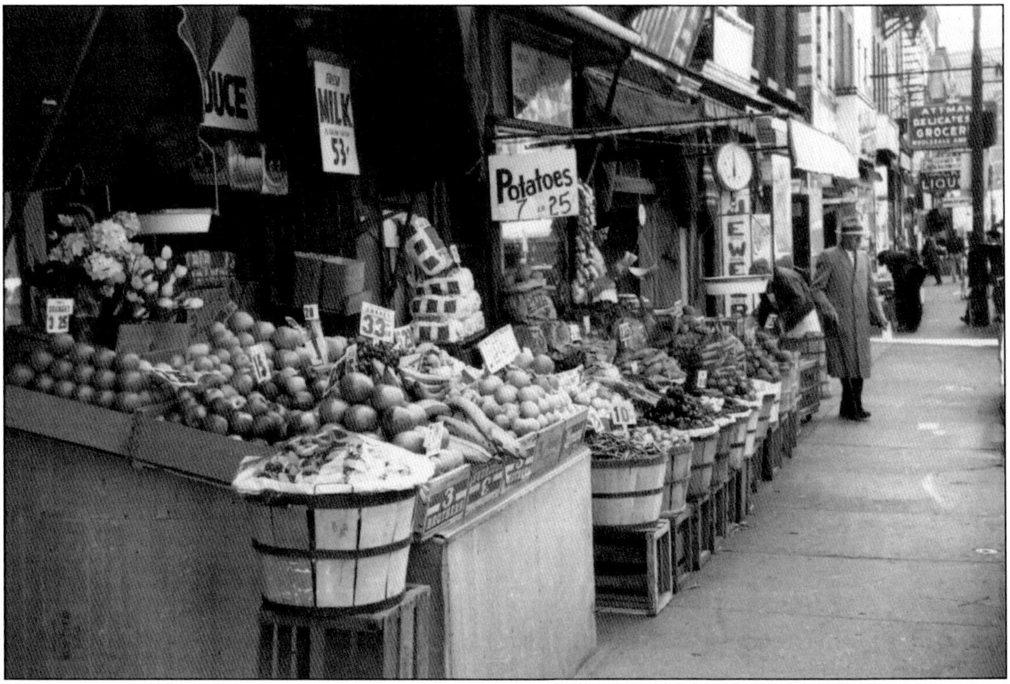

Lombard Street functioned as the commercial artery of East Baltimore. Customers could find anything in its shops. Sol Tulkoff, whose family owns Tulkoff's Products, Inc. (pictured above in 1963), described Lombard Street nostalgically: "The aroma of pickling spices, aroma of fresh grated horseradish, fruit aromas: oranges, melons, while all the wonderful aromas still linger in the memories of former visitors and customers." The bottom photograph shows Lombard Street from Tulkoff's around 1960. (Above, photograph by John McGrain; both, courtesy of the JMM, (above) 1995.187.20; (below) 1990.83.1.)

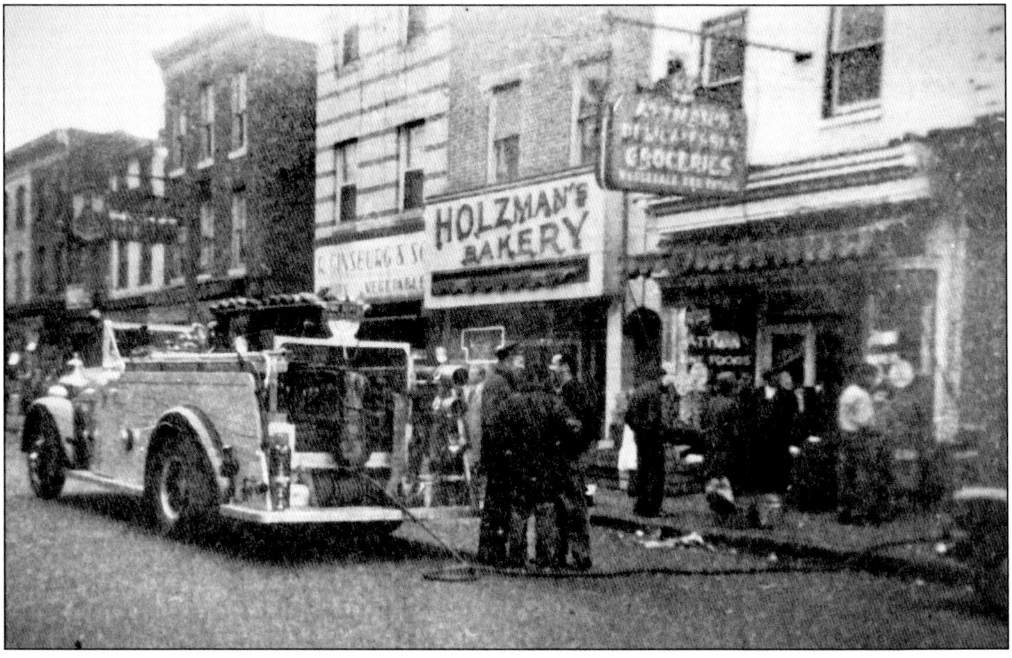

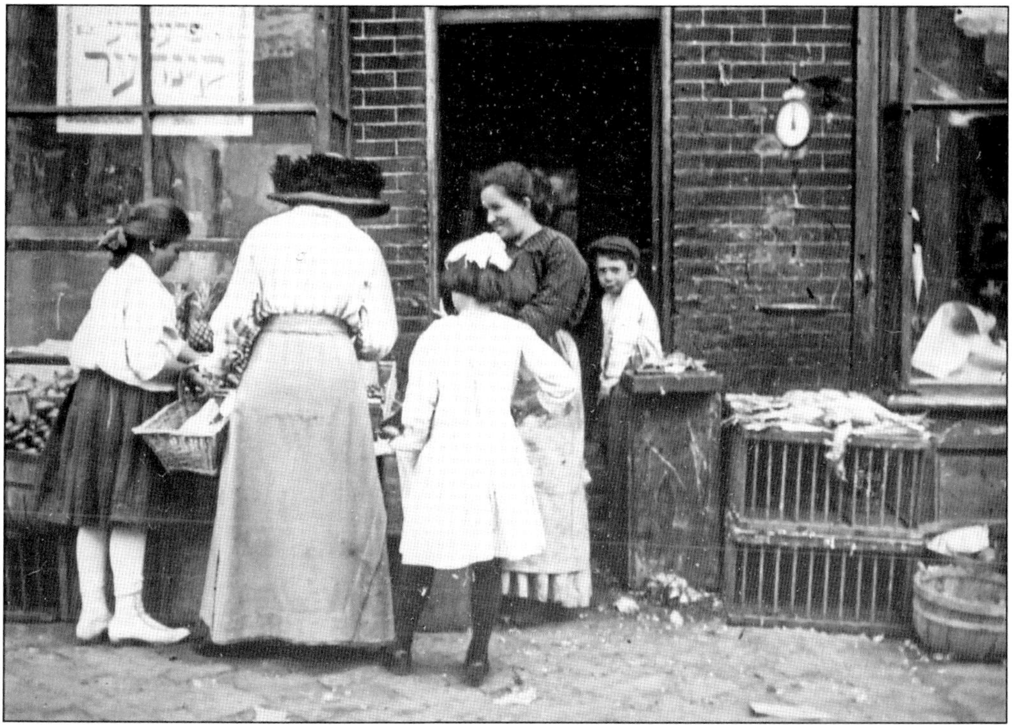

These images of Lombard Street and the Yiddish market date to the late 19th century. (Courtesy of the JMM and the Ross J. Kelbaugh Collection, (above) 1988.226.3a, (below) 1988.226.5a.)

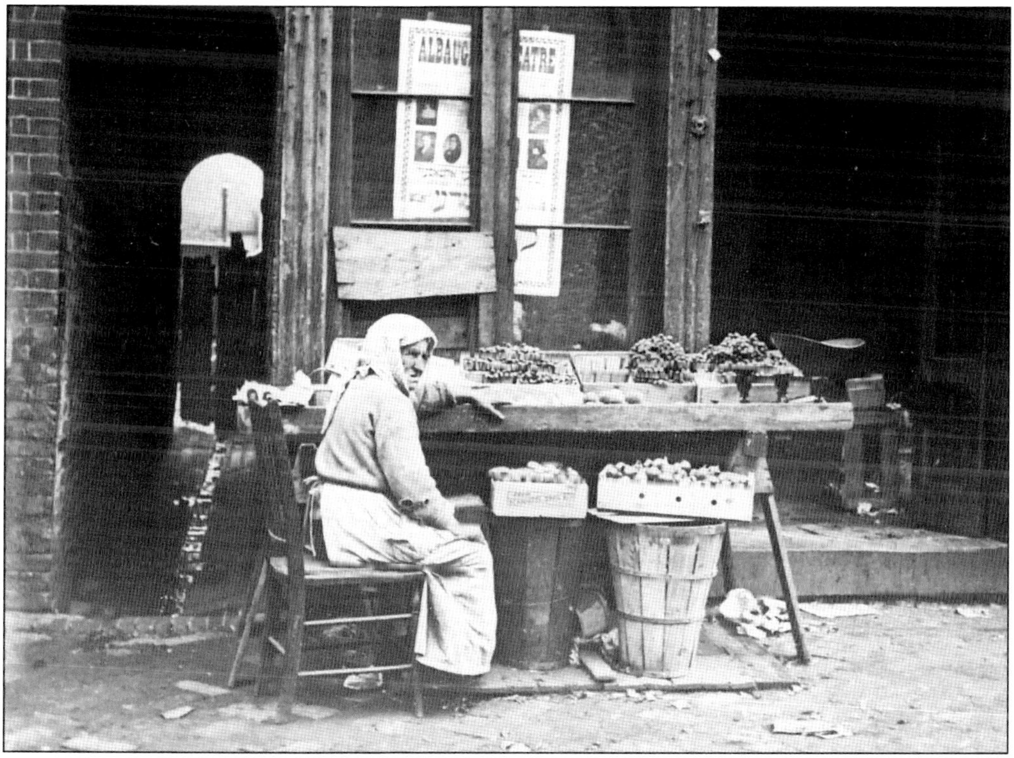

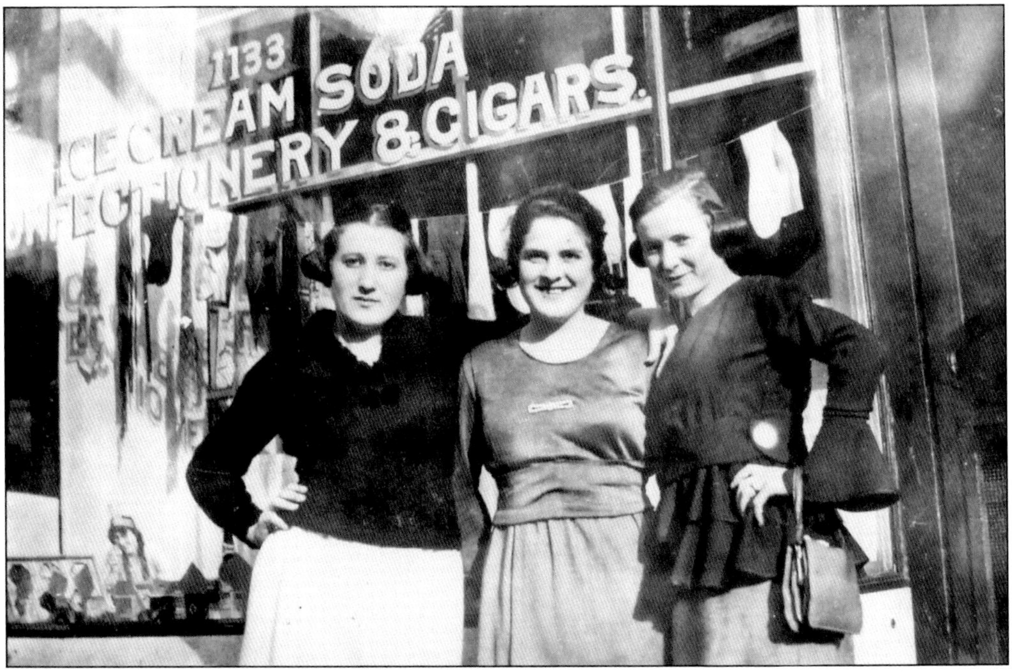

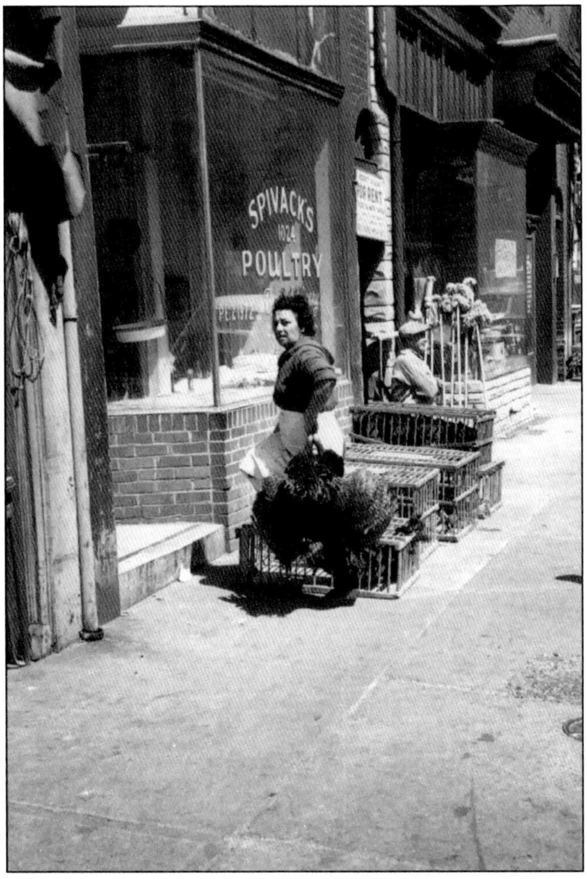

"And of course all the chicken stores had chicken coops on [Lombard] street," recalled Paul Wartzman. "People would come down on Saturday night; that was the big shopping night. The chicken coops were out on the street and they'd come down and buy the chickens. And of course up the street . . . there was a *schochet* [a slaughterer who follows Jewish dietary laws]. . . . In any event, Briney had her store and she would sit. She was a big, heavy set woman and her apron, I'll never forget it, was always full of blood, I guess from the chicken. And she would sit on coops sometimes and she had a stoop also she would sit on." (Photographs by John McGrain, 1963; courtesy of the JMM, (above) 1989.213.1a, (left) 1995.187.13.)

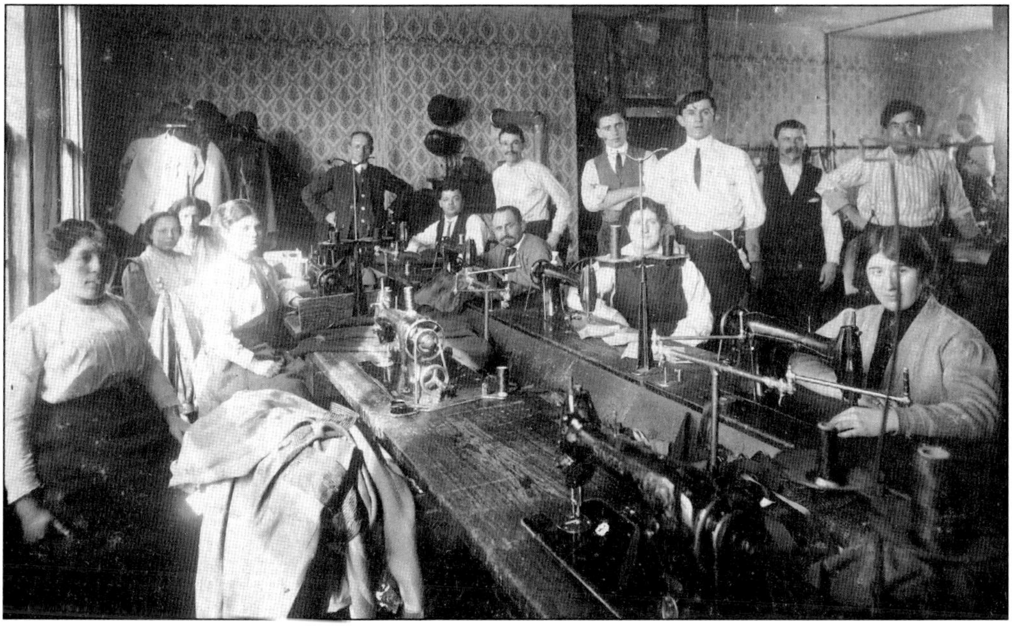

Jacob Goldberg had a factory on Fayette Street in the early 1900s. Eva Cohen is at the machine in the lower left-hand corner. In 1901, more than 400 sweatshops operated in East Baltimore. Many functioned in the same crowded apartments where multigenerational families lived. These sweatshops produced more than half the clothing manufactured in Baltimore. (Courtesy of the JMM, 1990.69.2.)

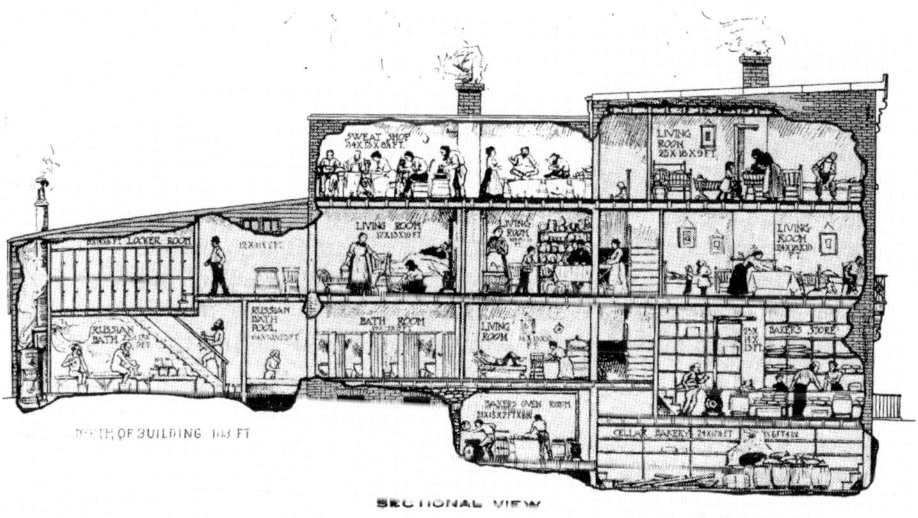

The Changing Location of the Clothing Industry 407

Sectional View of Building containing Sweatshop. **Source: B.I.S., 1903.**

While the row houses in East Baltimore originally started off as single-family homes, many were transformed into multiuse buildings by the beginning of the 20th century. This cross-section of a 1903 tenement includes a sweatshop, a Russian bath, a bakery, and five apartments. (Courtesy of the Maryland Bureau of Industrial Statistics.)

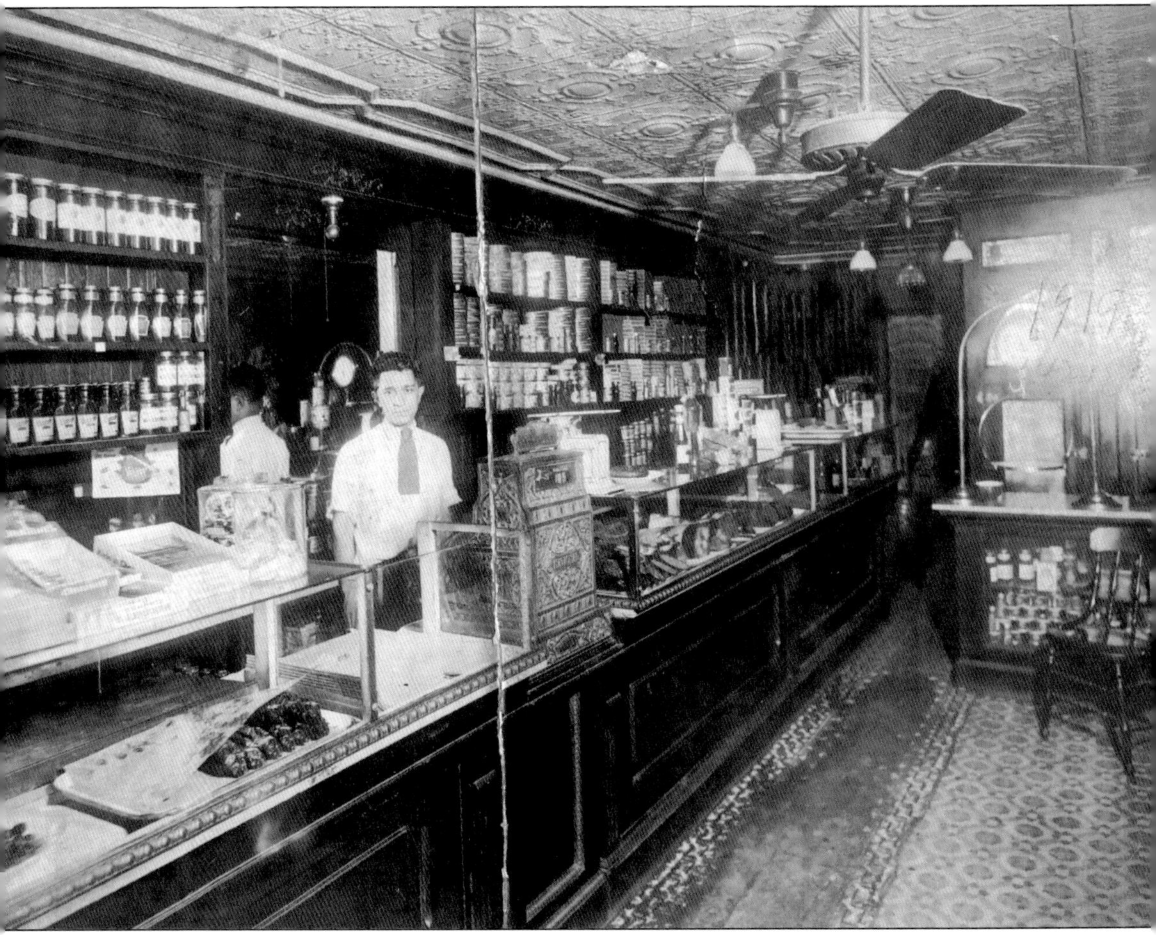

In this 1919 photograph, Harry Cohen stands in the delicatessen he owned on Fayette Street. In its heyday in the 1920s and 1930s, East Baltimore was alive with many independent and family-run stores. Over time, the neighborhood changed, and "everything started moving northwest," in the words of Seymour Attman, late owner of Attman's Delicatessen on Lombard Street. Before World War II, there had been a "conglomeration of people on the street. Plus, you had your peddlers, pushcarts, trucks on the streets, and food stores had their stalls out front." By the 1940s, more Jews joined the burgeoning middle class and moved out of East Baltimore as more affordable housing opened in the suburbs. Meanwhile, supermarkets changed people's shopping habits. Lombard Street gradually lost business. Today only three delis remain on the block of Lombard, which was renamed "Corned Beef Row" in the 1970s. (Courtesy of the JMM, 1988.132.1.)

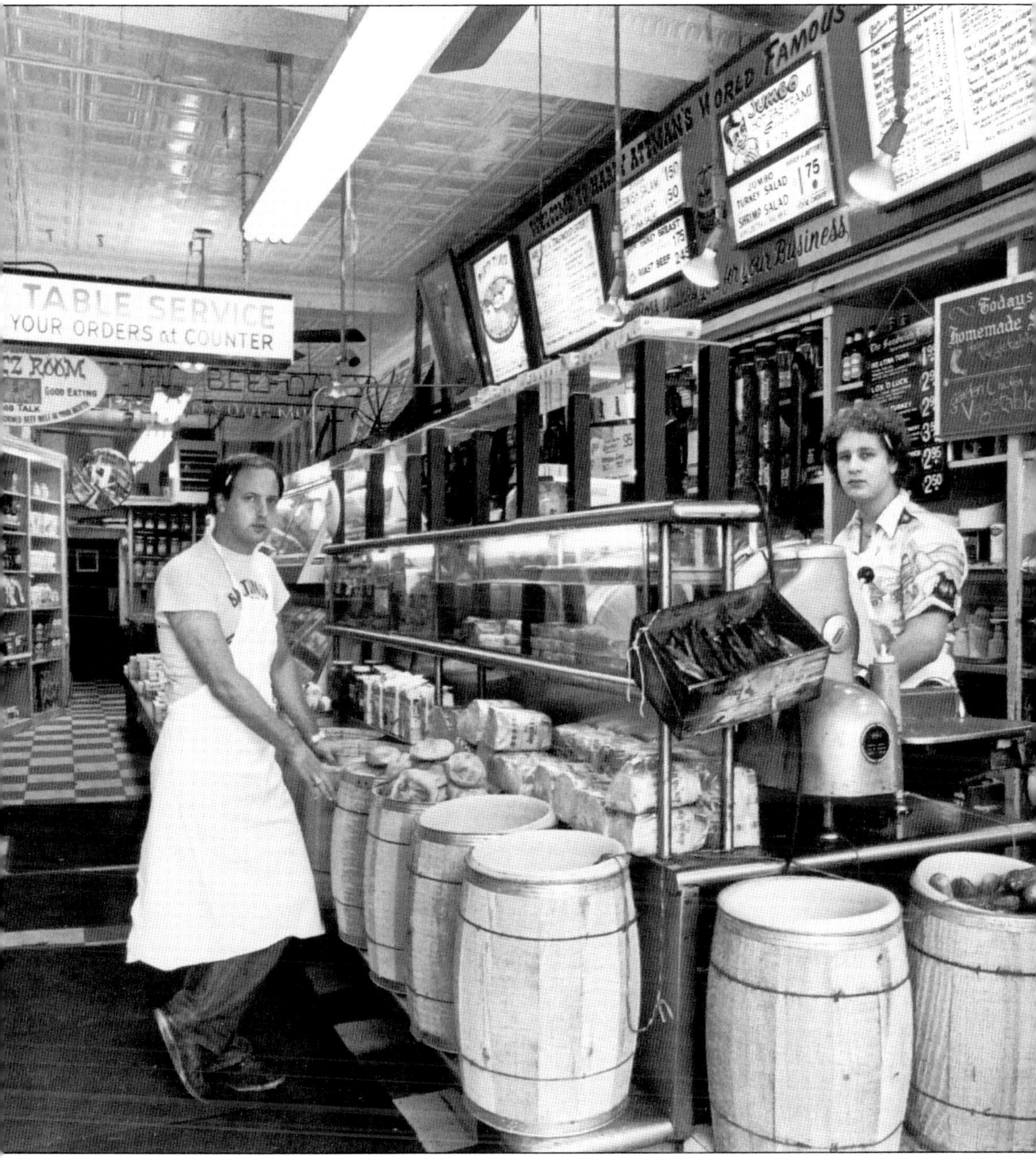

Attman's Delicatessen is one of the few vestiges of old East Baltimore. Founded in 1915 by Russian immigrant Harry Attman, the deli is still very much alive with the flavor of the groceries, shops, and restaurants that once lined Lombard Street. The menu is full of classics: hot corned beef, roast brisket, pastrami, pickles, and the "Baltimore-style" hot dog, which is wrapped in bologna in a seeded bun. The family business has passed from father to son for three generations and continues to flourish today. This photograph of Attman's interior was taken by Elinor B. Cahn in 1984. (Courtesy of the JMM, 1985.31.2.)

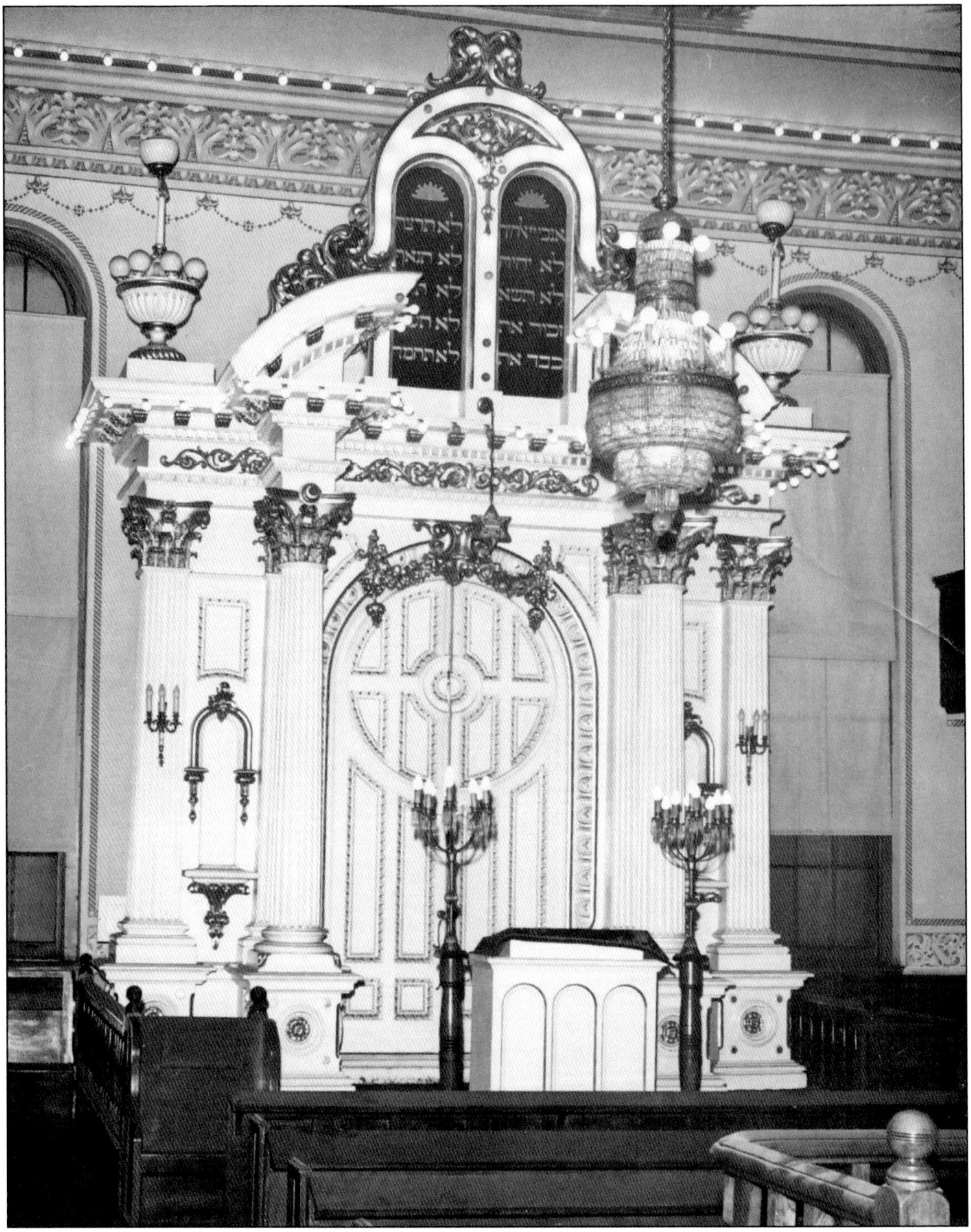

In the early 20th century, the heaviest concentration of Jews lived in East Baltimore. However, Jewish families lived across the city, including South Baltimore, not far from Locust Point. This Torah Ark was originally constructed for the South Baltimore synagogue Oheb Shalom around 1872. When Temple Oheb Shalom moved uptown in 1894, the Ark was transferred to another South Baltimore congregation, Anshe Emunah Congregation. Anshe Emunah had been chartered in 1887 and was originally located at 313 South Hanover Street before moving down the block to 513–519 South Hanover. In 1955, it moved uptown and merged with Liberty Jewish Center. (Photograph by Jerry Esterson; courtesy of the JMM, 1992.243.1.)

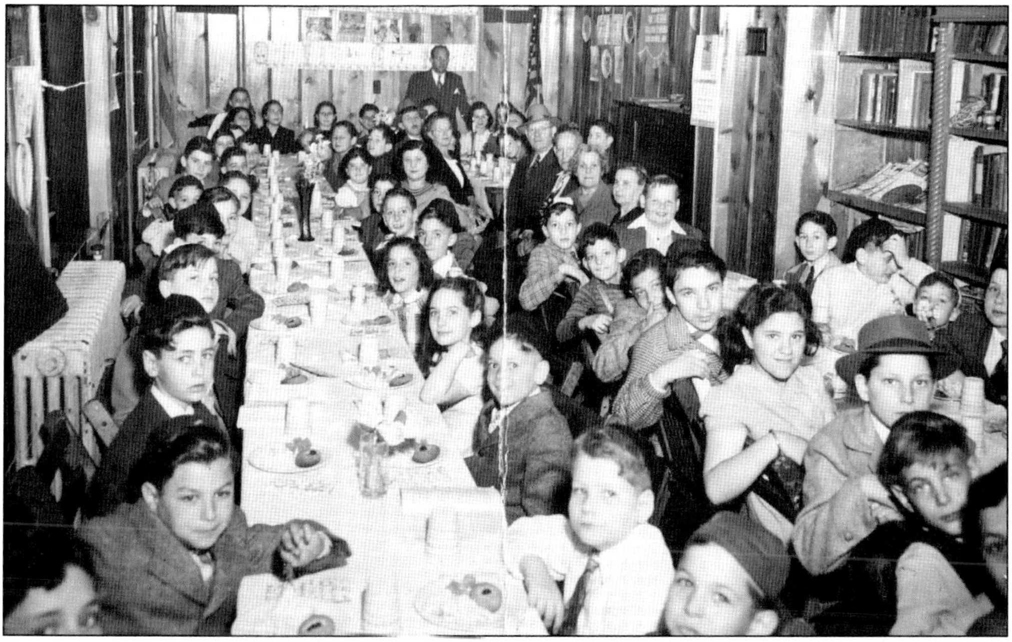

Southwest Talmud Torah holds a Passover Seder in 1944. Standing in the back of the photograph is Simon Bugatah, the principal at Southwest Talmud Torah. Jews in southwest Baltimore nicknamed their community "Little Jerusalem." (Courtesy of the JMM, 1991.36.8.)

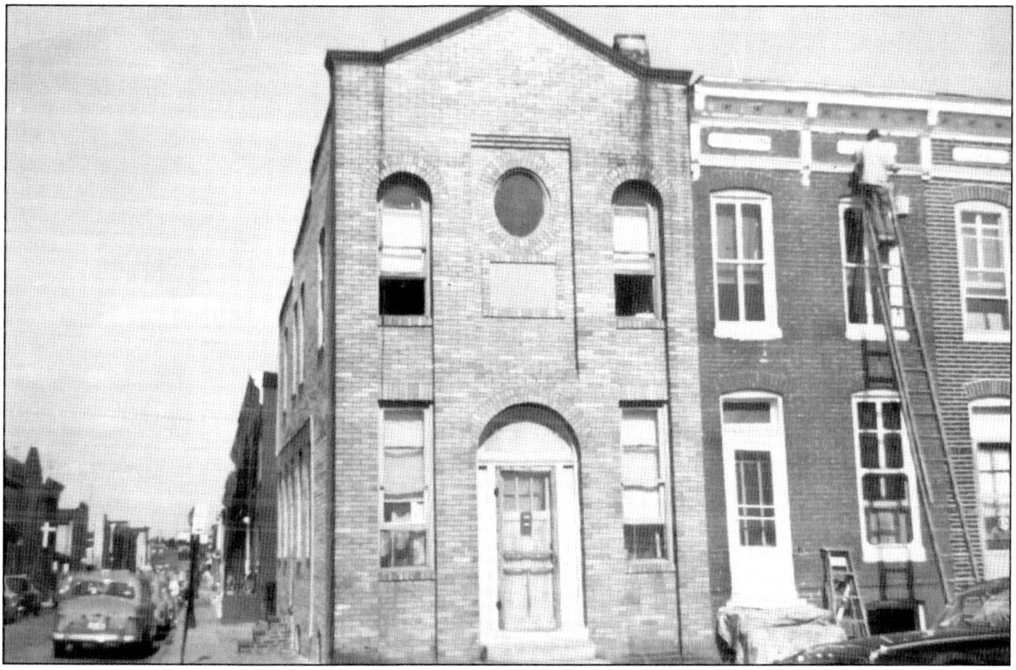

Ahavas Achim Congregation was founded in the early 1900s at 652 Lombard Street before moving to 427 Pulaski Highway, also in southwest Baltimore. In 1935, Ahavas Achim merged with another southwest congregation, Moses Montefiore Emunath Israel, which had been incorporated in 1888 and stood at 535 Smallwood Street. (Photograph by Menasha Katz; courtesy of the JMM, 1987.137.54.)

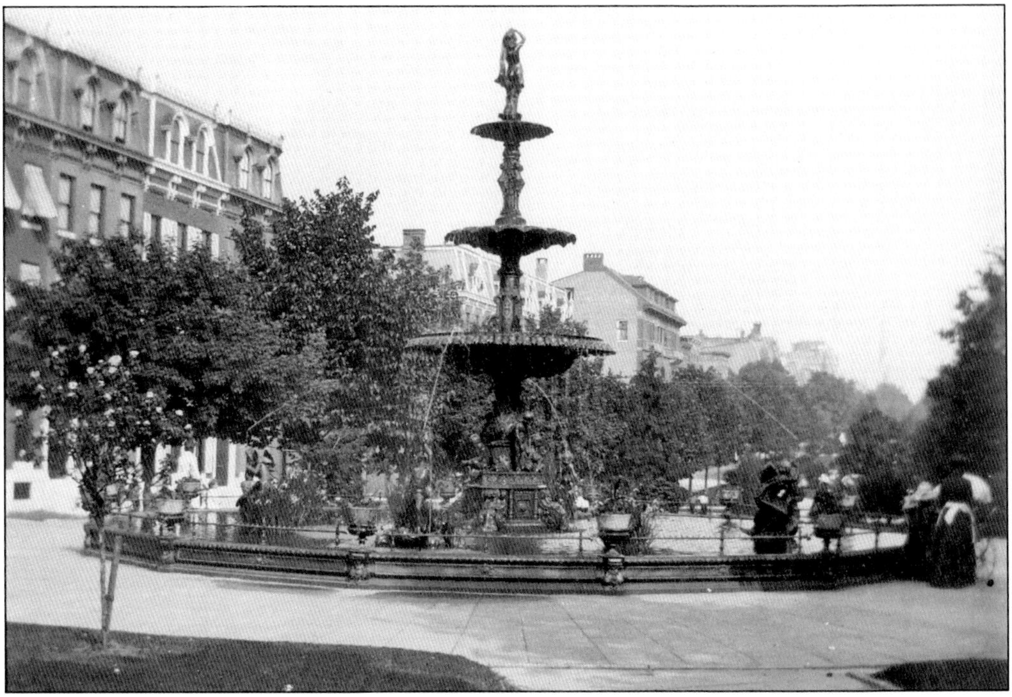

As Jews began to prosper, many left the crowded tenements of east and southwest Baltimore for the greener pastures of the northwest neighborhoods. Many German Jewish families purchased magnificent mansions on the grand, tree-lined boulevard of Eutaw Place. (Both, courtesy of the EPFL.)

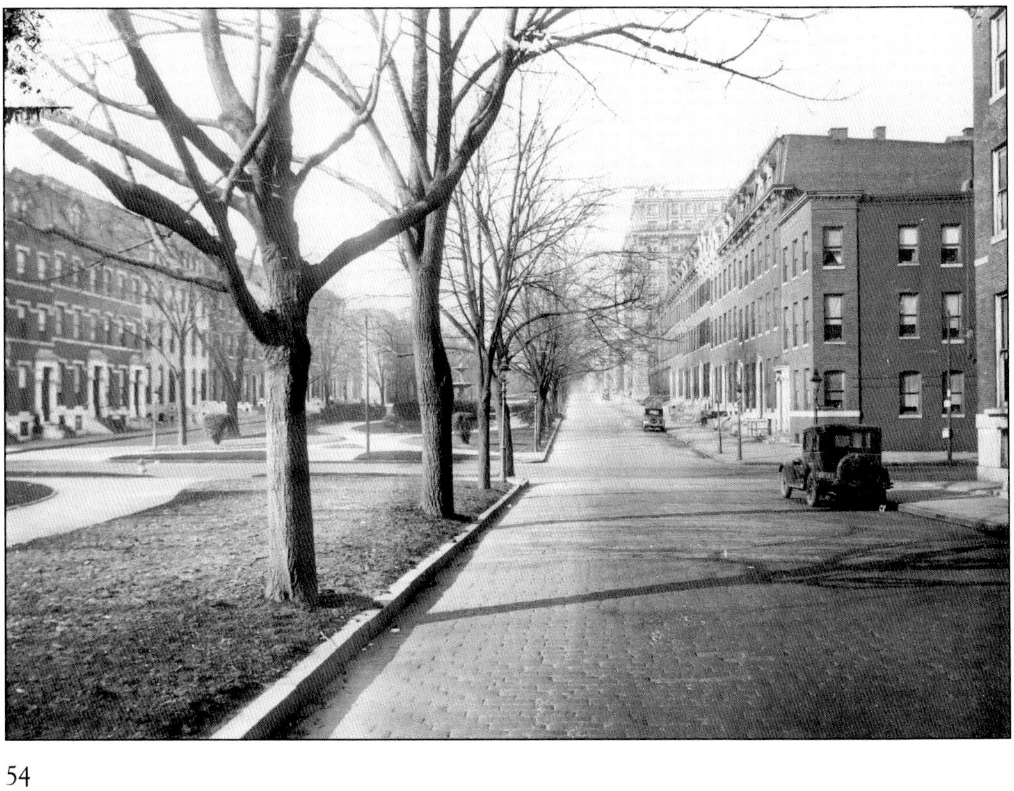

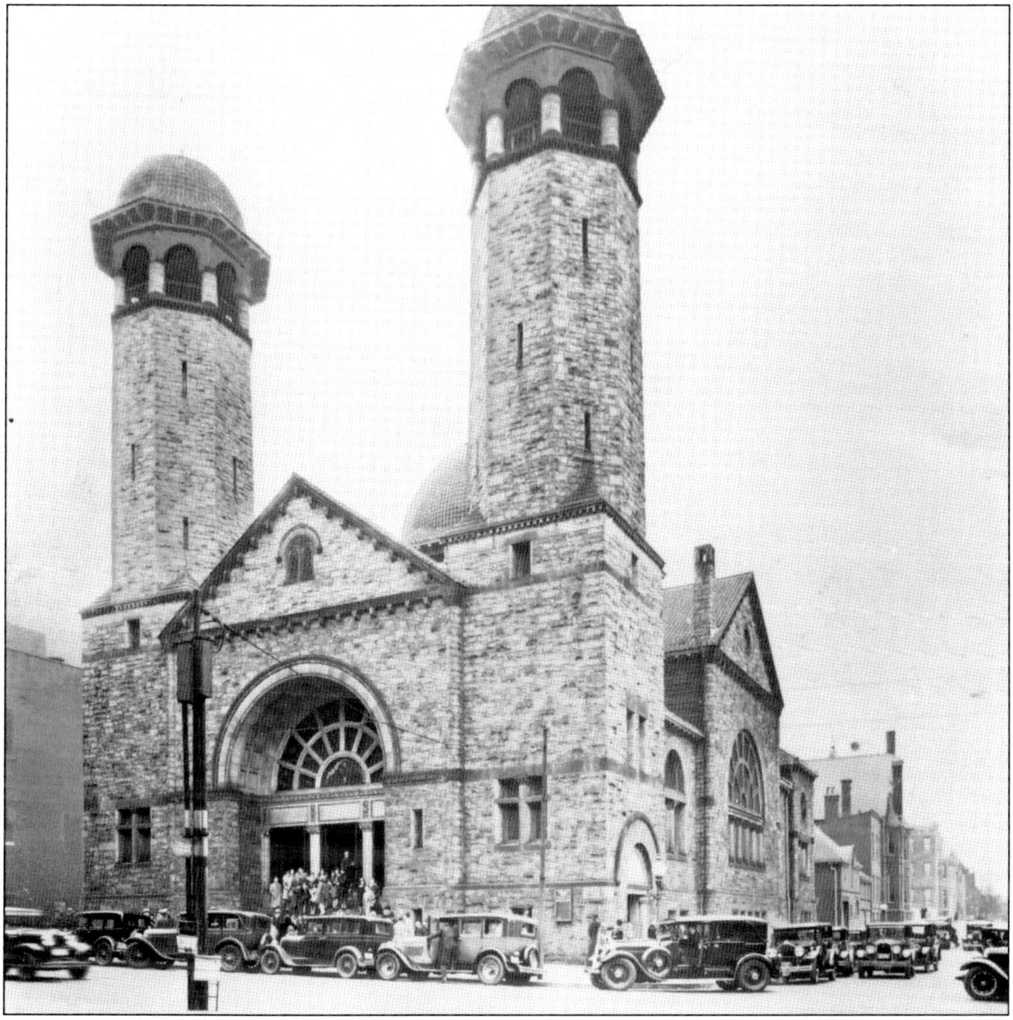

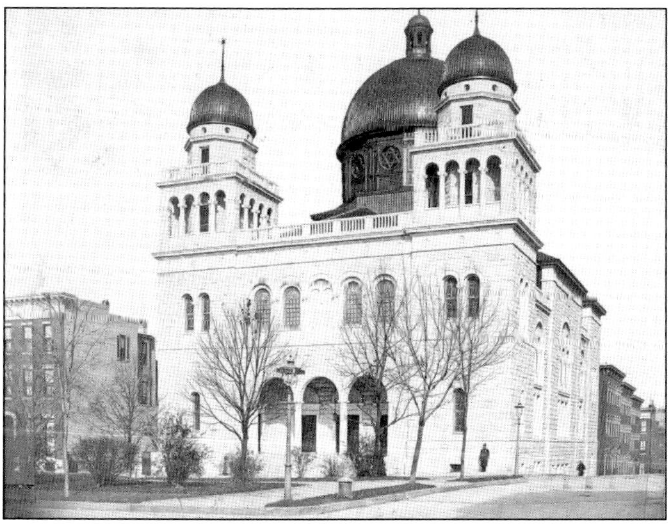

By 1905, the five oldest German Jewish synagogues had moved uptown, near Eutaw Place, including Baltimore Hebrew Congregation and Temple Oheb Shalom. (Courtesy of the JMM, (above) 1989.94.5a, (below) 1992.242.6.53.)

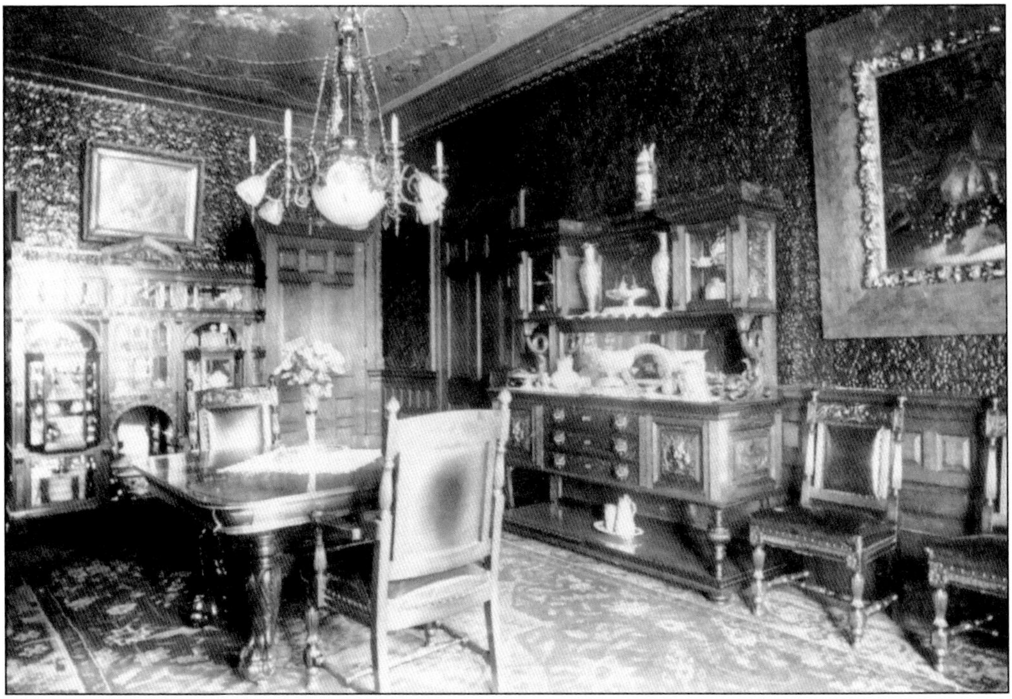

In this 1910s photograph, David and Ella Gutman Hutzler's Eutaw Place dining room features a china cabinet that replicated the facade of the family's Hutzler's "Palace" department store. The china cabinet was a present for their 15th wedding anniversary. (Courtesy of the JMM, 1991.24.1a.)

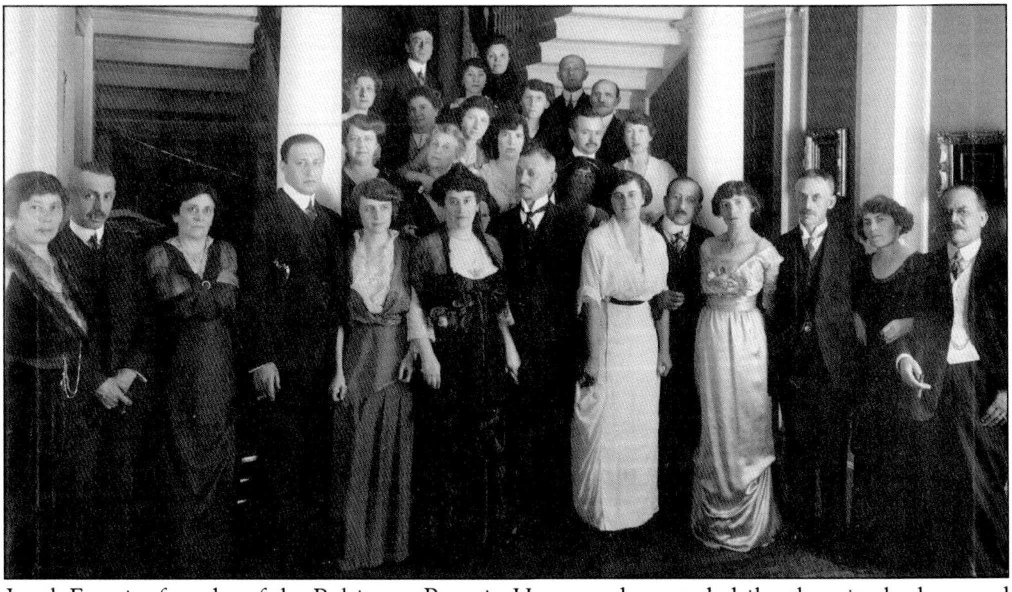

Jacob Epstein, founder of the Baltimore Bargain House and a noted philanthropist, had a grand home at Eutaw Place near Druid Hill Park. Among those pictured in this c. 1910 photograph are (first row, beginning fourth from left) A. Ray Katz; Ethel (Epstein) Katz; Lena Weinberg, Jacob Epstein, Marian (Epstein) Lansburgh, and Sidney Lansburgh. Also shown are Laura Epstein, Nathan Epstein, Adele Lansburgh, Irma Lansburg, and Rose (Epstein) Amram. Others are unidentified. (Courtesy of the JMM, 2004.78.67.)

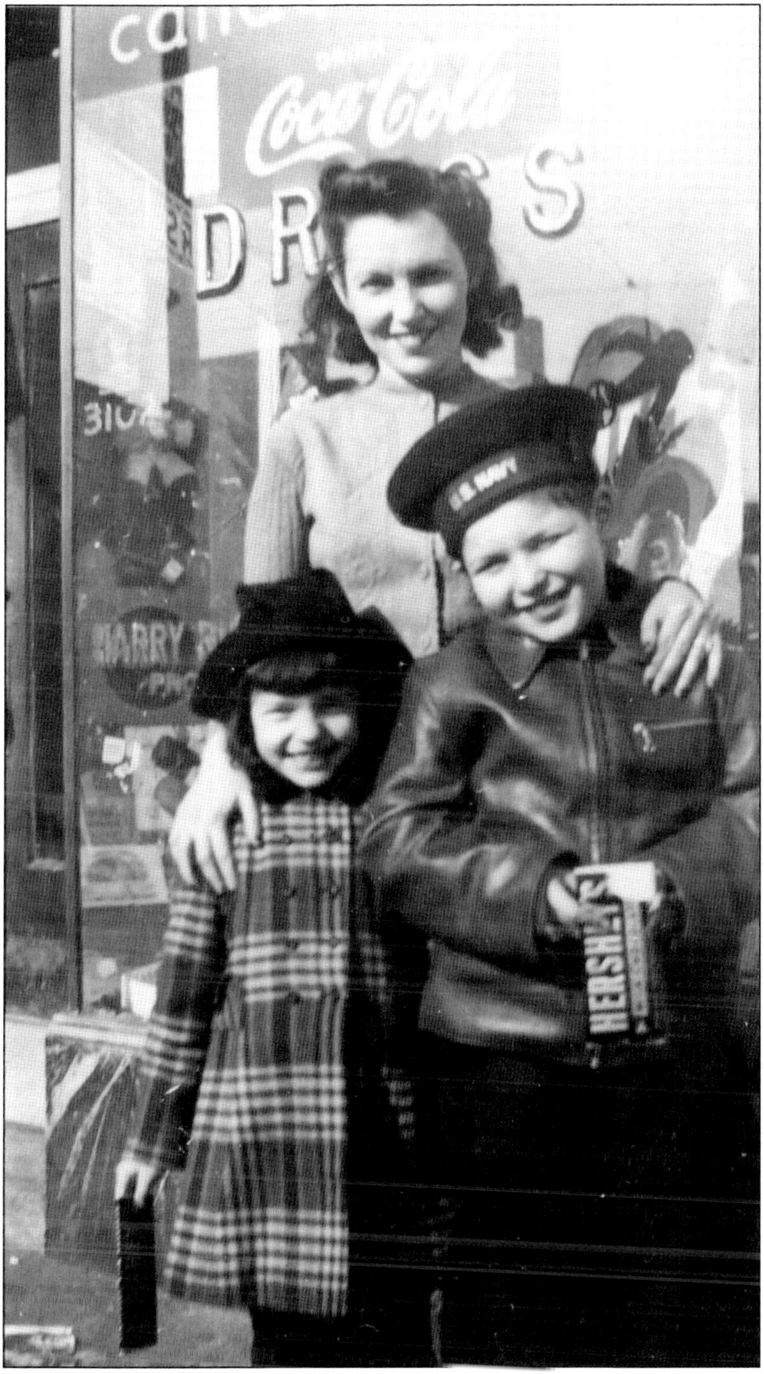

Hilda Lapides Rudy stands with her children Gail and Sheldon in front of Rudie's Pharmacy at 3100 North Avenue in the 1940s. Increasing numbers of less-affluent Jewish families moved into the less expensive areas contiguous to Eutaw Place. In 1921, Jack Levin's family moved to Smallwood Street near North Avenue. He recalled this move, saying, "When we moved into Smallwood, from our backyard all the way to Windsor Hills was totally undeveloped. We used to camp out, pick strawberries." (Courtesy of the JMM, 1989.78.8.)

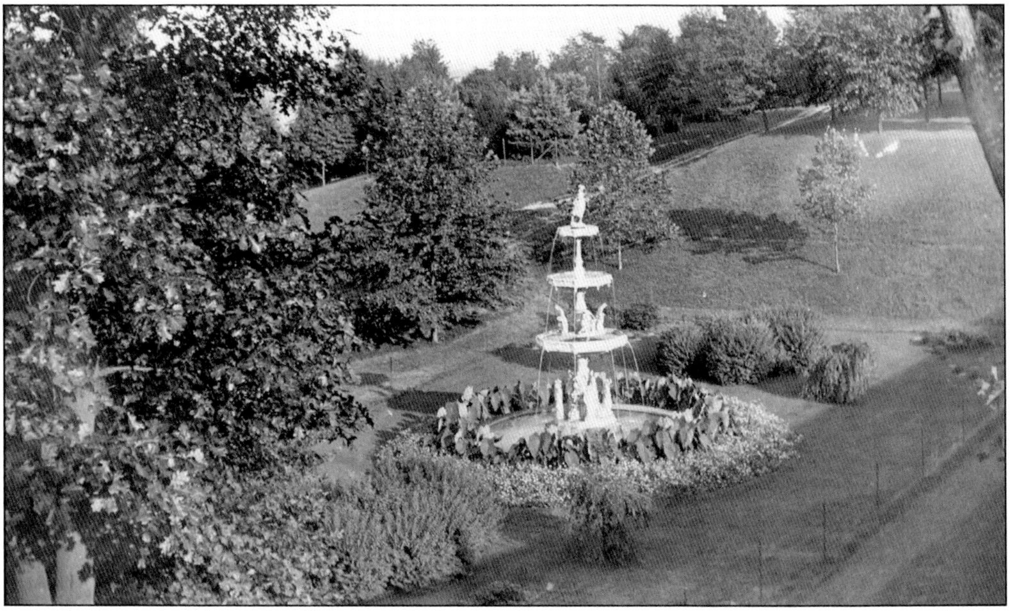

Two photographs of Druid Hill Park include one of Katy Berngartt (Plotnick) standing on a bridge in 1907. Druid Hill Park comprises 745 acres and was the first large municipal park in Baltimore, established in 1860. Much like Central Park in New York City in 1858, Druid Hill was developed as part of a nationwide movement to provide public green space for residents. (Above, courtesy of the JMM, 1989.167.9; below, courtesy of EPFL.)

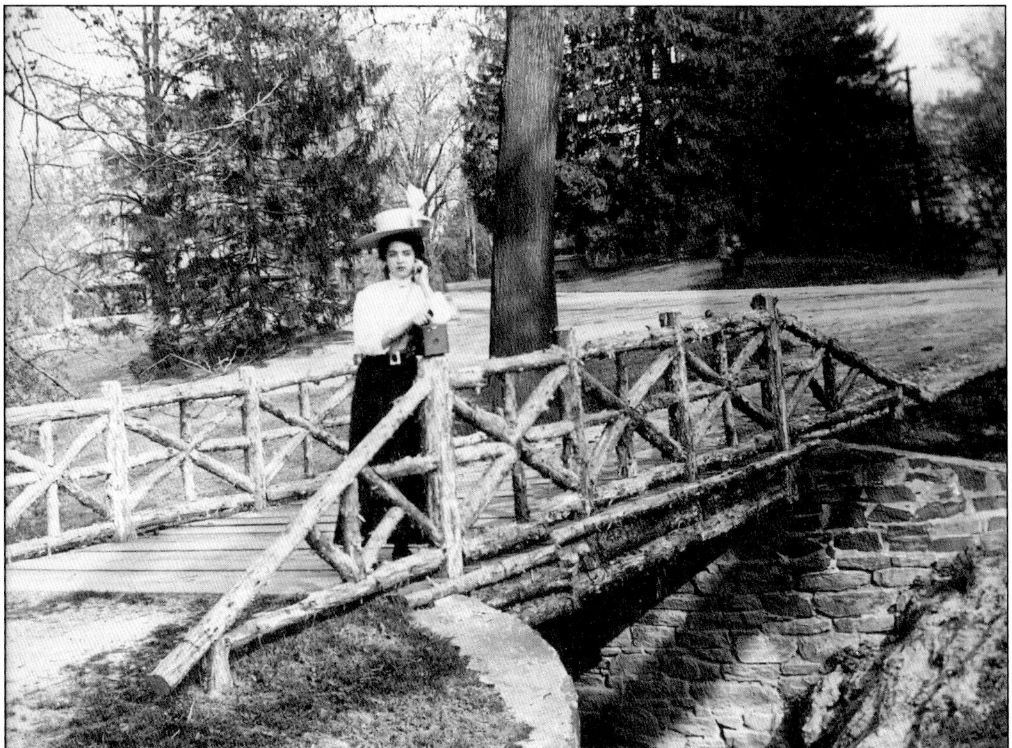

In 1932, Harry Adler II and Amalie Carol Adler pose with their nanny, Libby, across the street from their Park Circle apartment. (Courtesy of the JMM, 1989.167.9.)

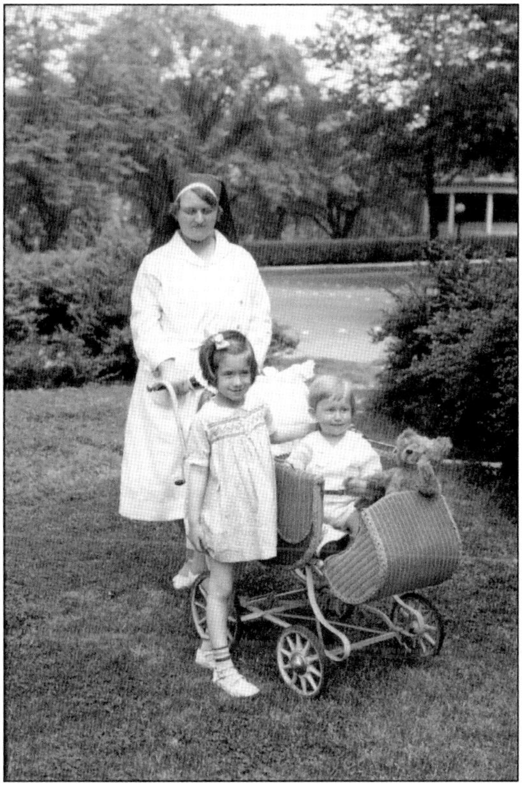

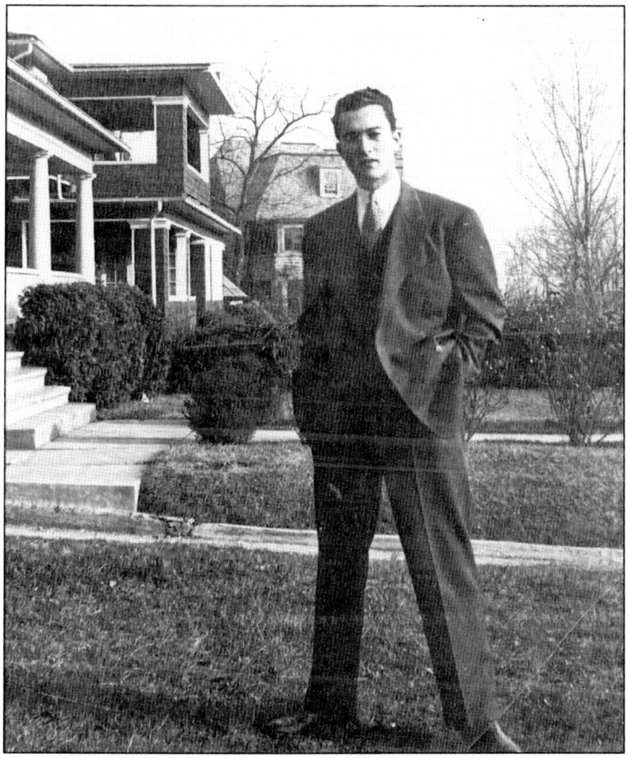

Berney Katzenberg Jr. stands outside his home in Forest Park in the mid-1930s. With its green yards and porch-fronted houses, Forest Park and its surrounding environs were affordable and desirable options for East European Jewish families moving out of East Baltimore. In 1921, the Beth Tfiloh Congregation was established on Garrison Boulevard. The Tifereth Israel Congregation started on Garrison near Forest Park Avenue. (Courtesy of the JMM, 1995.188.44.)

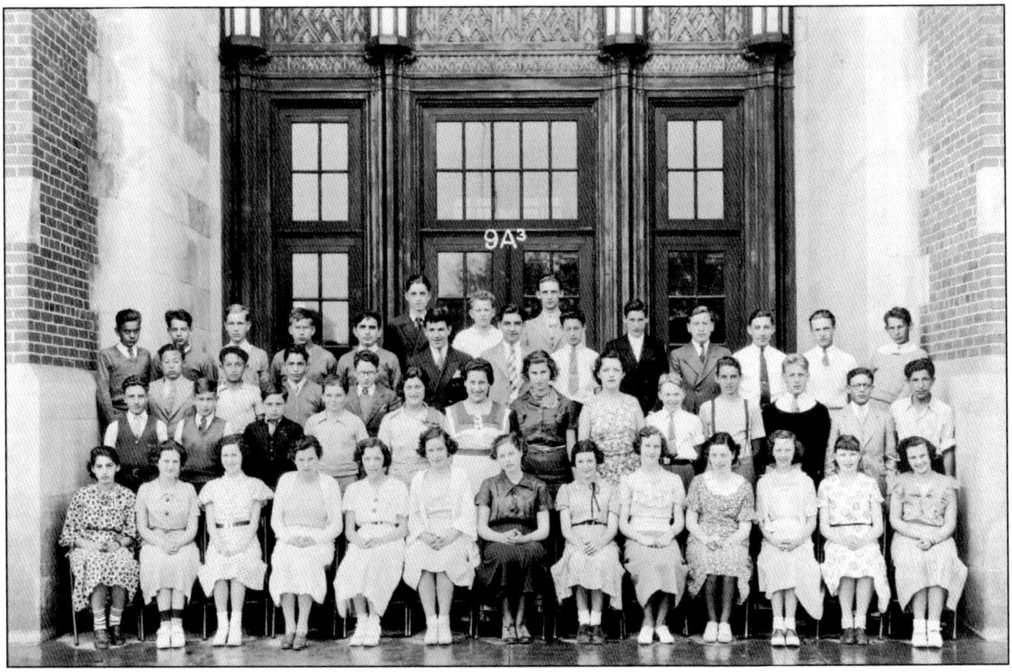

Milton Schwartz recalled the appeal of Forest Park: "It was a nicer neighborhood. . . . We saw grass. Remember, when I lived in the 1000 block of East Baltimore Street I had to go to Patterson Park, the 2100 block, before I saw a blade of grass if it didn't grow between a piece of cement." Shown above is the graduating class of Forest Park's Garrison Junior High School in 1935. (Courtesy of the JMM, 1987.19.14.)

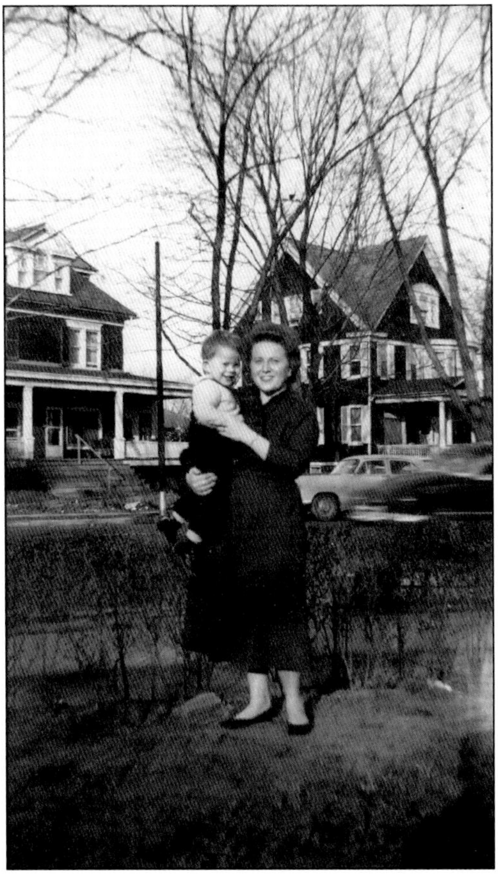

In 1956, Penina Kirek stands with her daughter, Yael, in her front yard on Garrison Boulevard. (Courtesy of the JMM, 1996.90.9.)

Shaarei Zion Synagogue was erected on Park Heights Avenue north of Park Circle in 1920. By the time World War I had ended, many Jewish families had begun moving into Lower Park Heights Avenue. (Courtesy of the JMM, 1987.19.28.)

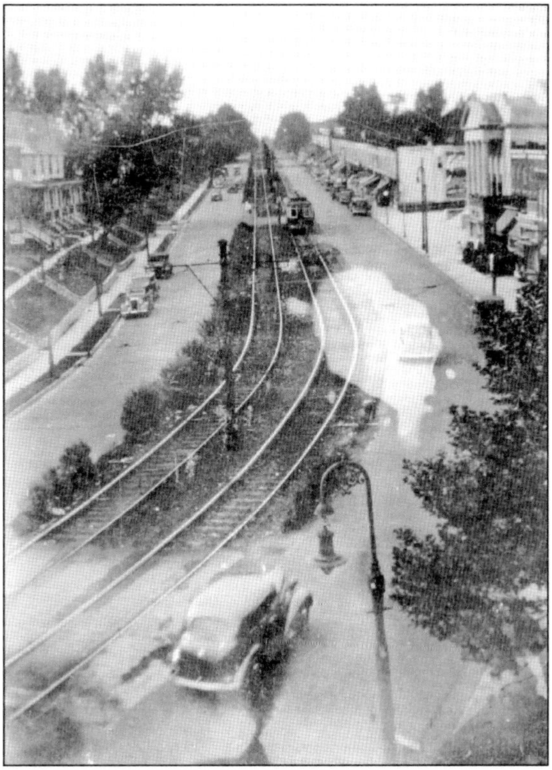

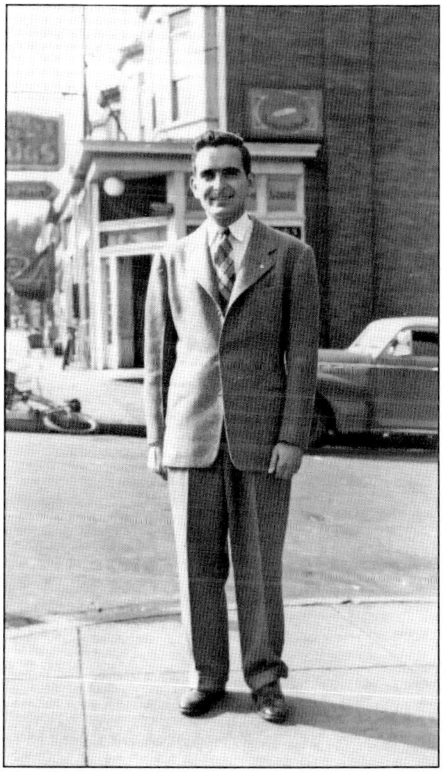

Stanley Berngartt stands in front of Sussman's Drug Store on Ulman and Park Heights Avenues around the 1940s. Today many families continue to live along Upper Park Heights Avenue, as well as in the suburbs, including Pikesville and Owings Mills. A Jewish community has remained active along Park Heights Avenue for over 30 years. This is due in part to the *eruv* (a defined enclosure wherein Orthodox Jews are permitted to carry certain objects during Shabbat), a bulwark of Jewish social institutions, and commitment from Jewish families. (Courtesy of the JMM, 1987.19.6.)

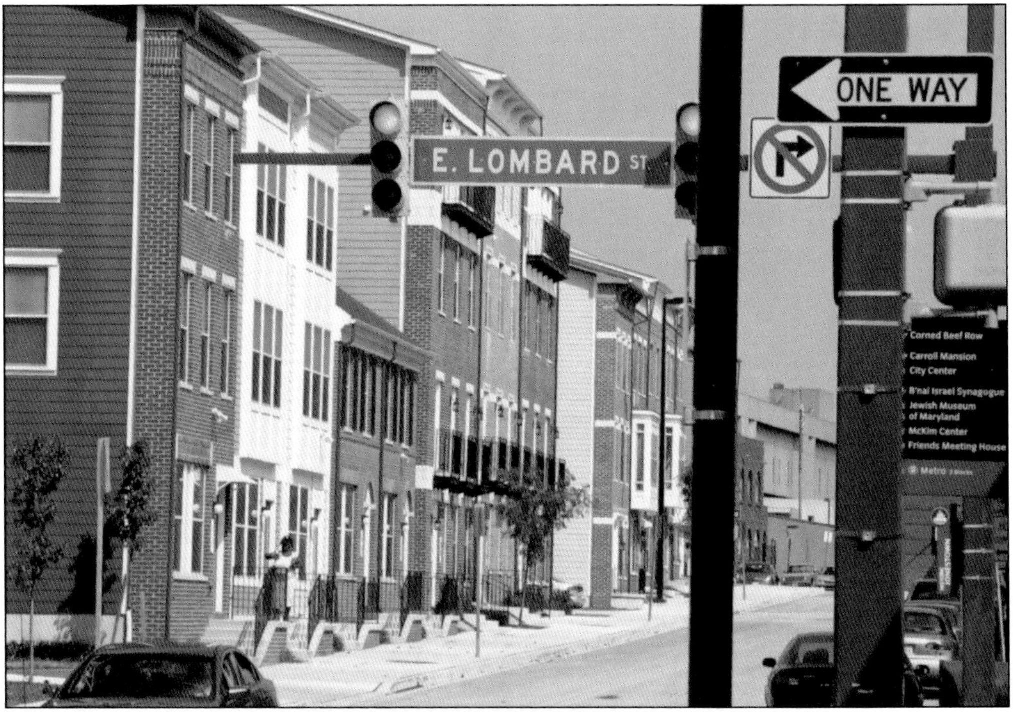

In recent years, a new trend has emerged in which some young Jewish families are moving back downtown. East Baltimore, now home to the Jewish Museum of Maryland, is being redeveloped. (Both, courtesy of the JMM.)

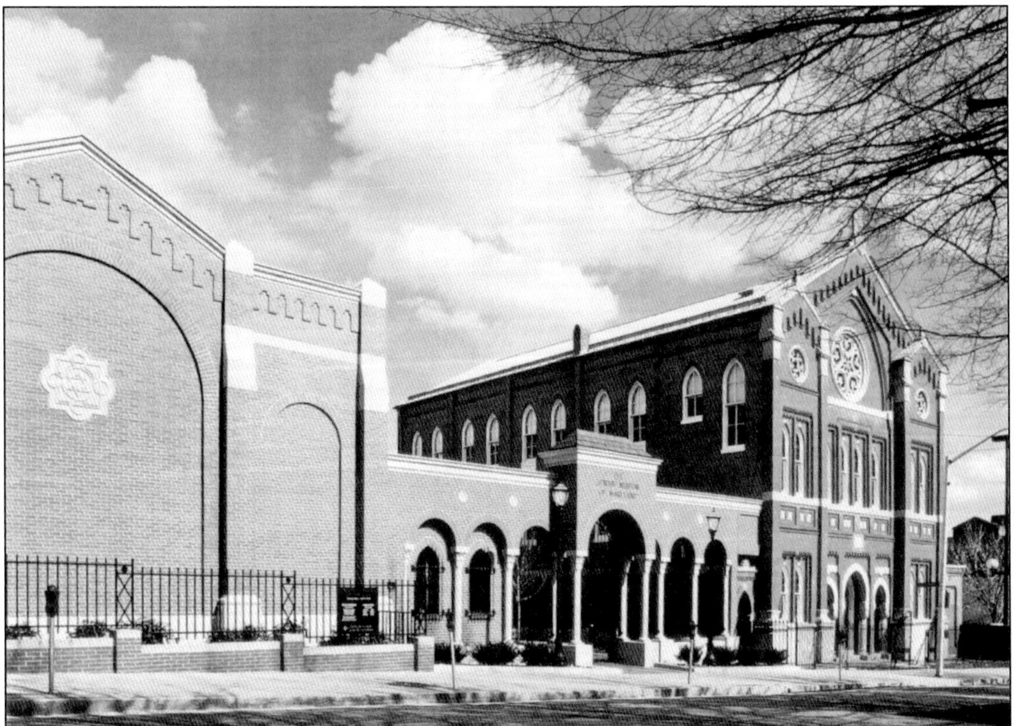

Four

Downtown Shuls, Uptown Synagogues

Baltimore's Jewish Houses of Worship

Perhaps nothing demonstrates the diversity of Baltimore's Jewish population more than its synagogues and congregations. Over the years, congregations have appeared, merged, disbanded, and occasionally even resumed after decades of hiatus. In 1945, there were 56 different Jewish congregations throughout the city. Even today, Baltimore's congregations reflect nearly every facet of Jewish culture and every mode of Jewish tradition. They range from Orthodox to Reconstructionist, speaking Russian to Yiddish to Farsi, and from loosely organized *chavurahs* (small groups) to congregations with more than 2,000 members. According to a 1999 population survey conducted by the Associated: Jewish Community Federation of Baltimore, 33 percent of 36,600 Jewish households identified as Reform; 33 percent as Conservative; and 21 percent as Orthodox. The remaining 11 percent identified as other, non-denominational, or secular.

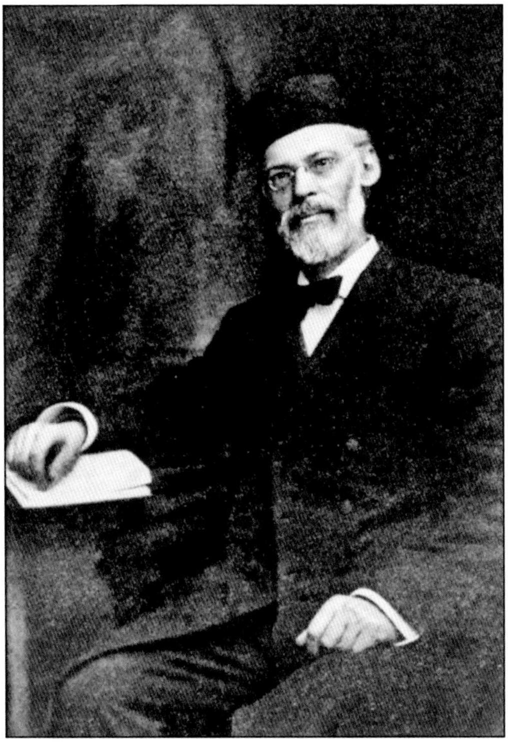

In 1893, Rabbi Dr. Schepsel Schaffer (1862–1933) became the spiritual leader for Shearith Israel Congregation. Schaffer was the only American delegate at the First Zionist Congress in Basle. (Courtesy of the JMM, 1999.121.1.)

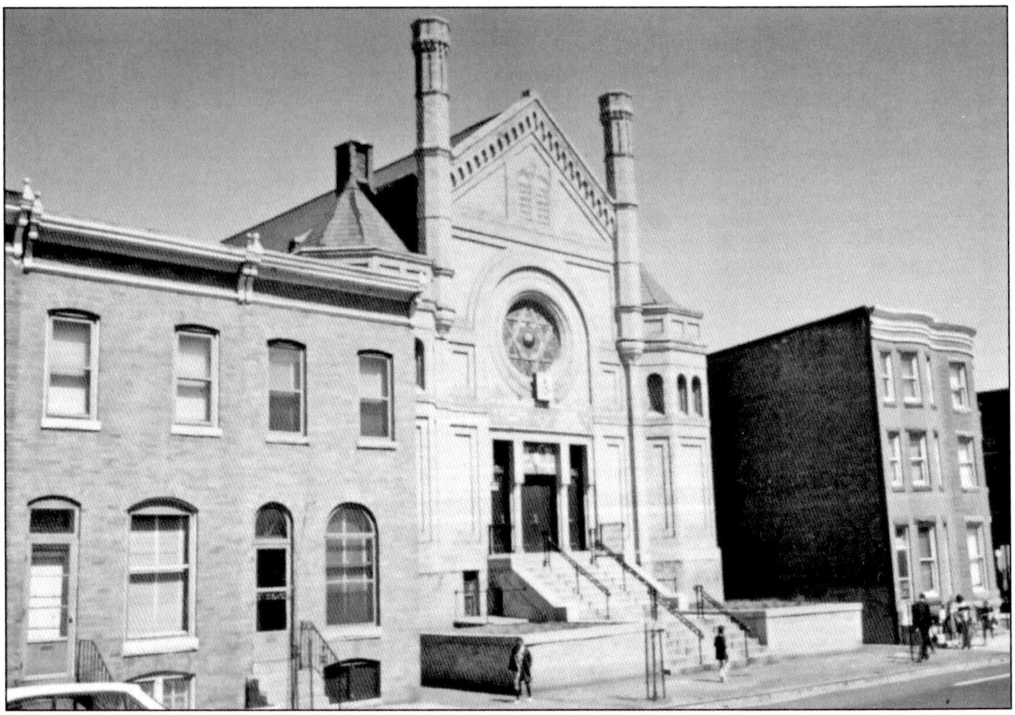

In 1903, the Shearith Israel Congregation moved to McCulloh and Bloom Streets. The congregation was one of the first to move to Park Heights Avenue and has remained in its current location since 1925. (Photograph by Milton Alpert, 1969; courtesy of the JMM, 1986.42.3.5.)

Shown in this c. 1862 carte de visite by J. H. Damph, Rabbi Henry Hochheimer served Baltimore Hebrew Congregation from 1849 to 1859 before leaving for the Fells Point Hebrew Friendship Congregation. He was a close friend of Rabbi Benjamin Szold at Temple Oheb Shalom and worked with Szold on a new version of the prayer book *Abodath Israel*. (Courtesy of the JMM, 1989.169.2.)

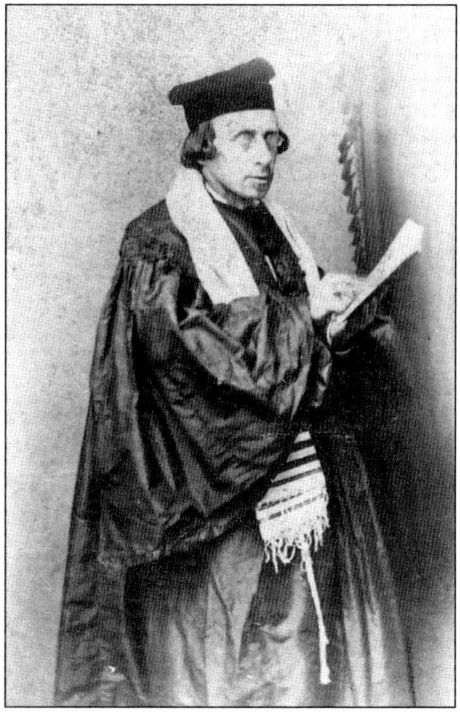

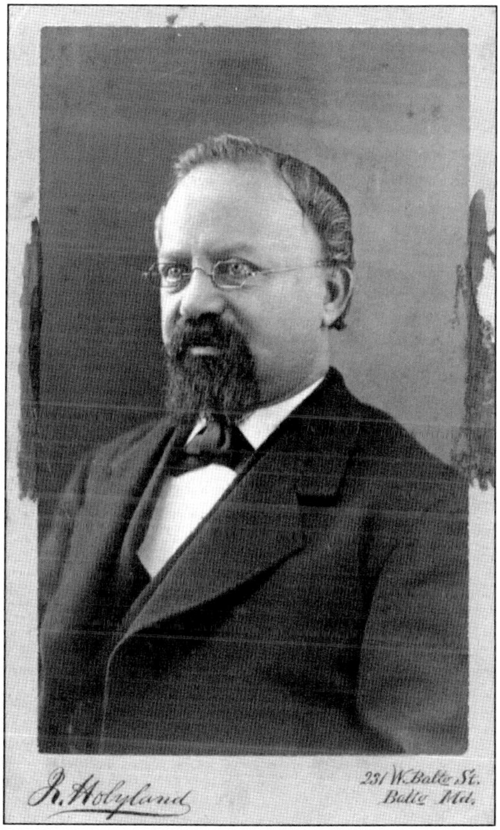

From 1868 to 1873, Rabbi Abraham Hoffman was the spiritual leader at Baltimore Hebrew Congregation. He left to become the superintendent at the Hebrew Orphan Asylum of Baltimore. (Courtesy of the JMM, 1989.187.1.)

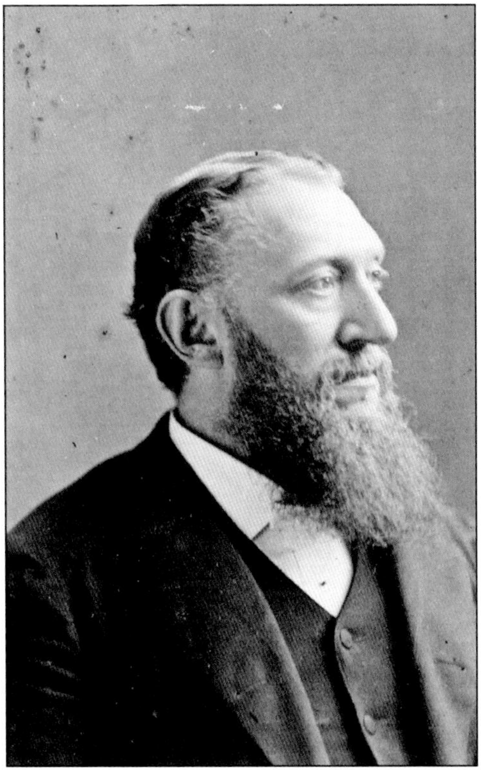

In 1865, the Baltimore Hebrew Congregation boasted 165 member families, but by 1884, there were only 48. In 1887, Rabbi Aaron Bettelheim (1830–1890), pictured to the left, and the congregation's president, Samuel Frank, decided that the best method to increase membership would be to follow the exodus of congregants to the northwest. In 1889, Baltimore Hebrew sold its first home and began construction at Madison Avenue. Rabbi Bettelheim passed away before the new synagogue opened in 1891. (Courtesy of the JMM and BHC, 1989.170.2b.)

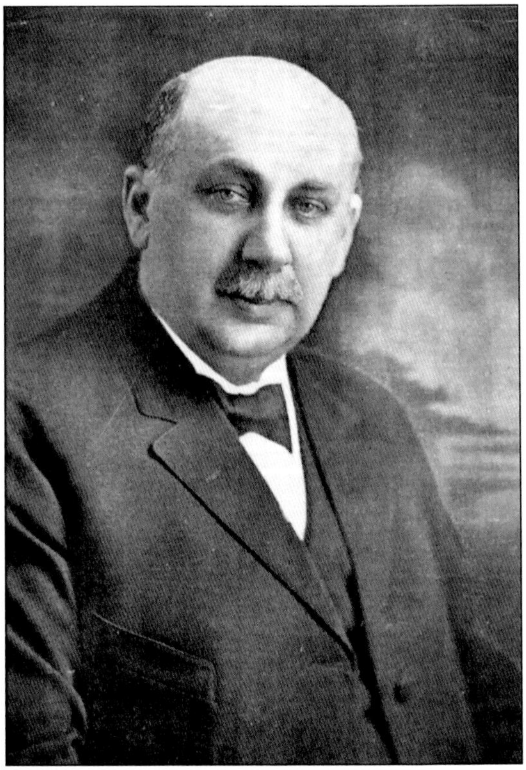

In 1891, Rabbi Adolf Guttmacher succeeded Rabbi Aaron Bettelheim at Baltimore Hebrew Congregation and served there until his death in 1915. (Courtesy of the JMM and BHC, 1989.170.1a.)

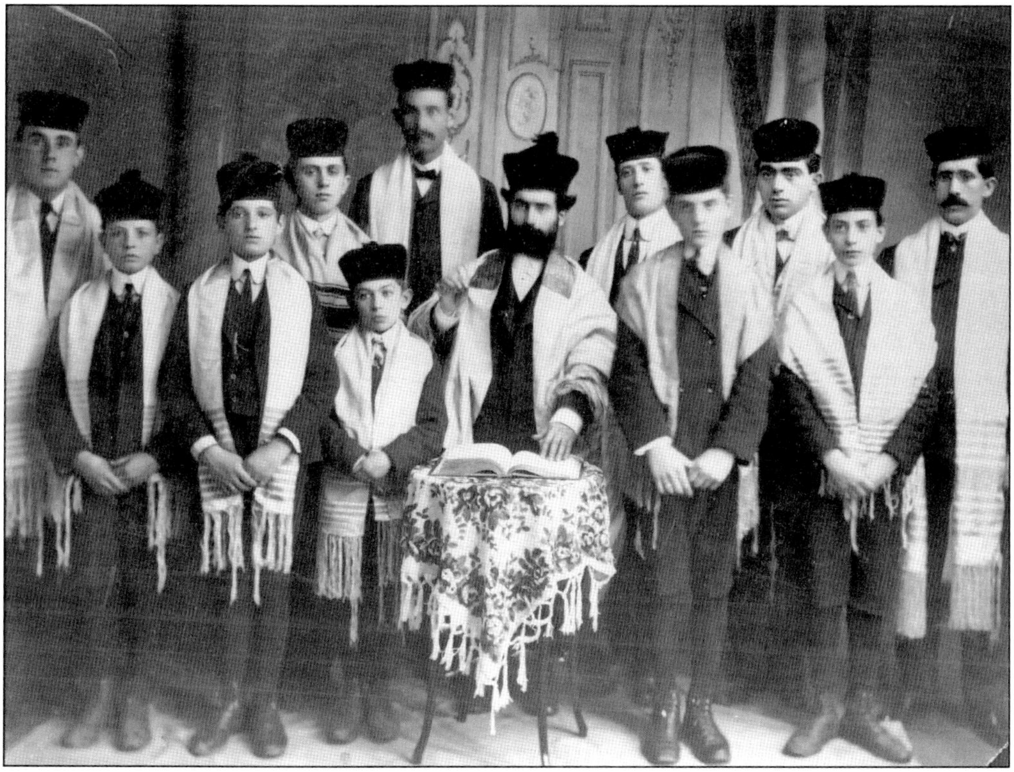

Cantor Reuben Graffman of Beth Jacob Anshe Veshear Congregation (established around 1919) stands with the boys' choir at the synagogue in East Baltimore in 1903. The congregation went out of existence around 1971. (Courtesy of the JMM, 1988.47.1.)

Also known as the Poppleton Street Synagogue, the Ahavas Shalom Congregation (established 1905) acquired a former church at 126 South Poppleton Street around 1916. It is pictured around the 1950s. Conversely, several former synagogues became churches. Notable examples of the latter include Temple Oheb Shalom's second home on Eutaw Place, now a Masonic temple, and Baltimore Hebrew Congregation's second synagogue on Madison Avenue, which became Berea Temple Seventh-day Adventist Church. Baltimore Hebrew's first synagogue on Lloyd Street served initially as a synagogue and then became a Catholic church before becoming a synagogue again. (Photograph by Menasha Katz; courtesy of the JMM, 1987.137.61.)

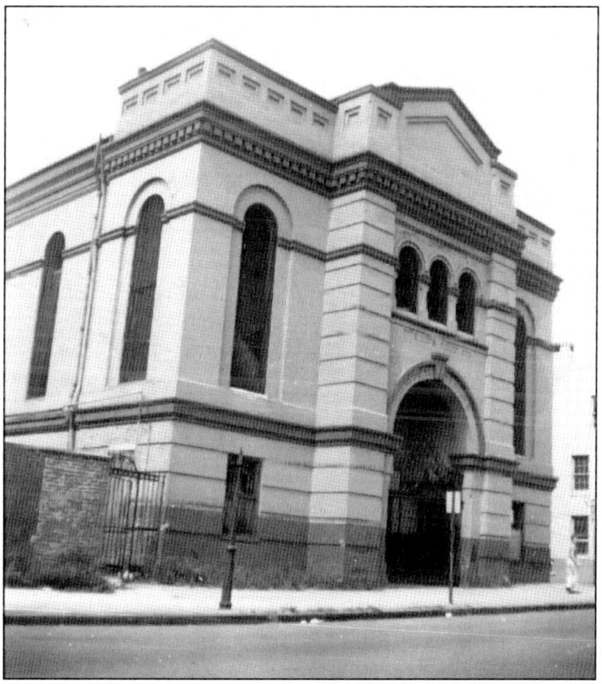

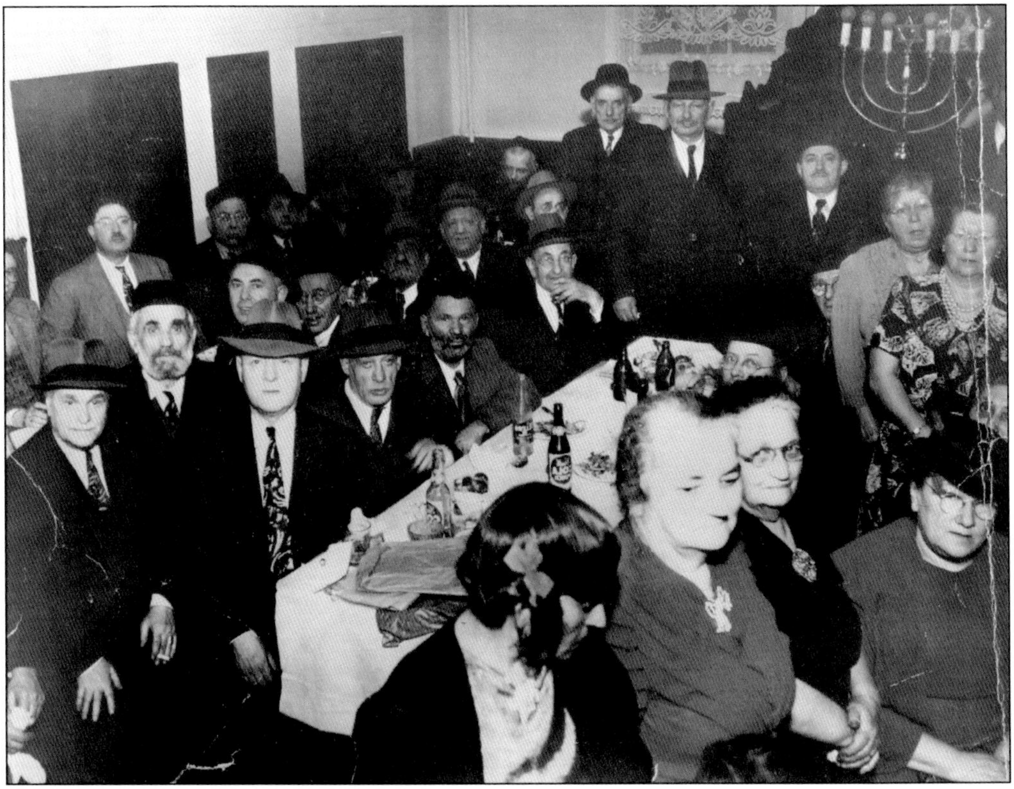

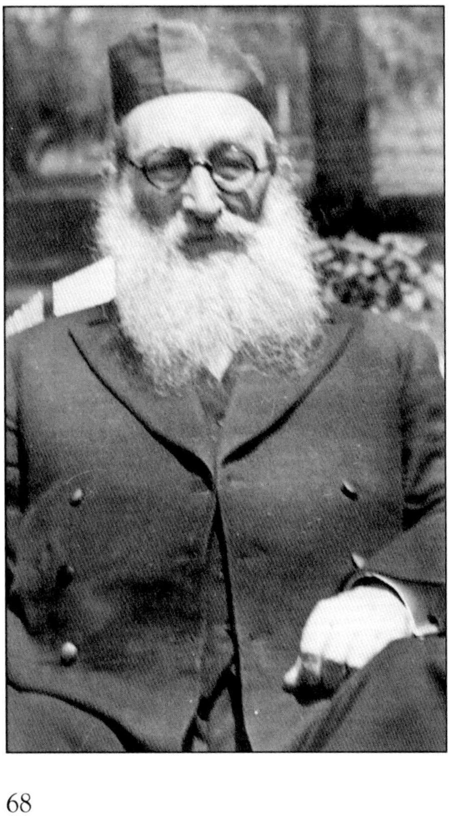

The Tzemach Tzedek Congregation started in 1913 but did not have its first synagogue until 1922 when it opened a new building at 2120 East Fairmount Avenue. Around 1956, the congregation merged with the Shomrei Hadath Nusach Ari Congregation, which was then absorbed into Khal Ahavas Yisroel Congregation in 1987. (Courtesy of the JMM, 1999.140.1b.)

Rabbi Abraham Nachman Schwartz (1871–1937) was considered "Baltimore's Chief Rabbi." Born in Lithuania, he left in 1905 and came to Baltimore in 1908 to serve at Shomrei Mishmeres Hakodesh Congregation, located in the historic Lloyd Street Synagogue. He officiated there until his death in 1937. Rabbi Schwartz helped establish the Union of Orthodox Rabbis of the United States and Canada (Agudas Harabonim). He assisted in arranging for the first printing of the Talmud in the United States during World War I and founded Baltimore's Hebrew Parochial School in 1917, now known as the Talmudical Academy. His wife, Golda Miriam, was one of the founders of the Bais Yaakov School for Girls. (Courtesy of the JMM, 1996.113.71.)

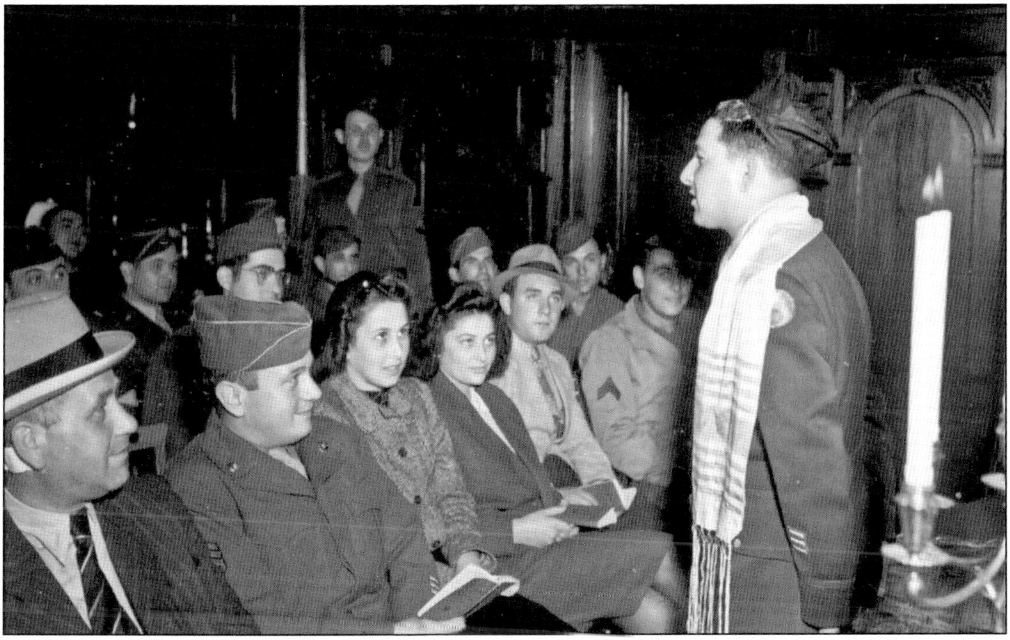

Rabbi Manuel Poliakoff was the grandson of famed rabbi Abraham Nachman Schwartz and served as the rabbi of the Beth Isaac Adath Israel Congregation. Between 1943 and 1946, he served as a chaplain in the army and was awarded a Bronze Star for bravery in action as well as a service medal upon retirement. In this World War II photograph, Rabbi Poliakoff leads services for soldiers and civilians. (Courtesy of the JMM, 1996.113.35.)

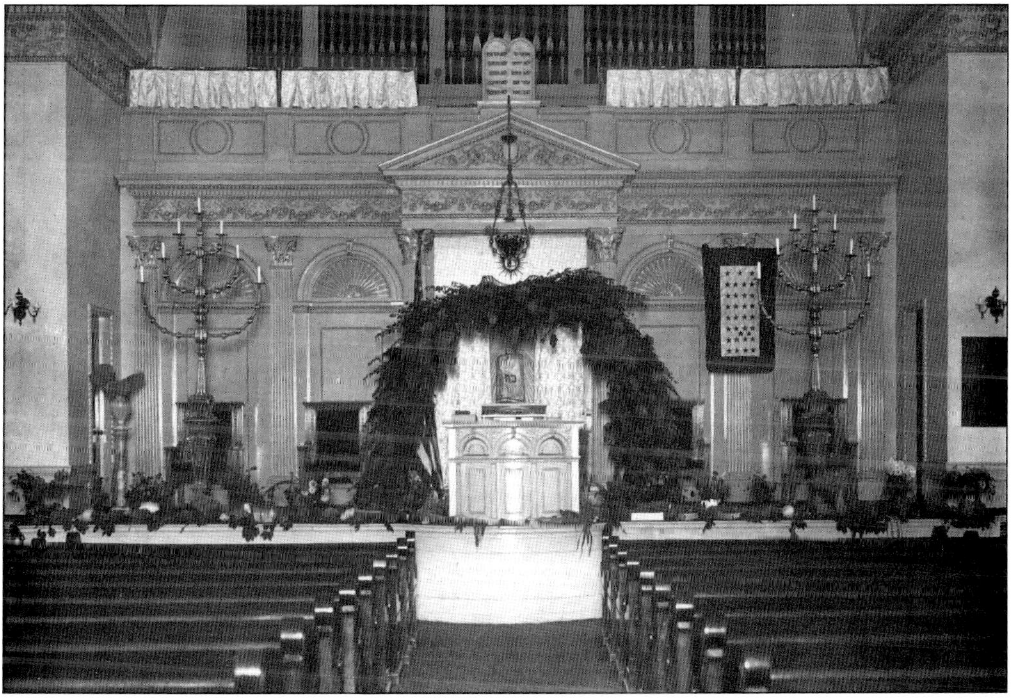

The Har Sinai Congregation left East Baltimore and moved uptown to Bolton Street near Eutaw Place. This interior shot was taken around 1918. (Courtesy of the JMM, 1985.90.2.)

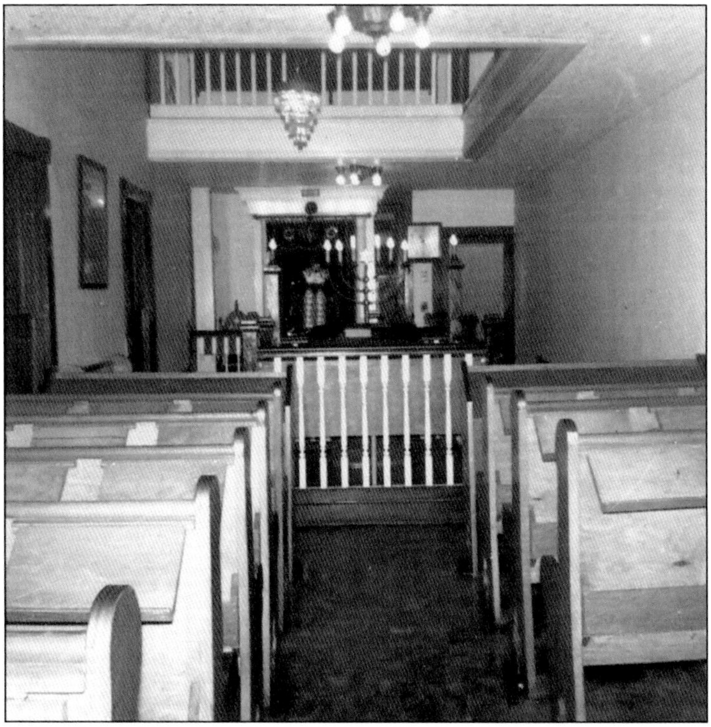

A few synagogues began in surprising locations, such as the Anshe Beth Jacob Congregation of Highlandtown (established 1927). A local story suggests that the congregation originally met in the early 20th century in a hall over a streetcar barn. It moved to its first synagogue on Eastern Avenue around 1927. Here is its second home on Highland Avenue, where the congregation remained until it disbanded around 1960. (Courtesy of the JMM, 1982.14.23a.)

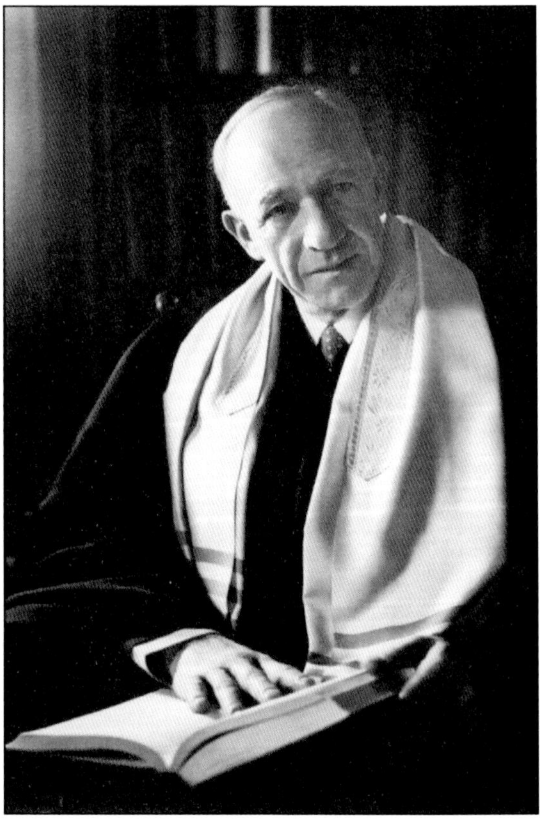

Rabbi Morris Lazaron (1888–1979) served the Baltimore Hebrew Congregation from 1915 to 1949. He helped found the National Conference of Christians and Jews in 1932. He was a U.S. Army chaplain in World War I and officiated at the burial of the Unknown Soldier of World War I in 1921. (Courtesy of the JMM, 1988.12.36.)

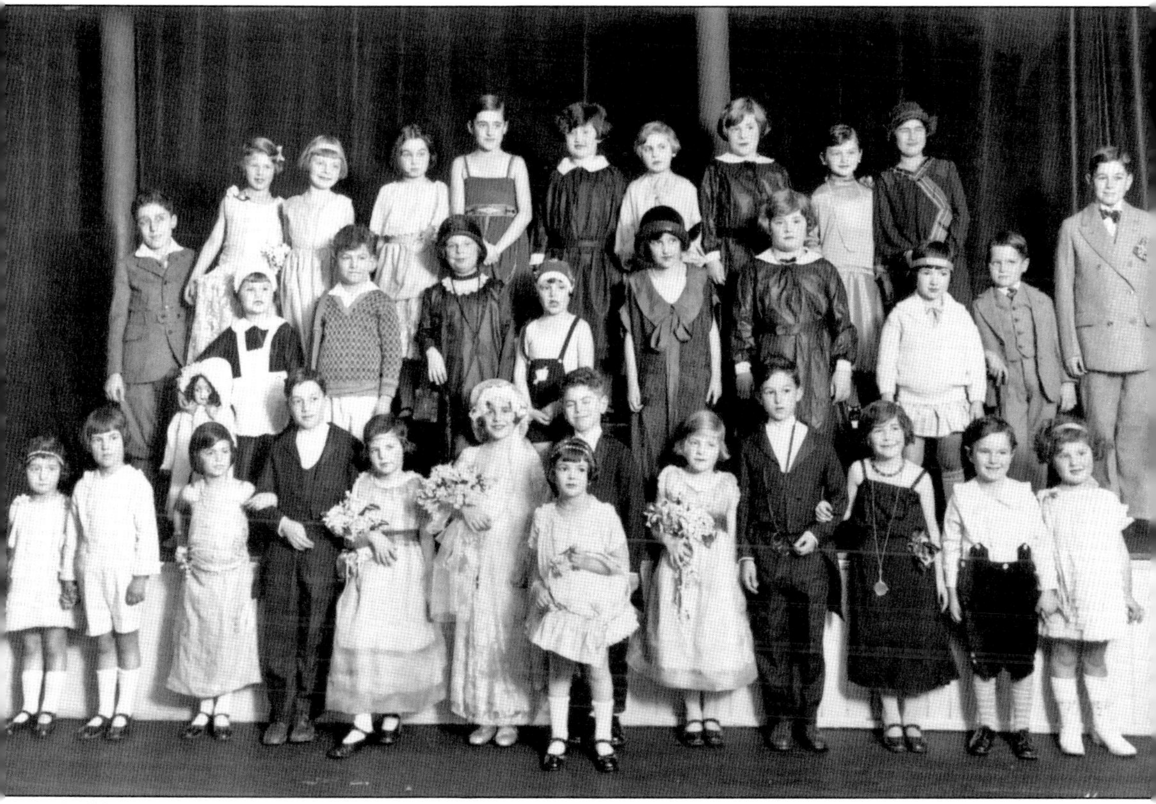

Rabbi Lazaron's son, Morris Lazaron Jr. (age 6), is the groom at a Tom Thumb wedding at the Baltimore Hebrew Congregation in November 1923. Allyne Katzenstein (age 5) acts as the bride. (Courtesy of the JMM, 1989.94.2a.)

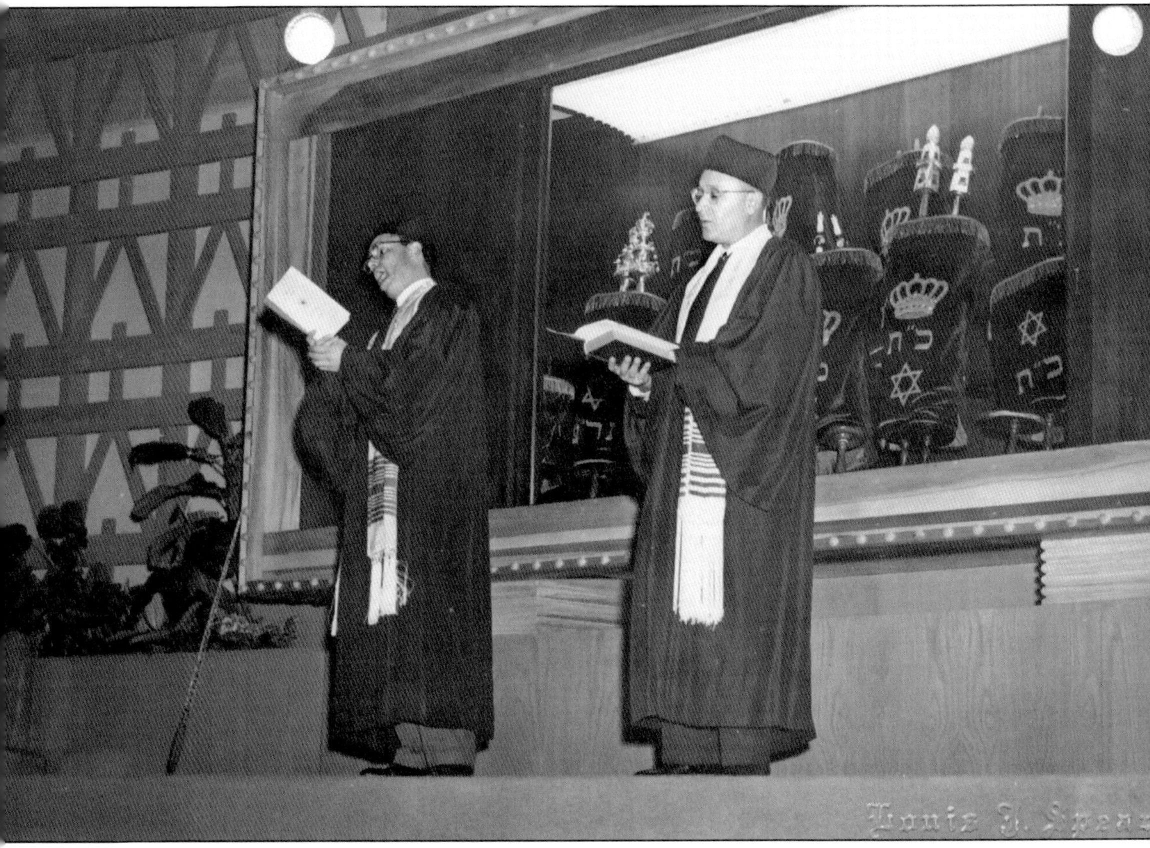

Rabbi Morris Lieberman (1909–1970) was the spiritual leader of the Baltimore Hebrew Congregation from 1937 to 1970, in addition to serving as an army chaplain from 1942 to 1946. Cantor Joseph Rosenfeld was with Baltimore Hebrew from 1945 to 1981. Rabbi Lieberman oversaw Baltimore Hebrew's move from Madison Avenue to its current home on Park Heights Avenue. He was also the first executive director of the Baltimore Jewish Council. An early advocate of racial justice, he organized interfaith demonstrations and was a lifelong member of the NAACP. Rabbi Lieberman (right) and Cantor Rosenfeld (left), in a photograph by Louis F. Spear, lead the dedication service at the congregation's new home at Park Heights Avenue in 1951. (Courtesy of the JMM, 1994.5.13.)

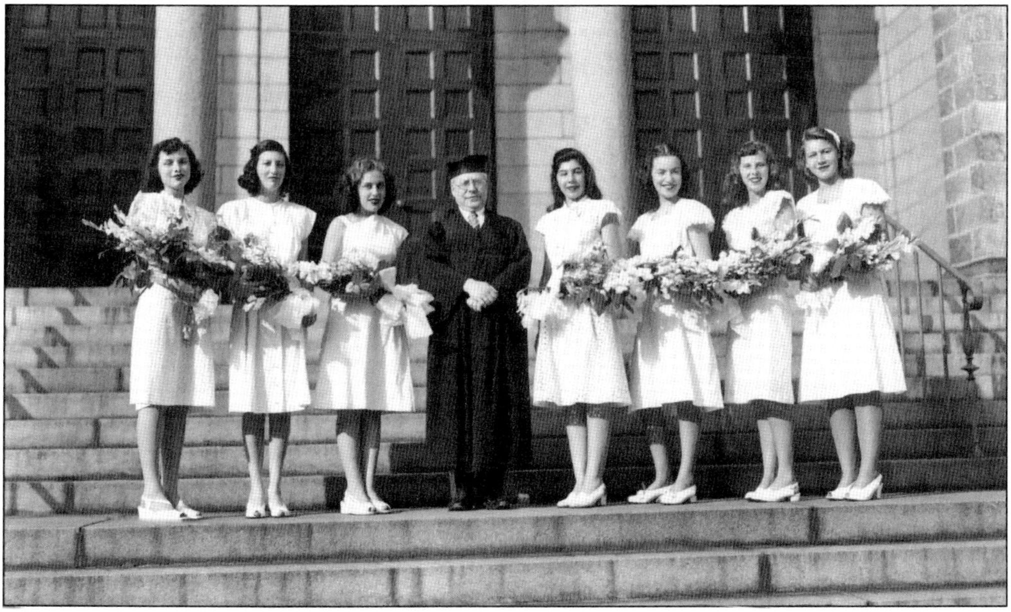

Chizuk Amuno Congregation's 1945 confirmation class is seen at its third home on Eutaw Place. Baltimore Hebrew Congregation members broke off to found Chizuk Amuno in 1871 in response to the reforms instituted at Baltimore Hebrew. They constructed their first synagogue in 1876, which is still in use today by the B'nai Israel Congregation. (Courtesy of the JMM, 1996.32.2.)

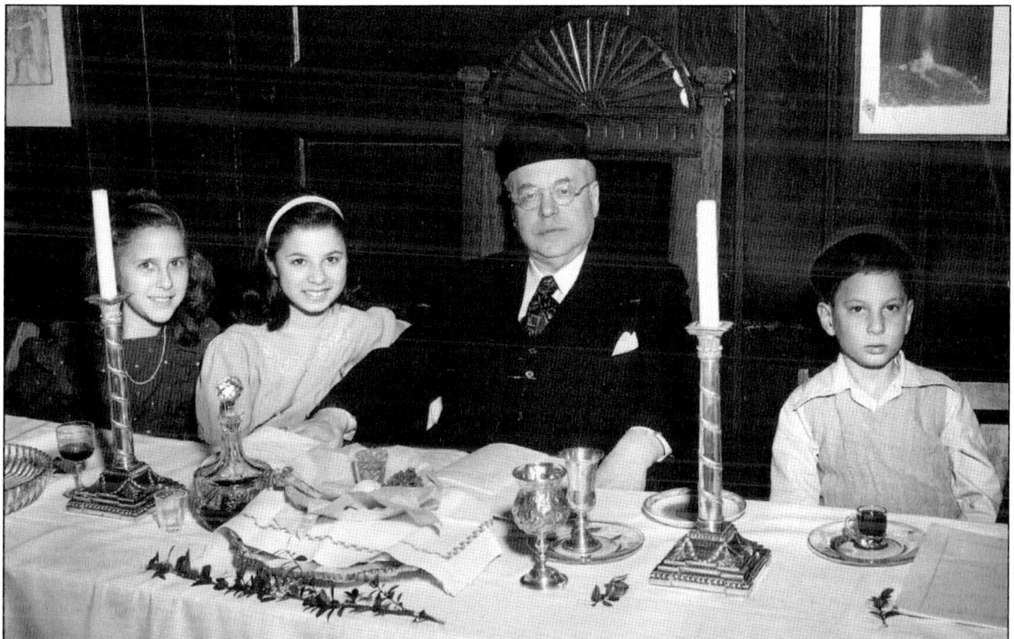

Rabbi Adolf Coblenz (1887–1949) is shown with three children during the Passover Seder at the Chizuk Amuno Congregation School in 1947. Born in Lithuania, Rabbi Coblenz came to Baltimore in 1920. He remained with Chizuk Amuno until 1946 and oversaw its move from Mosher Street to Eutaw Place in 1922. He served as the president of the Baltimore Zionist District from 1932 to 1934. (Courtesy of the JMM, 1991.7.1.)

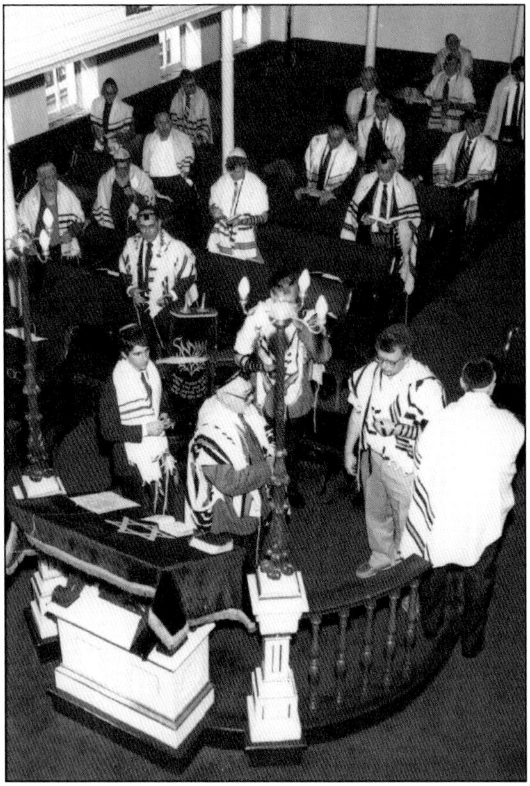

In this 1989 photograph, a baby-naming ceremony is celebrated at the B'nai Israel Synagogue. Established in 1873, B'nai Israel is today the only active congregation in East Baltimore. It purchased Chizuk Amuno Congregation's first home in 1895. While the synagogue is part of the Jewish Museum of Maryland, the congregation operates independently of the museum. The building is listed on the National Register of Historic Places. (Courtesy of the JMM, 1989.97.1.)

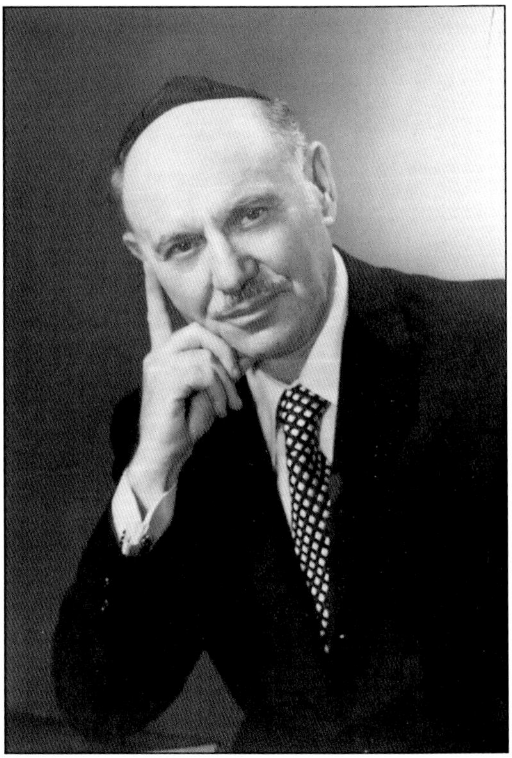

Rabbi Samuel Pliskin served the B'nai Israel Congregation from 1939 to 1978. (Courtesy of the JMM, 1988.3.1.)

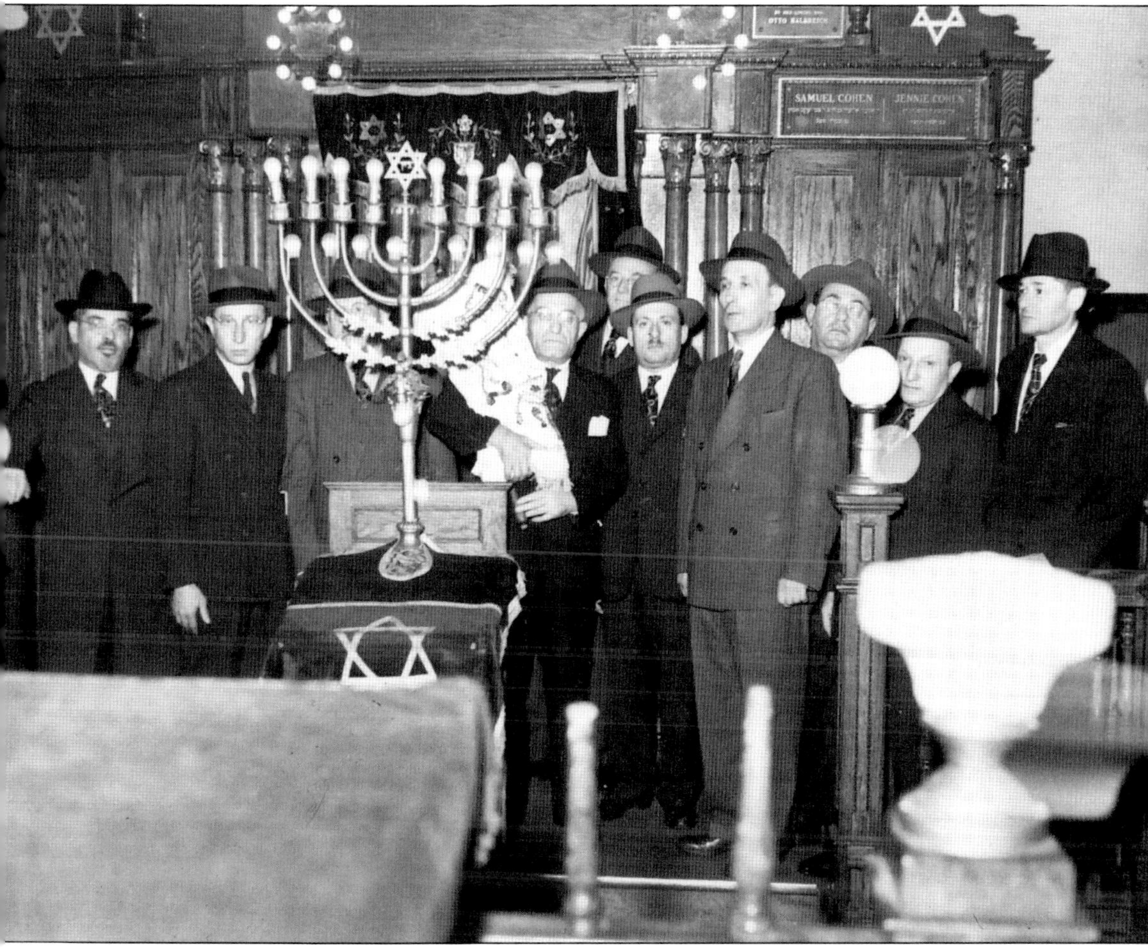

The Anshe Sphard Congregation dedicated its new synagogue at 4 North Broadway in 1937. Anshe Sphard first started off as Chevra Anshe Sphard Congregation around 1887. Like many other new immigrant congregations of the time, the synagogue began as a "row house shul," in which it adapted a private home for use as a house of worship. Anshe Sphard later moved its synagogue to Broadway in 1936. It merged with the Ohr Knesseth Israel Congregation (established 1894) in 1950, forming the Rogers Avenue Synagogue in 1951. (Courtesy of the JMM, 1996.28.10.)

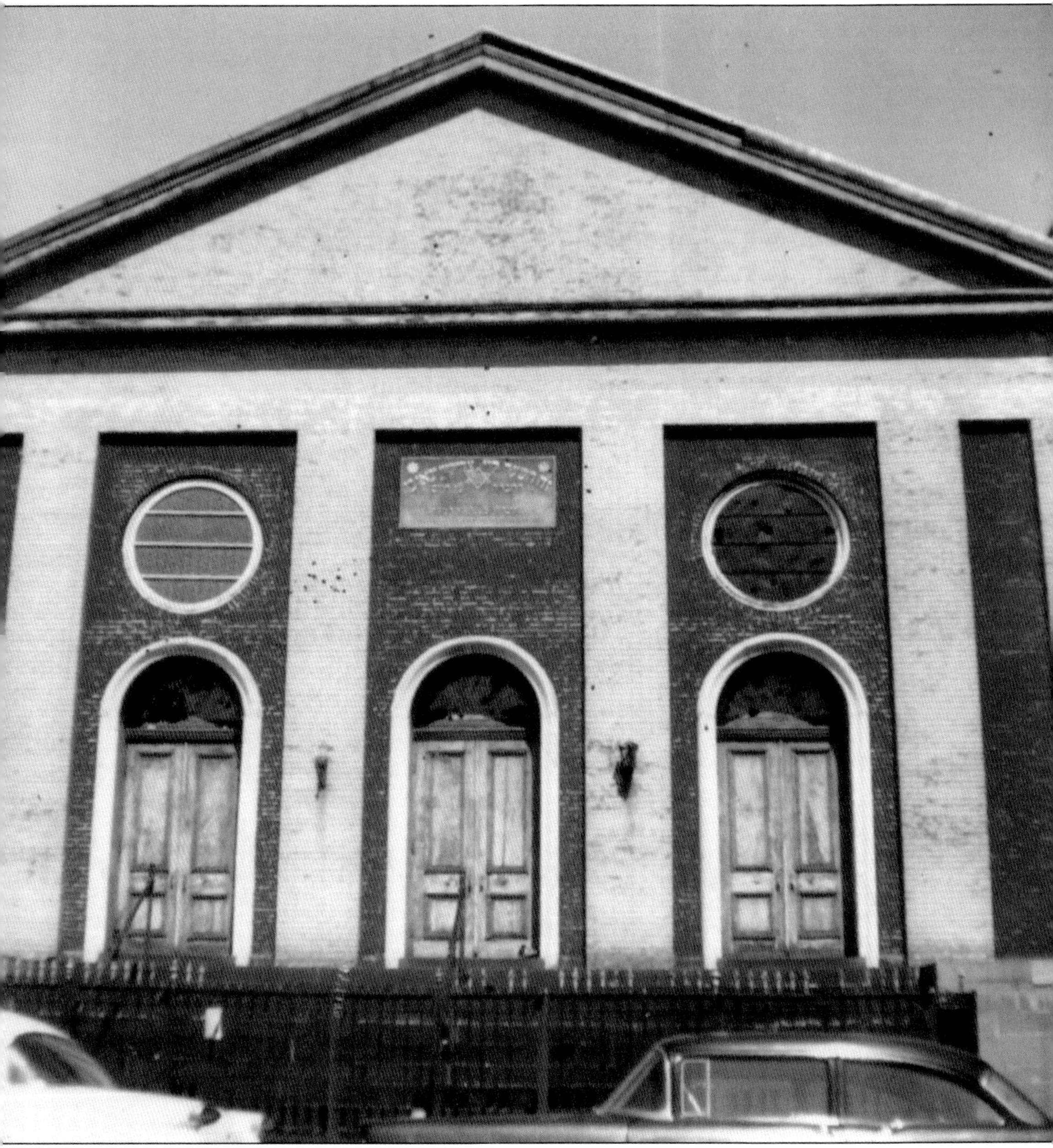

The Aitz Chaim Congregation (established 1887) moved into 15–21 South Eden Street in 1902 (shown around the early 1950s), which had previously been the home of the Oheb Israel Congregation (originally Fells Point Hebrew Friendship). The synagogue was one of a number of landsmanshaft shuls, synagogues named after the founding members' town of origin. Aitz Chaim was often referred to as the Prushnitz Shul as well as the Eden Street Shul. Other examples include the Ohel Yaakov Congregation, also known as the Bialystoker Shul after Bialystok, Poland. It was later known as the Frantsoizishe (French) Shul for its supposed pretentiousness. Mikro Kodesh Congregation (established 1886) was called the Pokroyer Shul for Pokrov, Russia, and Anshe Wolyn (established 1894) literally translates to "the people of Volhynia." (Photograph by Menasha Katz; courtesy of the JMM, 1993.85.2.)

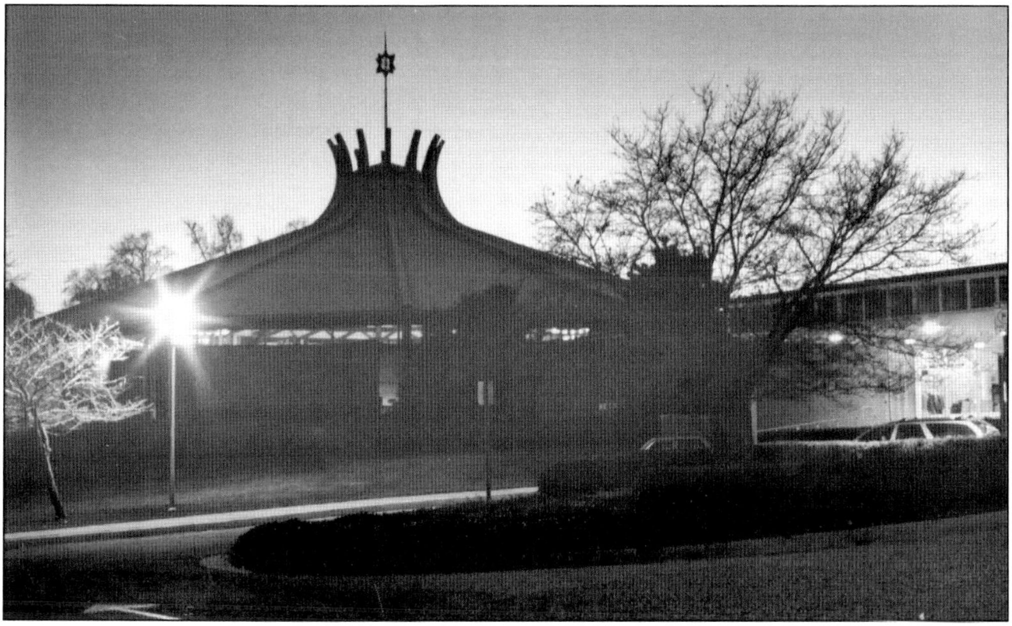

While many congregations followed their congregants to new neighborhoods, the creation of the Beth Tfiloh Congregation (established 1921) helped to establish Forest Park as a viable Jewish community. It moved to its current home on Old Court Road in 1966. Son of renowned cantor Yosele Rosenblatt, Rabbi Samuel Rosenblatt (1902–1983) was Beth Tfiloh's first spiritual leader, serving the congregation from 1927 to 1972. (Photograph by Ann Sue Grossman, 1992; courtesy of the JMM, 1992.142.7.)

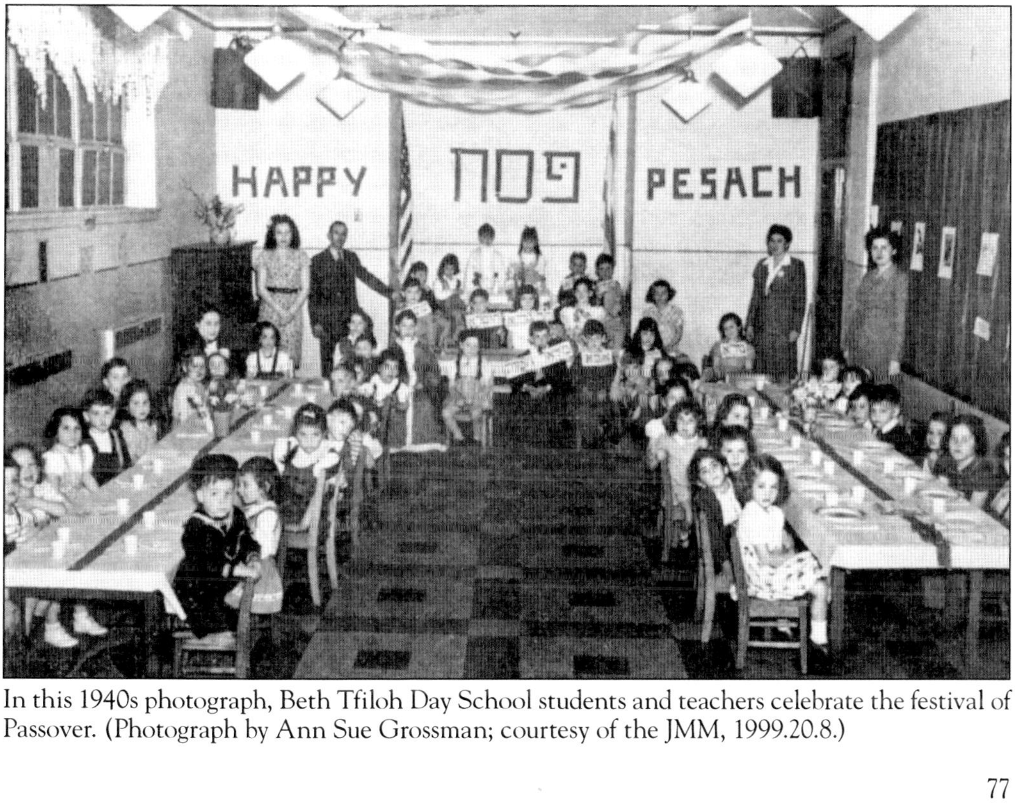

In this 1940s photograph, Beth Tfiloh Day School students and teachers celebrate the festival of Passover. (Photograph by Ann Sue Grossman; courtesy of the JMM, 1999.20.8.)

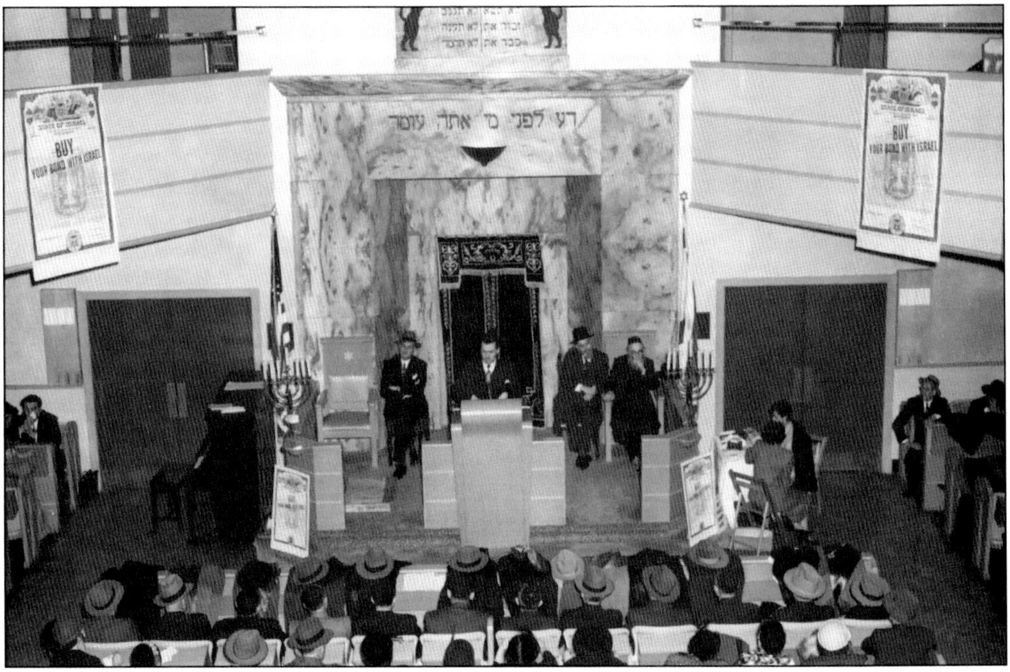

Rabbi Benjamin Bak (speaking) and Moses I. Speert (at right), chairman of the Baltimore Israel Bond Committee, attend a reception at Tifereth Israel Synagogue honoring Rabbi Isar Yehuda Unterman in 1952. Tifereth Israel Congregation organized in 1926 at 3218 Garrison Boulevard near Forest Park before merging with Har Zion Congregation (established 1918) and Petach Tikvah Congregation (established 1922). (Photograph by Nat Lipsitz; courtesy of the JMM, 1991.136.14.)

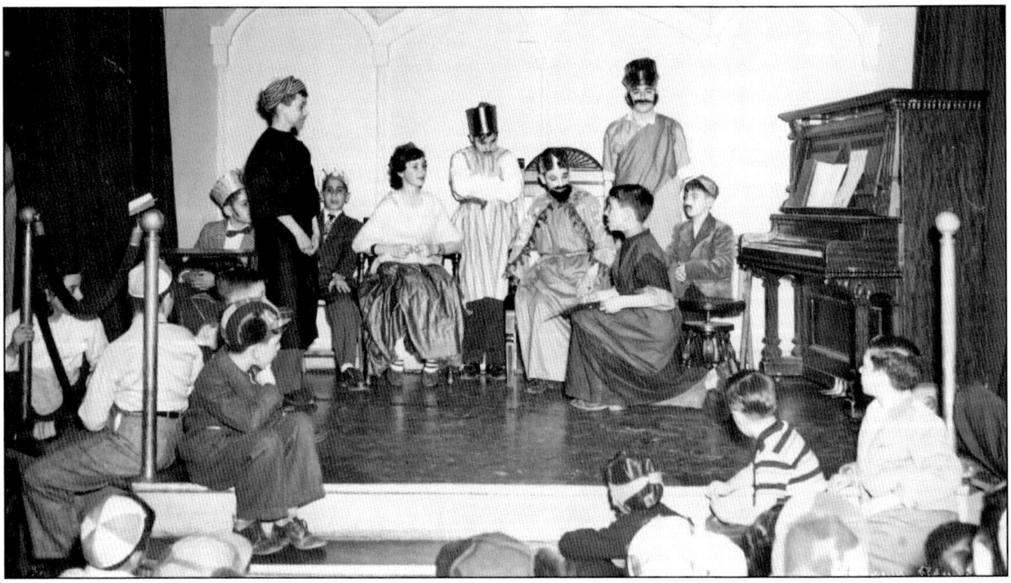

In this photograph from 1951, the Agudath Achim Anshe Sphard Congregation (established 1921) celebrates the festival of Purim with a pageant performance at its synagogue on Park Heights Avenue. In 1970, the congregation merged with Randallstown Synagogue Center in Baltimore County. (Courtesy of the JMM, 1992.108.1.)

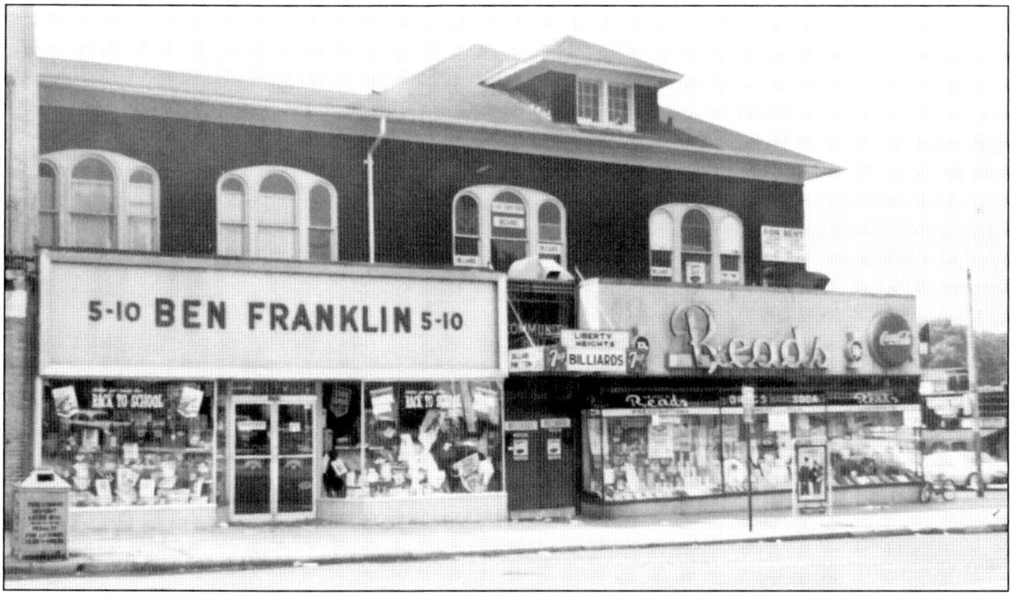

The Beth El Congregation (established 1947) used a community hall on the corner of Liberty Heights and Gwynn Oak Avenues until 1949. It was not until 1959 that it finally began building a synagogue on Park Heights Avenue near Hooks Lane, where the congregation still worships today. Beth El was the first congregation in the area to be organized as part of the Conservative movement. (Photograph by Menasha Katz; courtesy of the JMM, 1987.137.51.)

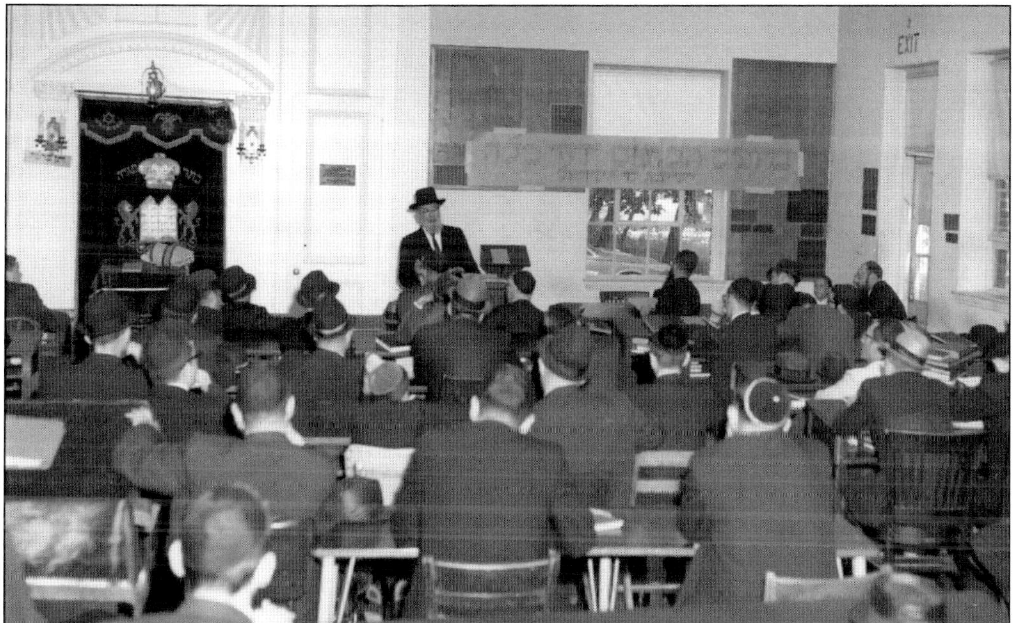

Born in Lithuania, Rabbi Jacob Ruderman (1900–1987) was a child prodigy in the Talmud and wrote *Avodas Levi*, a study of complex issues in the Talmud, at age 19. In Baltimore, he became known as the "Rosh HaYeshiva" or "Head of the School" after establishing Ner Israel Rabbinical College in 1933; he is shown around 1970. (Photograph by Arthur Kravetz; courtesy of the JMM, 1988.142.7.)

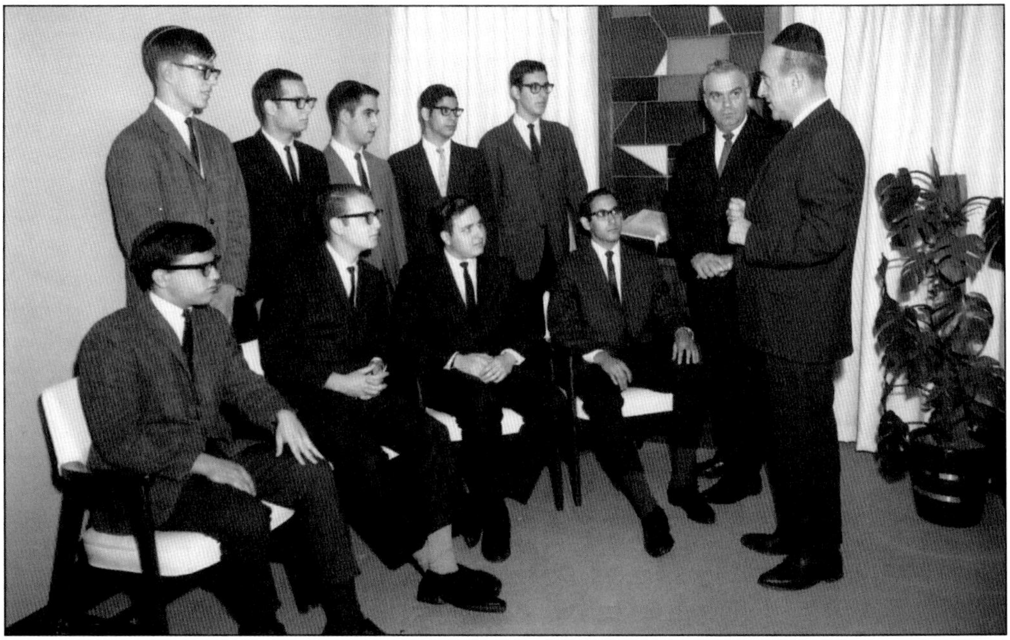

Rabbi Samuel Vitsick (1914–2000) was the first chaplain at Sinai Hospital for 35 years. He founded the Synagogue Center in Baltimore as well as Yeshivas Hagraz Bengris, a Talmudical graduate school, in Jerusalem. Rabbi Vitsick (on the far right, standing) and Rabbi Joseph Schecter (second from the right) are shown talking to a group of young men in October 1966. (Courtesy of the JMM, 1988.142.18.)

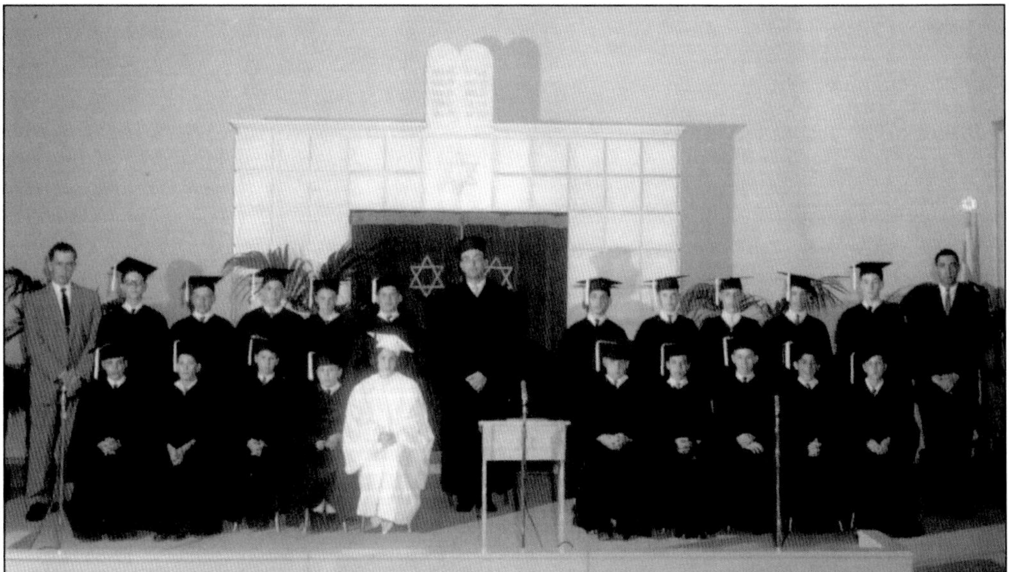

While Liberty Jewish Center began meeting in 1952 on Liberty Heights Avenue, the congregation traces its roots to the Anshe Emunah Congregation (established 1887) and the Aitz Chaim Congregation (established around 1887), both located in East Baltimore. In 1961, the new synagogue merged with the two older congregations. In 1959, Jack Classon photographed the Liberty Jewish Center graduation class with Rabbi Jacob Max (center). (Courtesy of the JMM, 1987.168.17.)

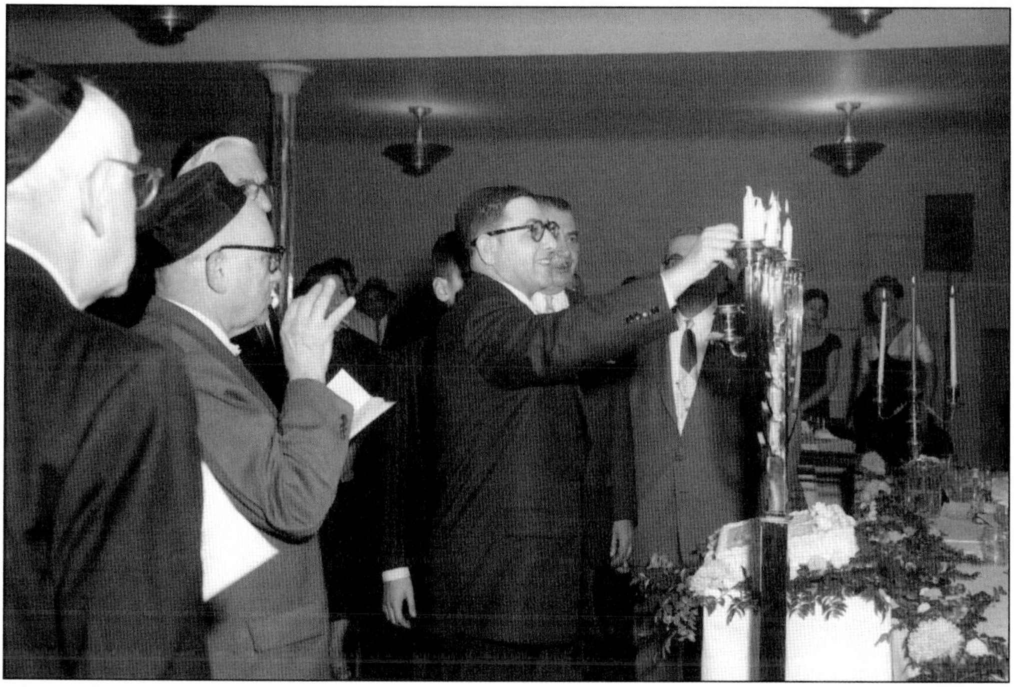

The Beth Isaac Congregation began in 1923 on Springhill Avenue between Park Heights and Reisterstown Road. The congregation merged with Adath Israel Congregation (established 1914) in 1948. The congregation was known as the Milbrook Congregation. Rabbi Manuel Poliakoff lights the Chanukah candles in the 1950s at Beth Isaac. Cantor Samuel Klawansky stands second from the left. (Courtesy of the JMM, 1996.113.89.)

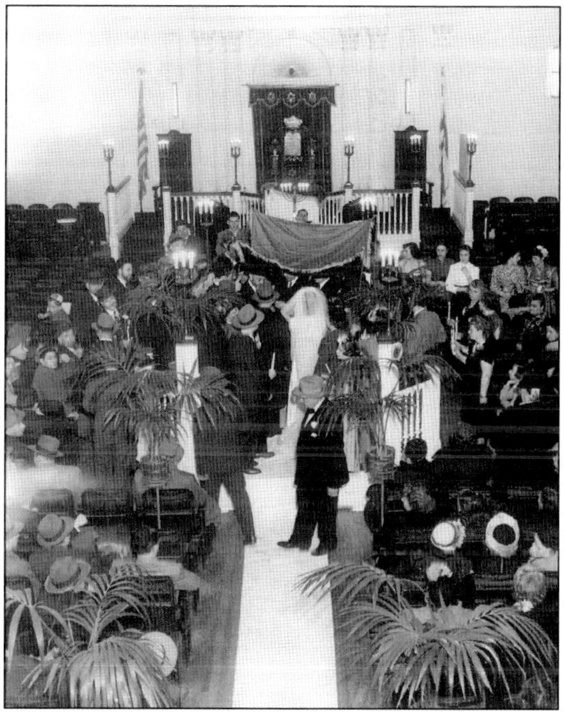

On March 13, 1949, Rabbi Ephraim Shapiro officiates at the wedding of Rabbi Simcha Shafran and Pauline Kahn at Agudas Achim Anshe Sphard Congregation. Founded in 1921–1922, Agudas Achim was the second congregation established on Park Heights Avenue, after Shaarei Zion Congregation in 1919. In 1970–1971, the congregation merged into the Randallstown Synagogue Center. (Courtesy of the JMM, 1997.70.2.)

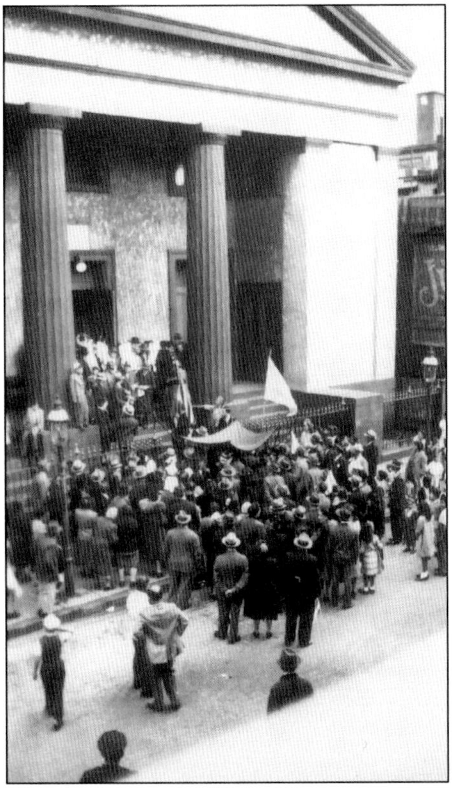

Knesseth Israel Anshe Sphard Congregation (established 1902) dedicates a Torah at their home on 27–31 High Street around 1935. According to two different newspapers, when the congregation's High Street building was demolished in 1954, the tractor cable broke multiple times as a result of how well the structure had been built. (Courtesy of the JMM, 1992.224.1.)

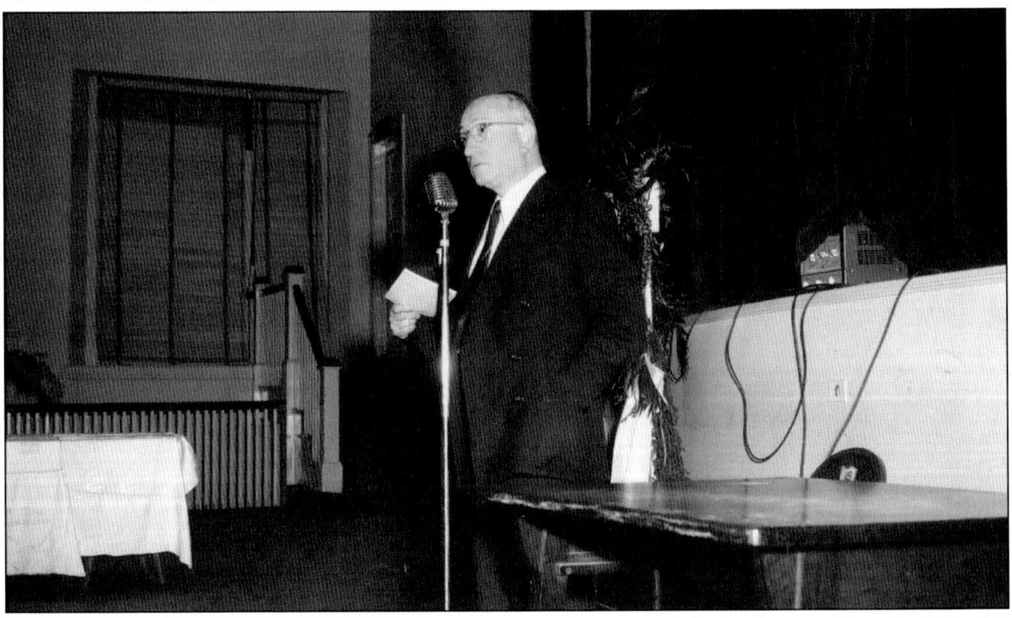

Dr. Louis L. Kaplan (1902–2001) was the executive director of the Baltimore Board of Jewish Education, president of Baltimore Hebrew College from 1930 to 1970, and president of the National Council for Jewish Education from 1939 to 1941. He wrote *A New Approach to the Teaching of the Torah*. Kaplan helped found Beth Am Congregation as an independent synagogue. Today the congregation is affiliated with the Conservative movement. (Courtesy of the JMM, 1992.108.5.)

Five

Making a Living
Jewish Businesses in Baltimore

In the early 20th century, a fascinating dichotomy of Jewish businesses developed in Baltimore. If a visitor traveled on the east side of the city to Lombard Street, he or she would encounter sidewalks overflowing with open-air markets, chicken coops, and family-owned delis and bakeries. If the same person then trekked to Howard Street on the west side of the city, he or she would find blocks of high-rise department stores and massive garment factories.

A surprising number of national companies have Baltimore Jewish connections. For example, Louis and Jacob Blaustein founded the Amoco Oil Company in the 1910s. Israel Myers started London Fog (originally Londontown Clothes) in 1923. Spice maker Gustav Brunn developed Old Bay Seasoning in the late 1930s. Jerold C. Hoffberger owned the National Brewing Company (makers of National Bohemian Beer and Colt 45). Even the Ouija board was manufactured and sold by William Fuld until the business was sold to Parker Brothers in 1966.

From peddlers and jobbers to mom-and-pop shops, to factory owners and executive officers, the Jewish community has remained linked to the economic prosperity of Baltimore.

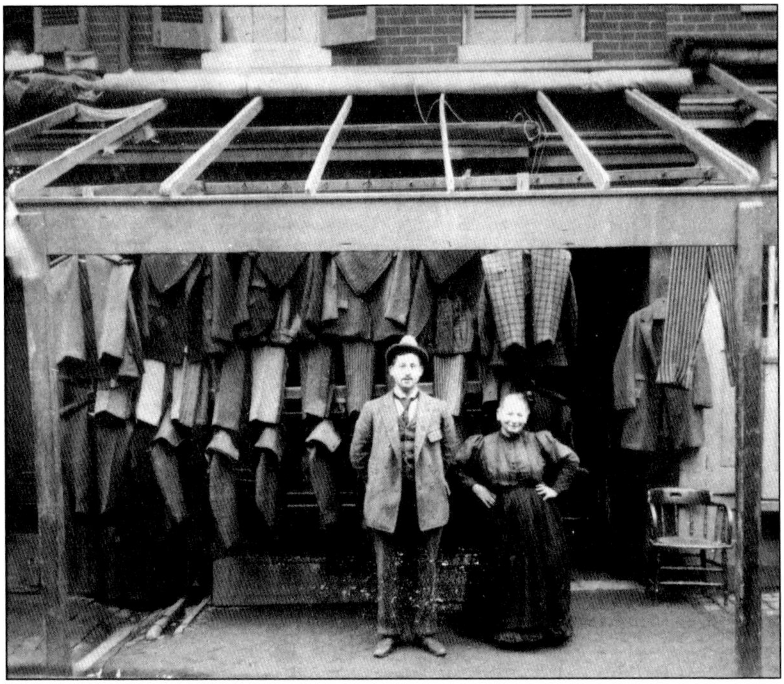

Amelia Kahn and her son, Samuel, operated their family's clothing store on Harrison Street in the 1880s. (Courtesy of the JMM, 1990.204.1.)

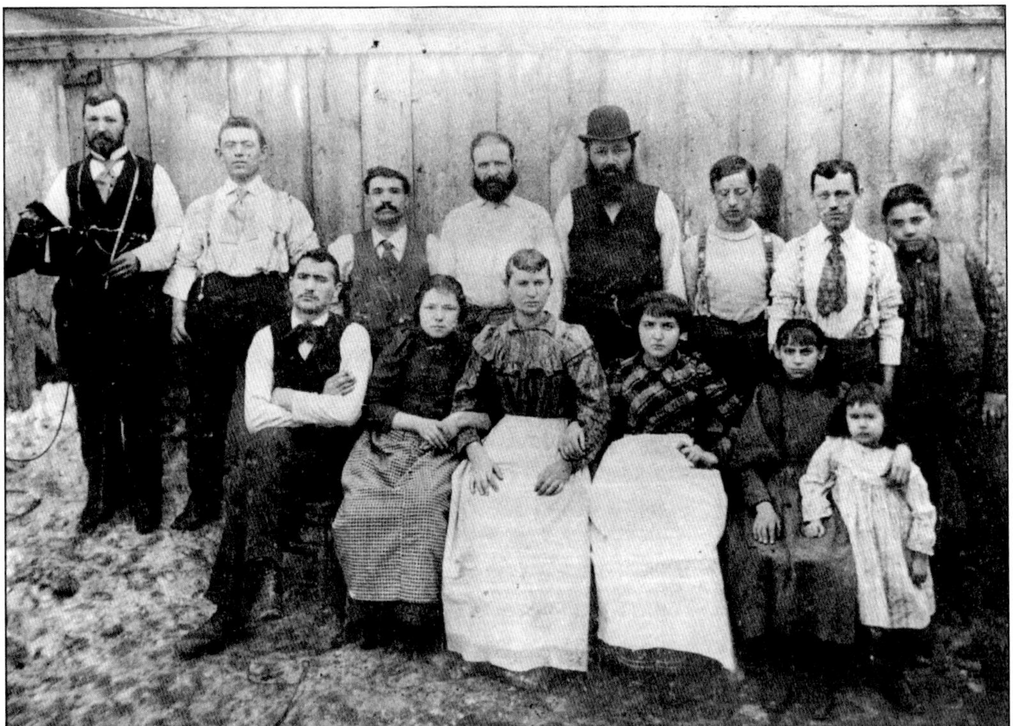

Moses Isaac Berman, in the second row with a measuring tape around his neck, operated a vest-making shop at 211 North Front Street. His family lived next door to the shop. A Russian immigrant, Berman had learned fine hand tailoring while serving in the Russian army for three years. This photograph dates to around 1893. (Courtesy of the JMM, 1984.201.1.)

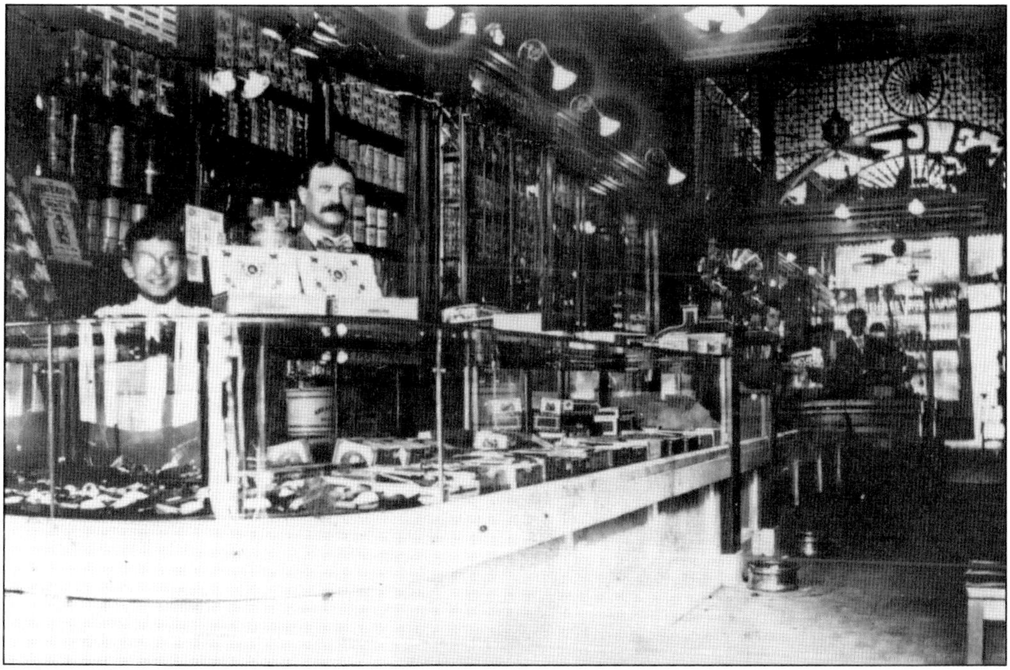

Fader's Tobacco Store was located at 210 Baltimore Street at the dawn of the 20th century. (Courtesy of the JMM, 1989.194.1.)

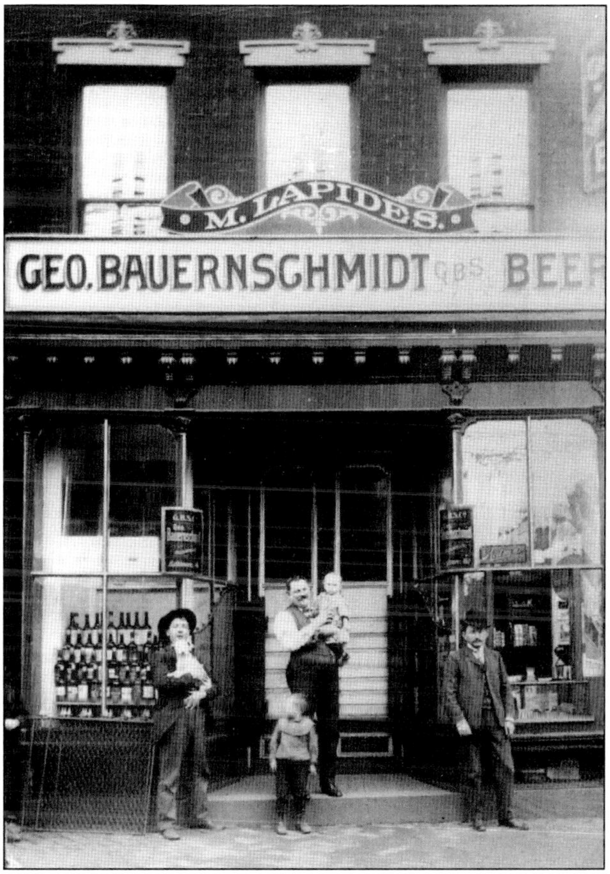

Max Lapides opened a saloon in Baltimore shortly after he immigrated to the city from Russia in 1897. In this photograph from around 1905, Lapides holds one son, Abe, while another, Joseph, stands at his feet. (Courtesy of the JMM, 1988.227.1a.)

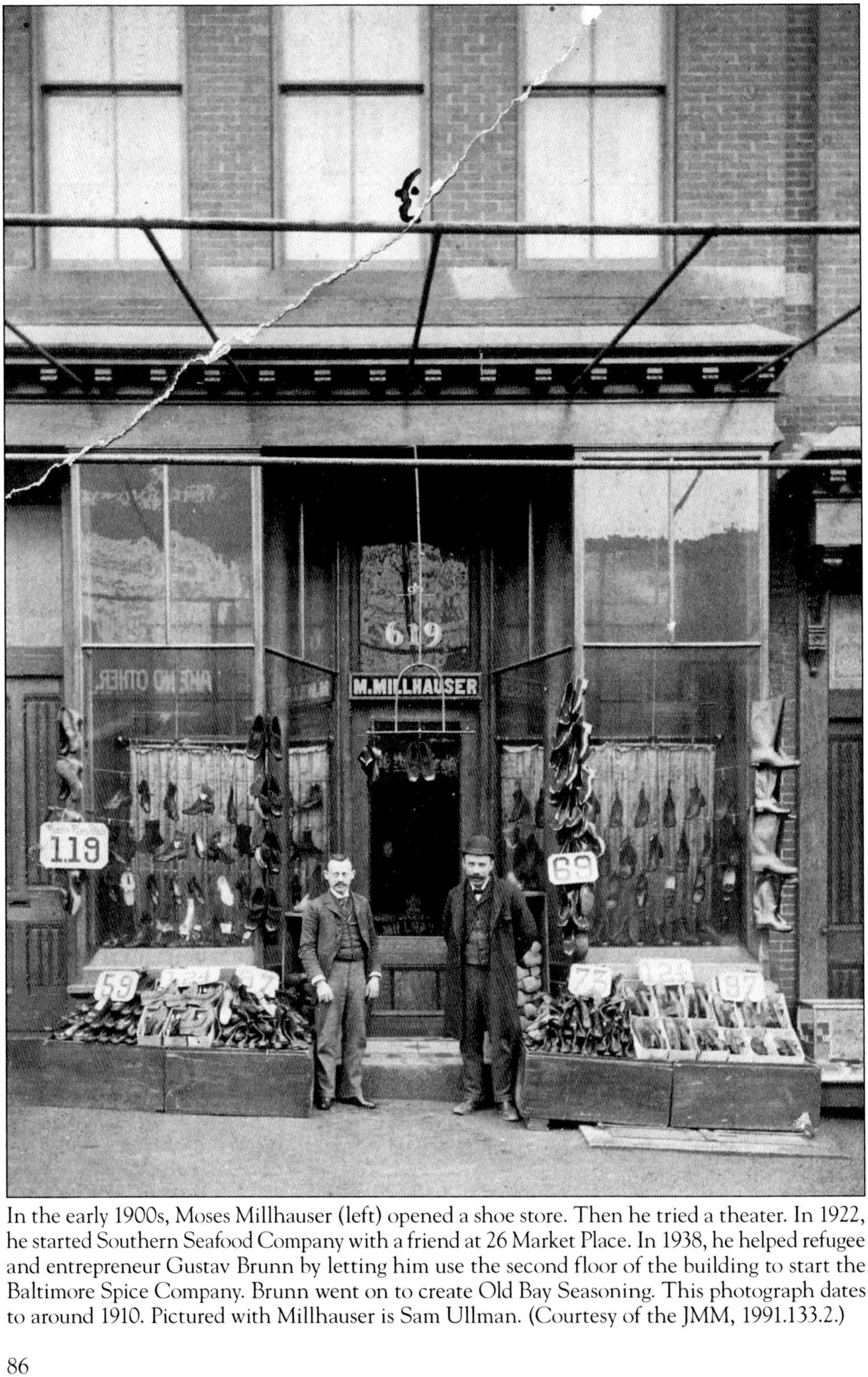

In the early 1900s, Moses Millhauser (left) opened a shoe store. Then he tried a theater. In 1922, he started Southern Seafood Company with a friend at 26 Market Place. In 1938, he helped refugee and entrepreneur Gustav Brunn by letting him use the second floor of the building to start the Baltimore Spice Company. Brunn went on to create Old Bay Seasoning. This photograph dates to around 1910. Pictured with Millhauser is Sam Ullman. (Courtesy of the JMM, 1991.133.2.)

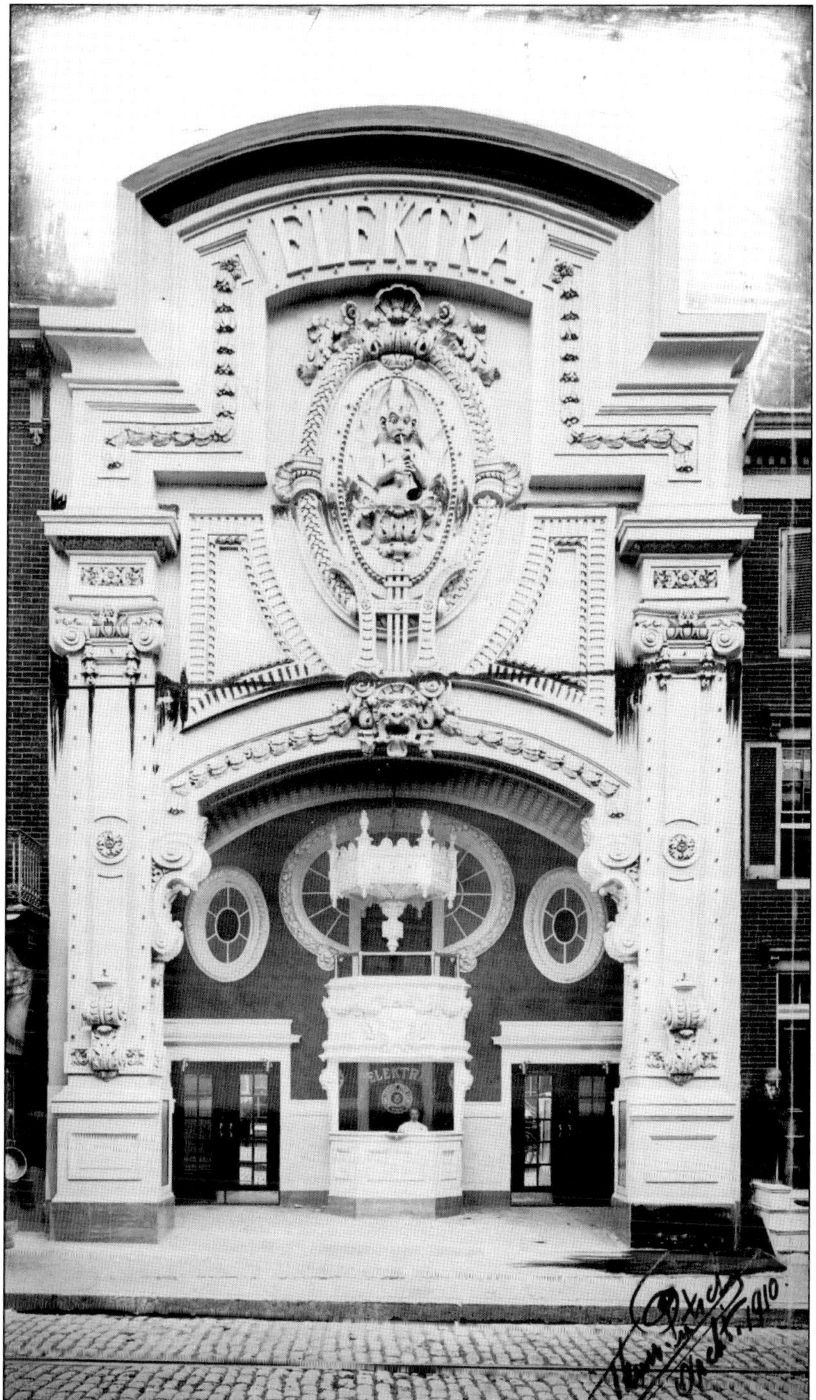

The Elektra Theatre, a moving picture and vaudeville house, began at 1039 North Gay Street in 1910. Run by Moses Millhauser, the theater offered silent films for 10¢ a ticket. Richard Millhauser recalled, "Pop used to tell me that he would sell tickets and then run back and collect [them]." This photograph dates to around 1910. (Courtesy of the JMM, 1991.133.4.)

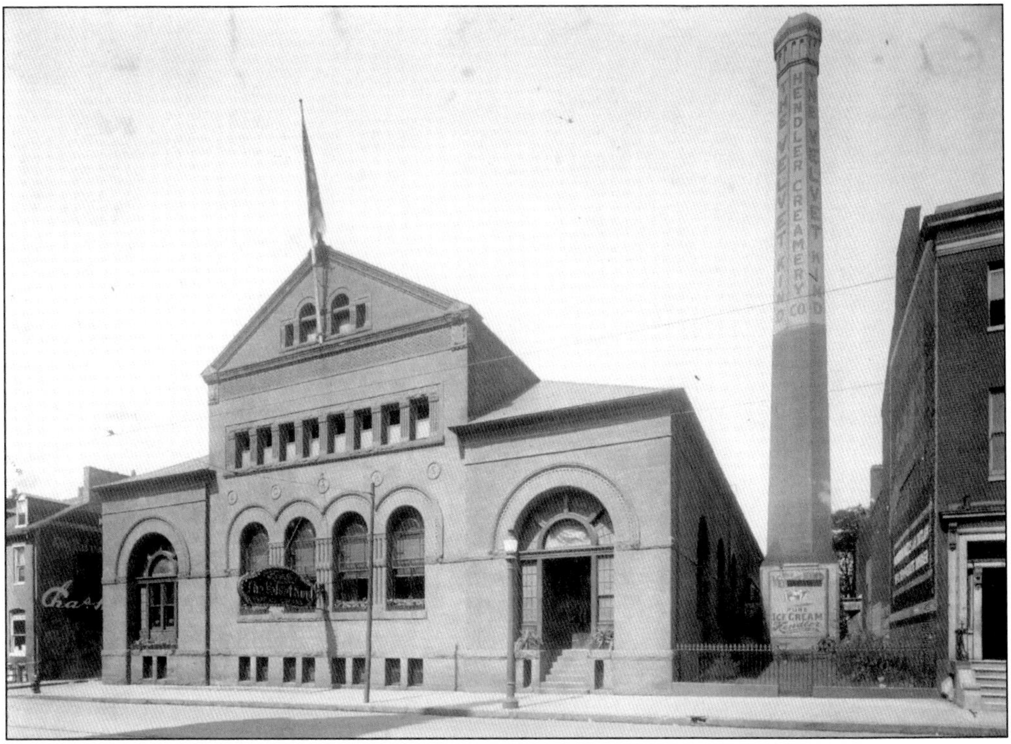

The Hendler Creamery Company's motto was "The Velvet Kind." Founded in 1905 by L. Manuel Hendler, the company began with just three flavors: vanilla, chocolate, and strawberry. Hendler's son, Albert, recalled that additional flavors were developed over the years, including "ginger ice cream and peppermint ice cream." Their seasonal "Good Old Fashioned Eggnog" ice cream was a perennial favorite. Hendler's was bought by Borden in 1929, which dropped the Hendler name in the 1960s. Hendler's Richardsonian Romanesque building at 1100 East Baltimore Street still stands, and one of its offices was reinstalled as the boardroom of the nearby Jewish Museum of Maryland. Shown are the factories (above) and the company baseball team (below) in 1928. (Courtesy of the JMM, (above) 1996.148.6, (below) 1997.16.1.)

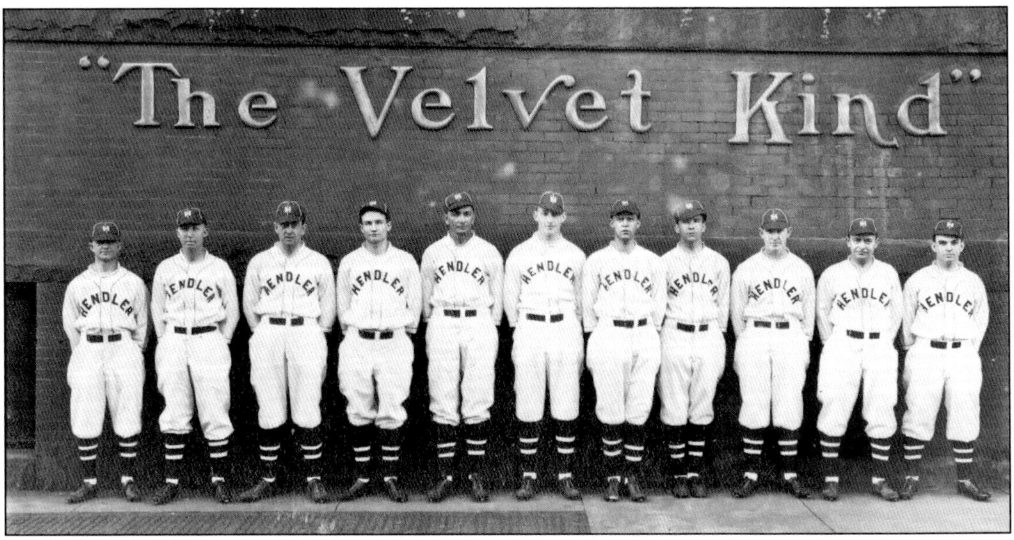

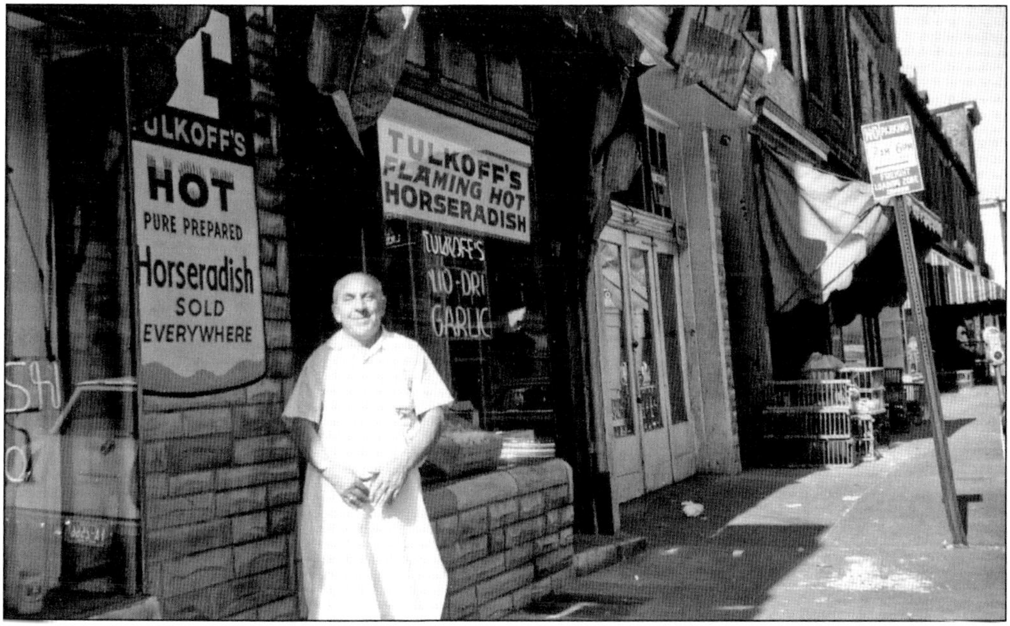

Harry Tulkoff (1899–1989) started Tulkoff's Products, Inc., which rose from a simple grocery stand to the largest supplier of horseradish in the country. When asked why he chose horseradish, Tulkoff responded, "You gotta have horseradish to be in the produce business." When describing his first sale, he said, "I never saw such beautiful stuff in my life. Weighed about 50 lbs . . . with the green tops and everything." (Courtesy of the JMM, 1992.189.004.)

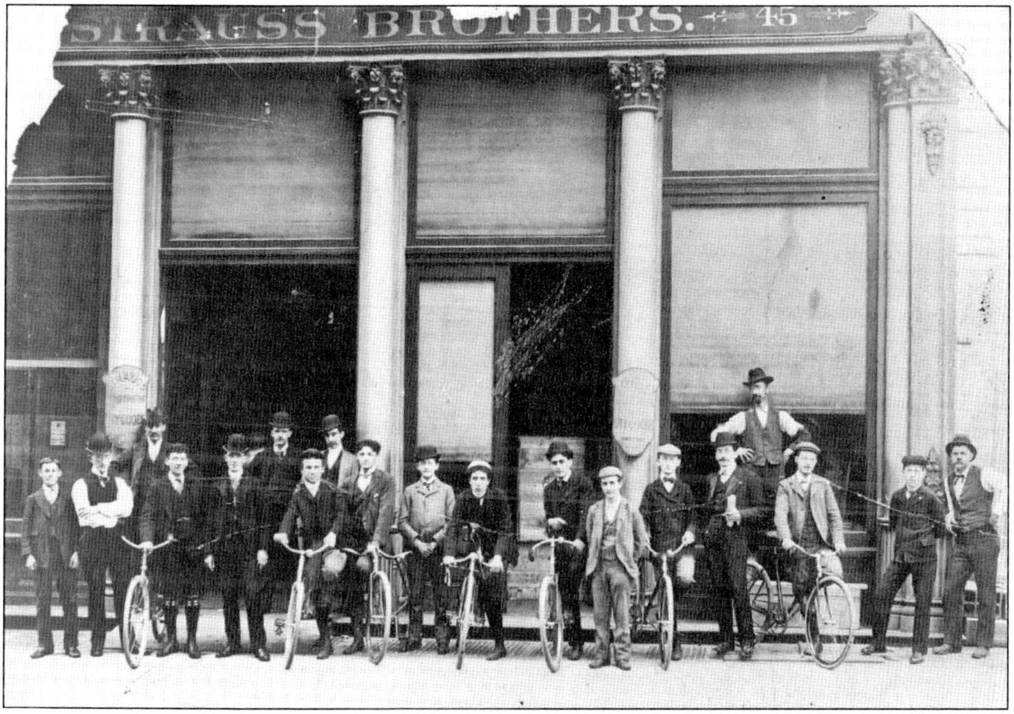

The Strauss Brothers Dry Goods store stood at 45 Hopkins Place in 1900. (Courtesy of the JMM, 1985.50.3.)

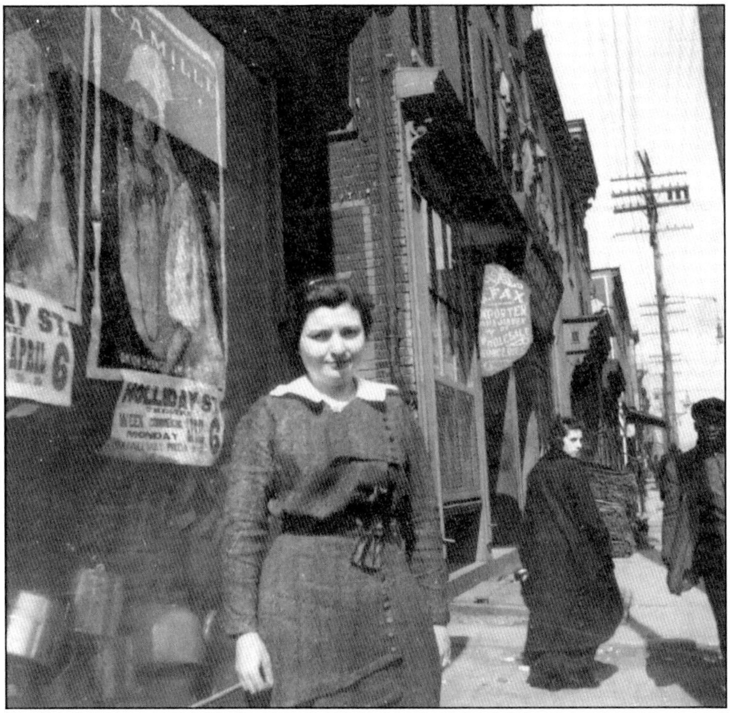

Bessie (Paymer) Grossman stands outside her family's dairy in 1913. Located on Pratt Street, the store was owned by her parents, Joseph and Ella Grossman. (Courtesy of the JMM, 1992.4.1.)

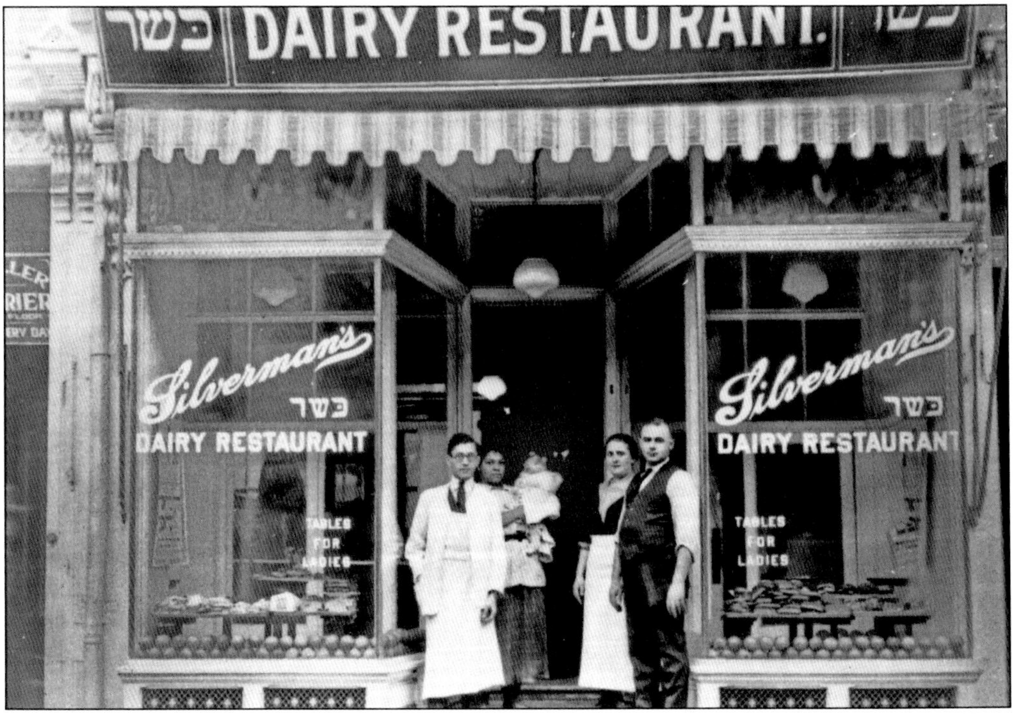

In this *c.* 1921 photograph, (from left to right) Harry Greenspan, an unidentified person holding infant Miriam (Waitsman) Silverman, and Tillie and Isadore Silverman stand in front of Silverman's Dairy Restaurant (a Kosher restaurant that did not serve meat), which was located at 1008 Baltimore Street. (Courtesy of the JMM, 1990.84.2a.)

Baltimore was known as "the city that tries to suit everyone." Most of the clothing factories were Jewish owned and produced men's garments. This 1913 illustration is from the Strouse and Brothers' booklet, *Rulers of the World*. (Courtesy of the JMM, 1991.51.2a.)

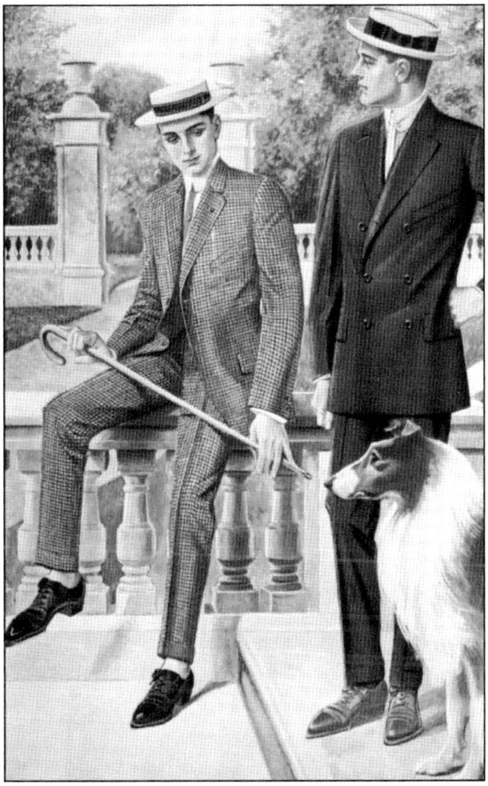

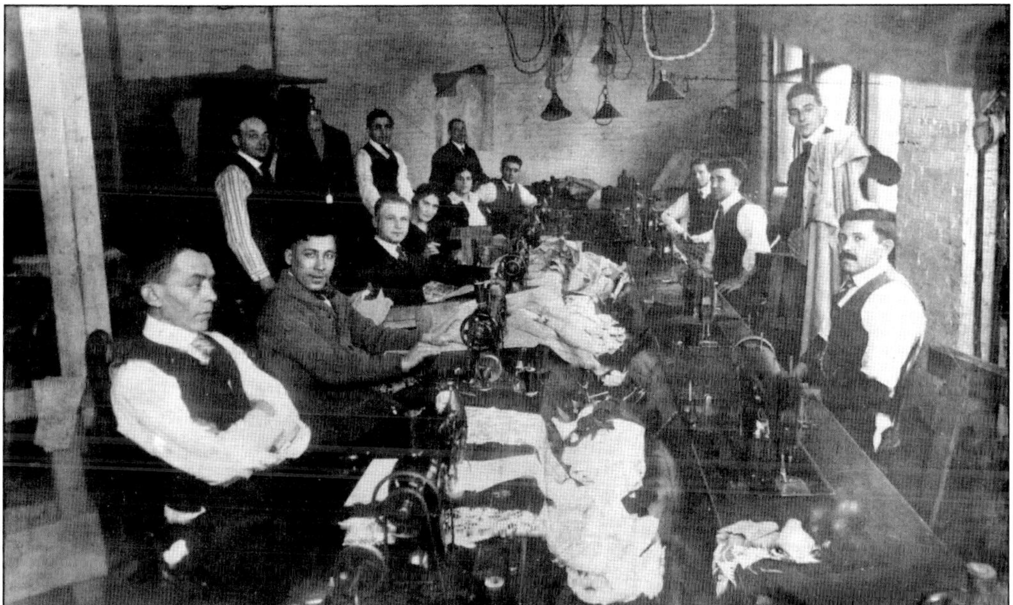

Started in 1855, Sonneborn and Company was the largest employer of clothing workers in Baltimore by 1919. Though it closed in 1931, its building still stands today on Baltimore's west side at Paca and Pratt Streets. Isidore Goldberg sits on the left side, second from the front, while working at Sonneborn around 1915. (Courtesy of the JMM, 1991.39.2.)

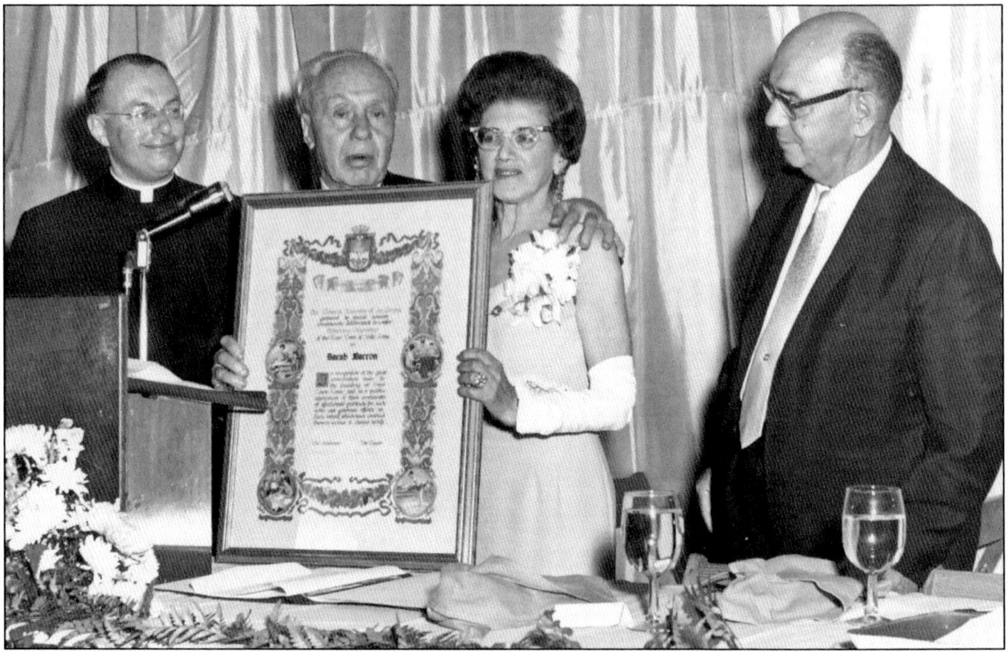

Sarah (Borinsky) Barron (1900–1993) came to Baltimore from Russia at the age of 12. She left school early to work in the clothing factories to support her family. As a minor working in Wohlmuth's, she used to hide in the scrap heap whenever a child-labor inspector visited. After she began working at Sonneborn, she joined the Amalgamated Clothing Workers of America (established 1914) and became heavily involved in the union movement. She was arrested 13 times and changed her last name from Borinsky to Barron to sound less "Communist." In 1967, she was honored at a dinner at the Pikesville Armory. (Courtesy of the JMM, 1993.58.4a.)

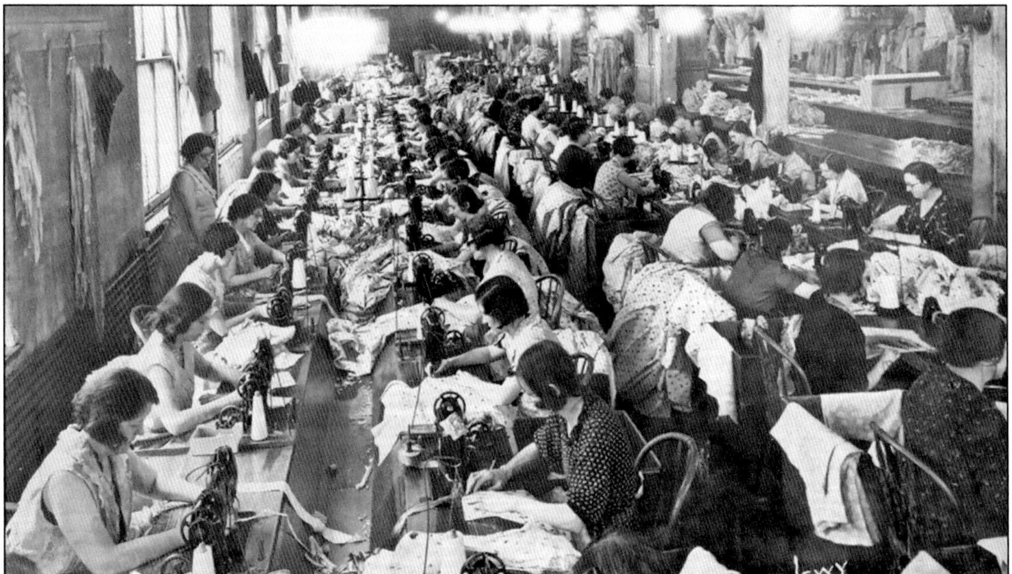

By the 1930s, conditions in most clothing factories, such as Katzenberg Brothers (seen here), had begun to improve. All of the factories, except for L. Greif, had unionized, but even L. Greif had adopted many of the union's resolutions. (Courtesy of the BMI.)

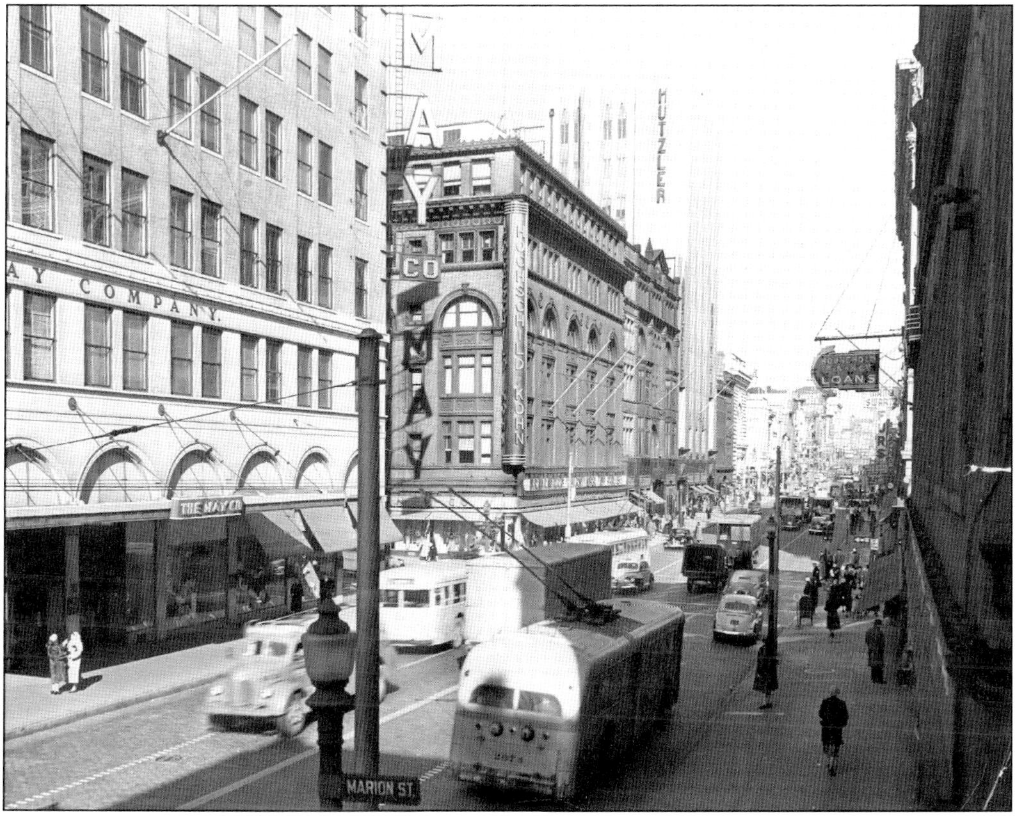

In 2001, the *Baltimore Sun* remembered Howard Street in its prime: "[Howard Street] was Baltimore's Fifth Avenue, the site of the city's leading department and specialty stores. You could buy everything from a grand piano to prestige furniture or furs on Howard Street. The cornucopia of Lexington Market and mass-market bargain houses added vibrancy to the area." (Courtesy of the EPFL.)

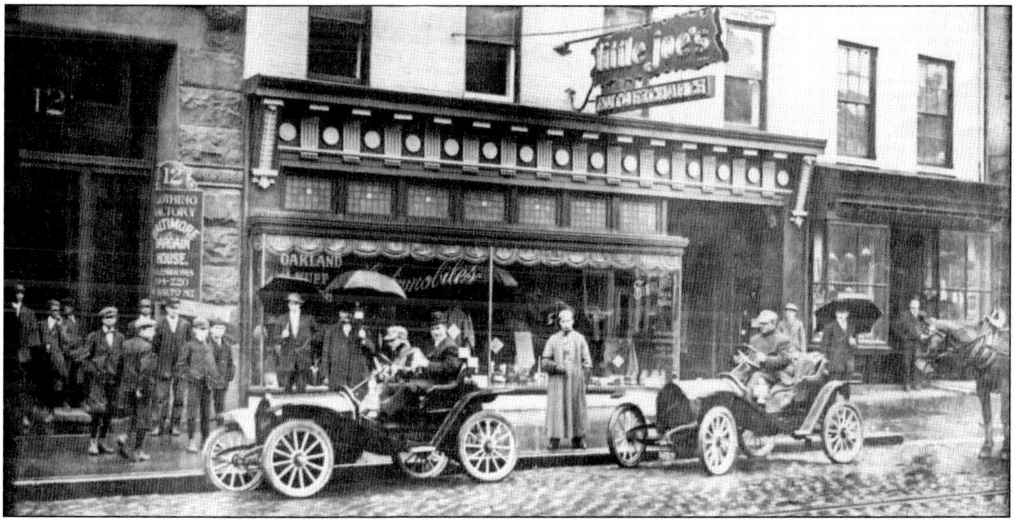

Little Joe's Automobile Exchange was a discount and sporting goods store located at Baltimore and Howard Streets. The eponymous store refers to Joe Wiesenfeld's diminutive stature. His relative Moses Wiesenfeld is shown driving the second car around 1911. (Courtesy of the JMM, 1990.2.56.)

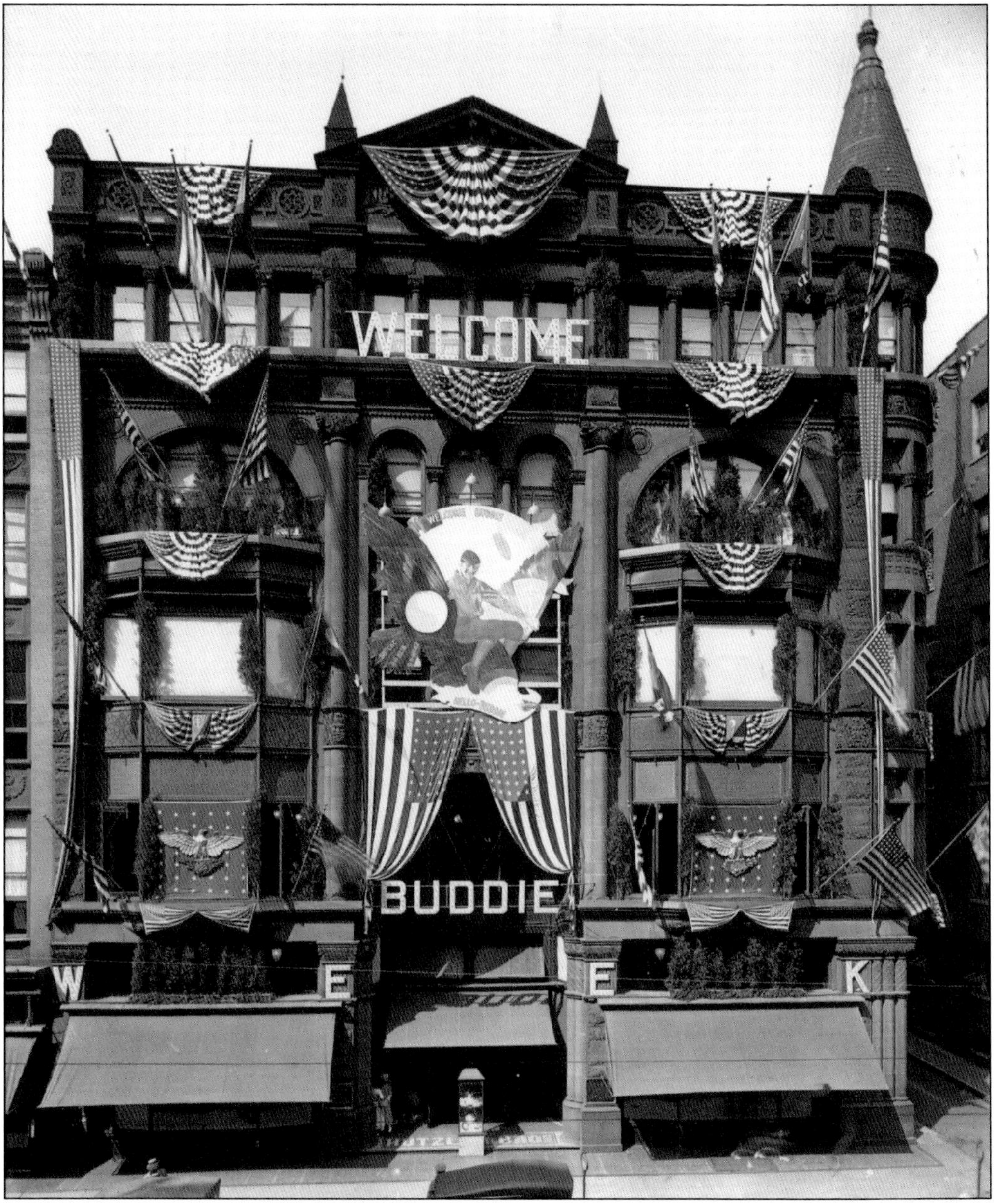

Moses Hutzler (1800–1899) immigrated to Baltimore from Bavaria in 1838 and started a store on Eutaw Street. His three sons—Abram (1836–1927), Charles (1840–1907), and David (1843–1915)—all followed him into the family business, opening and running additional stores. In 1888, they opened the Hutzler Palace Building, the second grand department store in Baltimore after Gutman's. Designed by Baldwin and Pennington, the Romanesque Revival building was called "one of the largest and best arranged buildings of its kind in the United States . . . a credit to Baltimore and her workmen and a monument to the enterprise and industry of its proprietors" by the *Baltimore Sun* when it opened. The Palace Store is shown decorated for "Buddie Week" around 1920. (Courtesy of the JMM, 2005.11.1.)

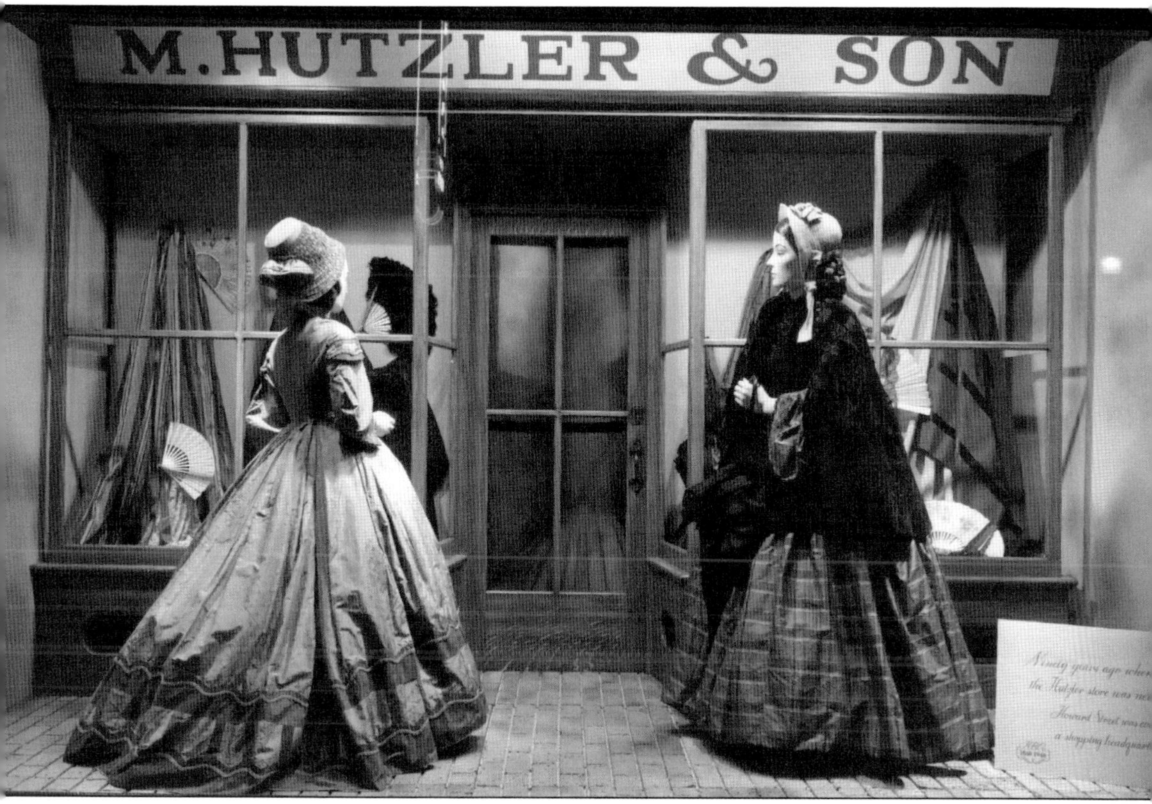

Hutzler's Department Store celebrated its 90th anniversary in 1948. The display sign reads, "Ninety years ago when the Hutzler store was new . . . Howard Street was even then a shopping headquarters." (Courtesy of the JMM, 1989.207.29.31.)

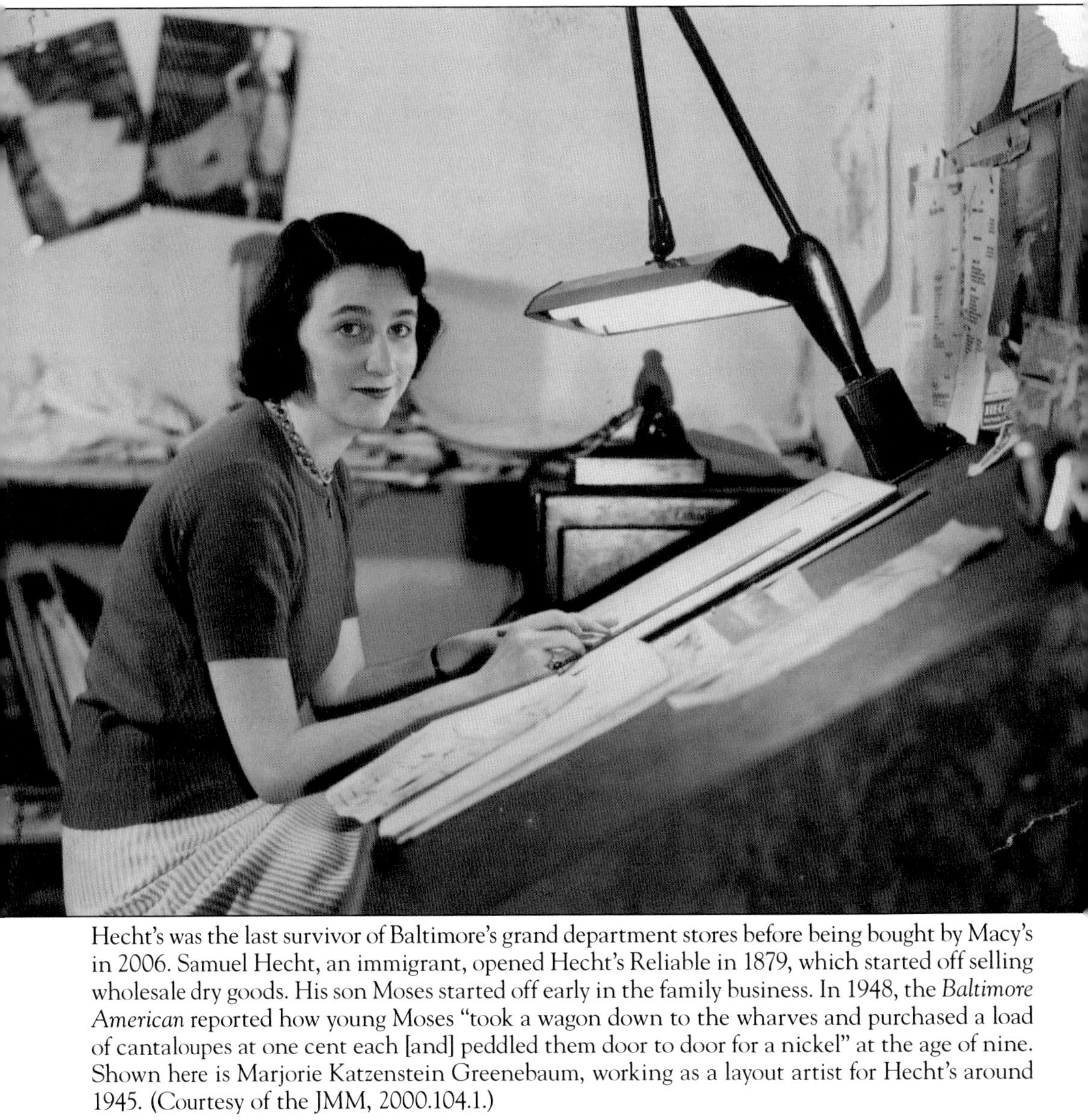

Hecht's was the last survivor of Baltimore's grand department stores before being bought by Macy's in 2006. Samuel Hecht, an immigrant, opened Hecht's Reliable in 1879, which started off selling wholesale dry goods. His son Moses started off early in the family business. In 1948, the *Baltimore American* reported how young Moses "took a wagon down to the wharves and purchased a load of cantaloupes at one cent each [and] peddled them door to door for a nickel" at the age of nine. Shown here is Marjorie Katzenstein Greenebaum, working as a layout artist for Hecht's around 1945. (Courtesy of the JMM, 2000.104.1.)

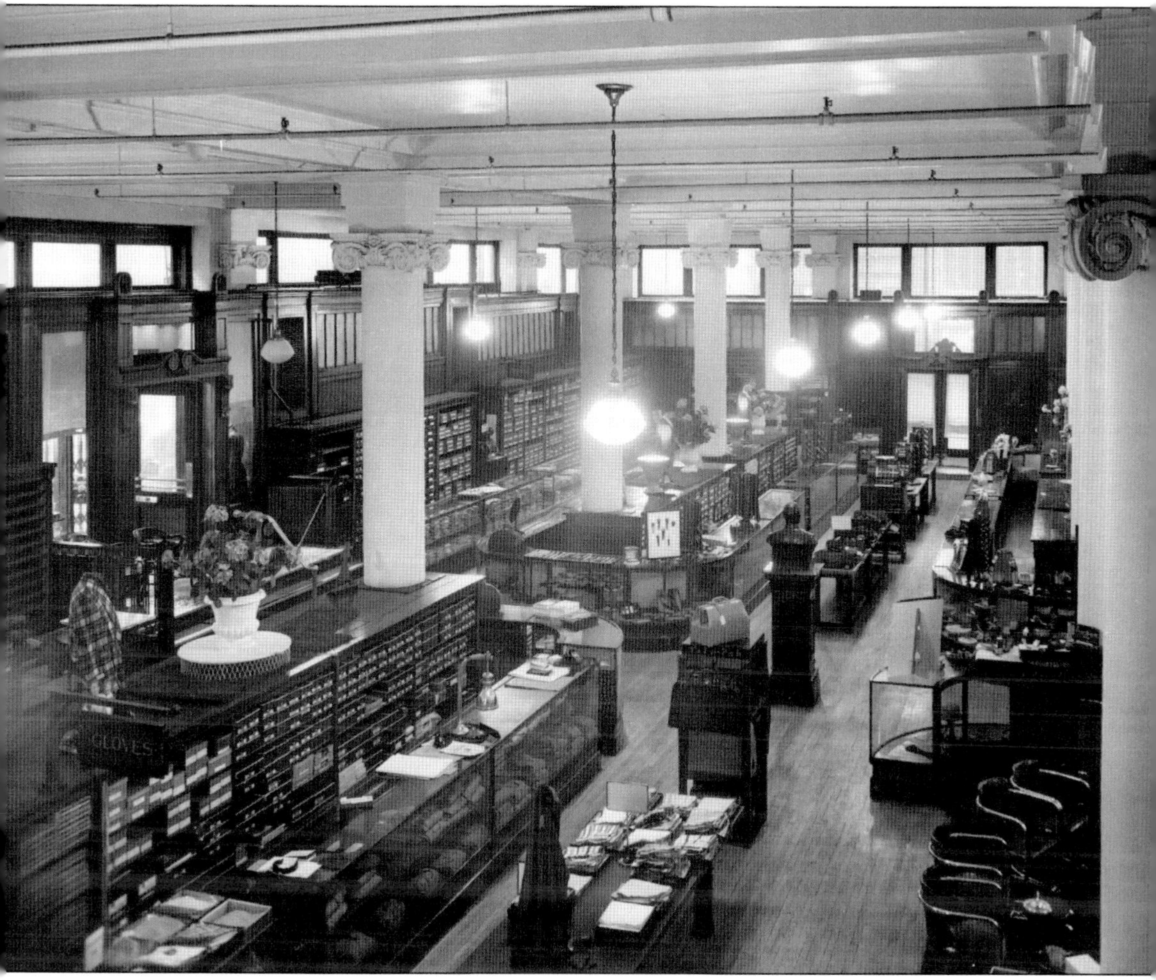

Isaac Hamburger, originally from Nudenberg, arrived in Baltimore at the age of 20. Initially, he worked as a clerk in a clothing store owned by Philip Herzberg before opening his own store on Harrison Street in 1849. By 1855, he had moved to Pratt Street and began wholesale trade in addition to retail. By the 1890s, there were branch stores in Washington, D.C., and Delaware. Hamburger opened his eponymous department store in 1894 on Howard Street. The store survived the Great Fire of 1904 by only one block. Hamburger's became known for menswear, carrying shirts, shoes, and hats on the first floor, sportswear on the second, and tuxedos on the third. This photograph dates to the 1940s. (Courtesy of the JMM, 1992.257.3.)

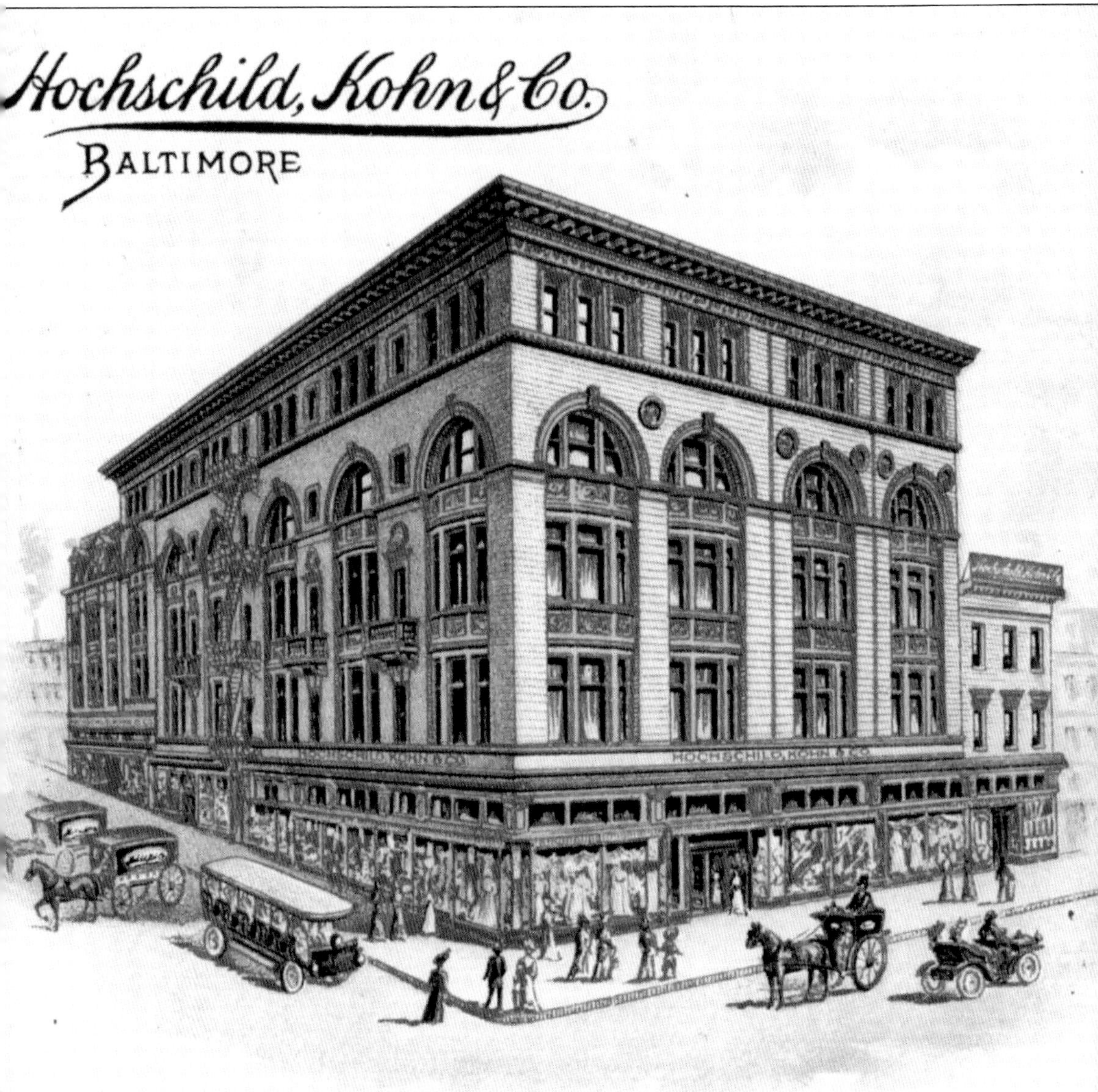

Bernhard Kohn opened a wholesale dry goods and notions business called B. Kohn and Brother after the Civil War. When both Max Hochschild and Kohn wanted the same plot at the corner of Howard and Lexington Streets, they decided to go into business together, opening Hochschild, Kohn, and Company in 1897. The store (shown in 1922) prided itself on its hospitality. Benno Kohn remembered overhearing a sales clerk saying to a customer, "No, we haven't had any for quite awhile and don't expect any soon." Upon hearing this, Benno raced over to ask, "What haven't we got and why can't I get it for you?" The customer responded, "Oh, we were talking about the weather—how long since we've had rain!" (Photograph by Hughes Company; courtesy of the JMM, 1994.106.17.)

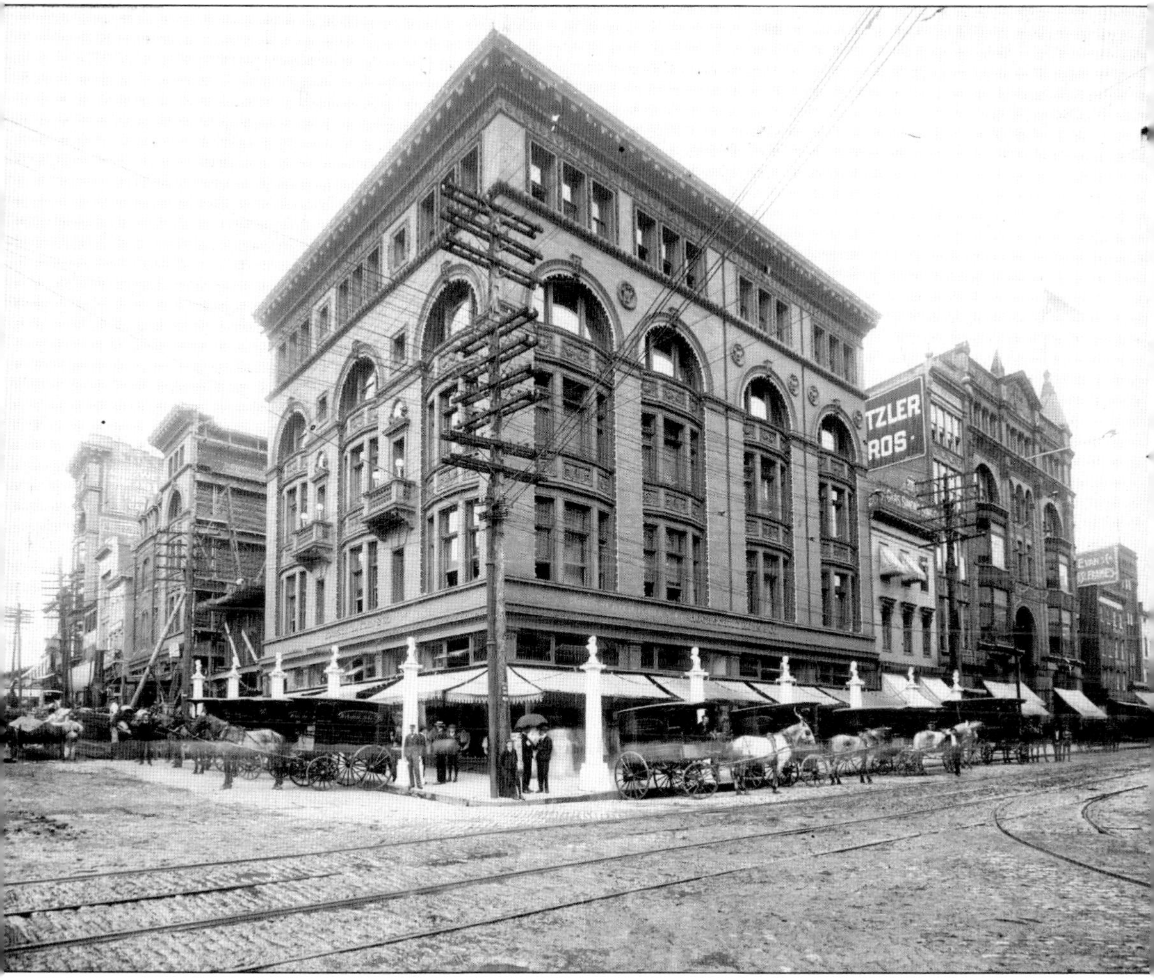

Walter Sondheim Jr. served as the senior vice president of Hochschild, Kohn, and Company when the store integrated its sales force. They were the first department store in Baltimore to employ an African American as a salesperson when Mamie Collins was promoted in 1959. When a group of students from Morgan State University protested discriminatory practices by organizing sit-ins at various department store restaurants, they were surprised to find themselves treated courteously at Hochschild's. After hearing that Hochschild's had integrated, the other department stores followed suit within days. (Courtesy of the JMM, 1987.226.6.)

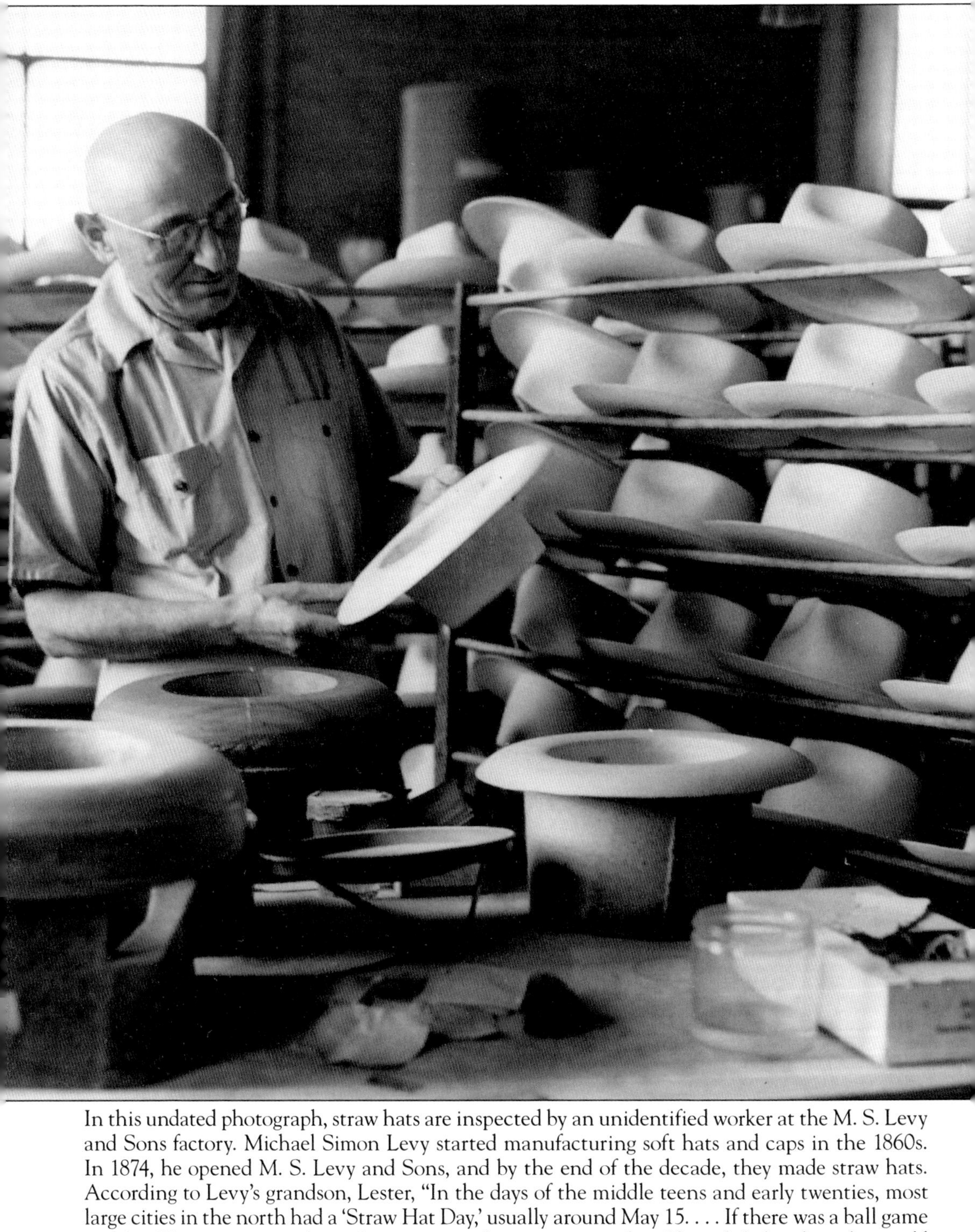

In this undated photograph, straw hats are inspected by an unidentified worker at the M. S. Levy and Sons factory. Michael Simon Levy started manufacturing soft hats and caps in the 1860s. In 1874, he opened M. S. Levy and Sons, and by the end of the decade, they made straw hats. According to Levy's grandson, Lester, "In the days of the middle teens and early twenties, most large cities in the north had a 'Straw Hat Day,' usually around May 15. . . . If there was a ball game on May 15, every man in the park was supposed to wear a straw hat. If one failed to do so, he would often be unfortunate enough to have his felt hat plucked from his head by the man behind him, who would send it skimming off into the ballpark." (Courtesy of the JMM, 2002.79.272.)

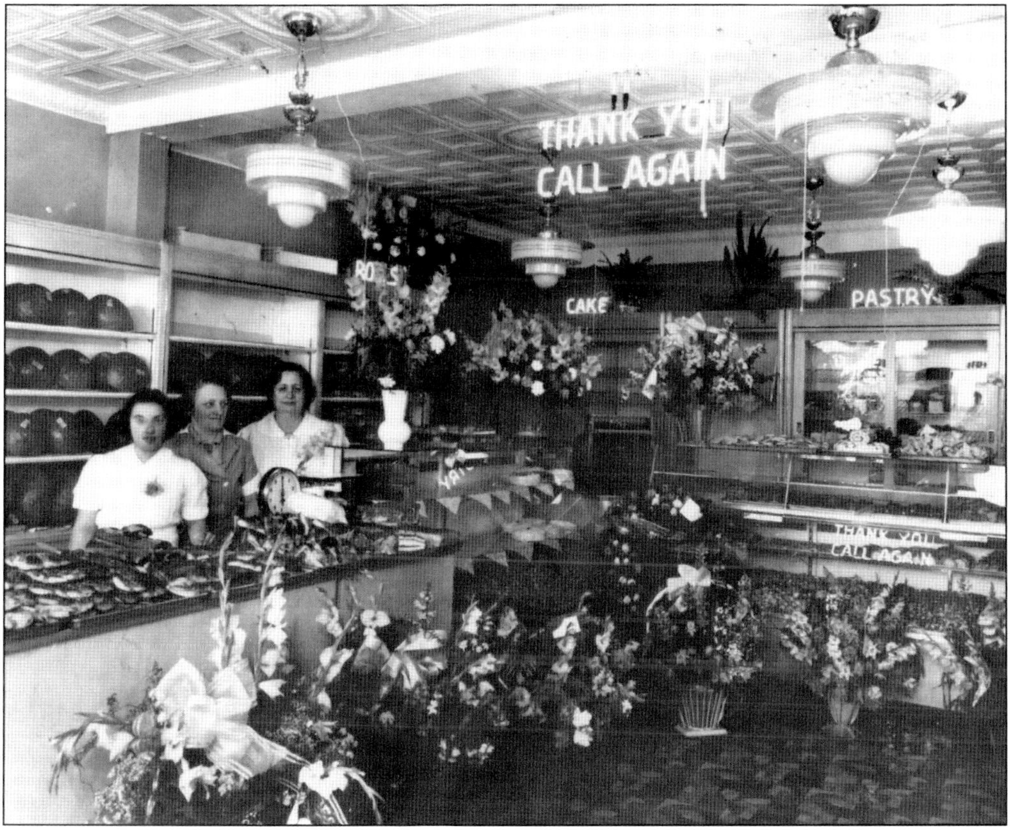

In 1939, Rose Crystal, one of the women pictured here, managed the grand opening of the family-owned Crystal's Fancy Bakery when it relocated to 1101 Lombard Street. (Courtesy of the JMM, 1987.203.1.)

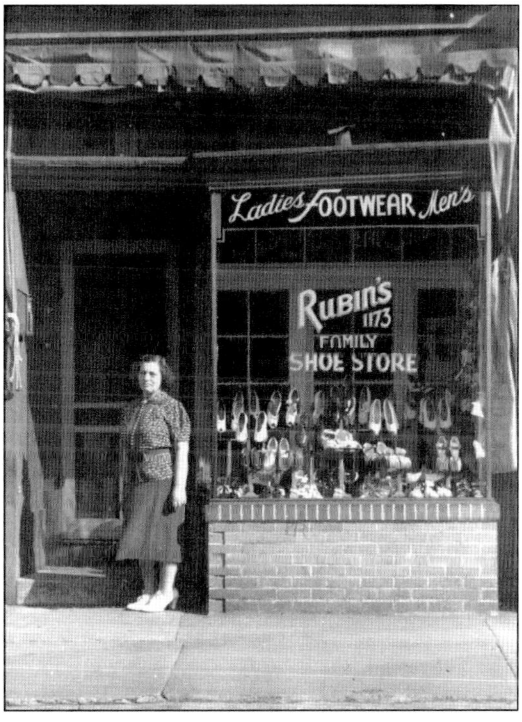

Around 1935, Yetta Rubin stands in front of her store, Rubin's Family Shoe Store, located at 1173 Lombard Street. (Courtesy of the JMM, 1990.187.1.)

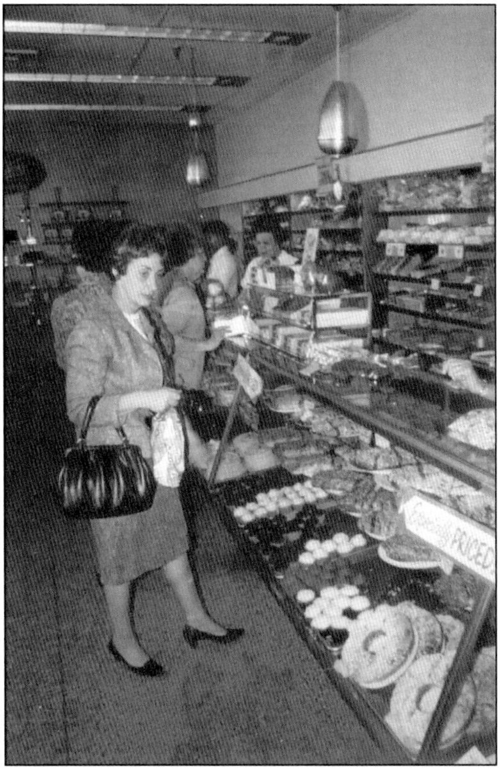

Dora and Ike Silber, parents of state senator Rosalie Silber Abrams, started Silber's Bakery in the early 1900s. Abrams recalled, "When I ran for office for the first time, and every time since, countless people would say to me, 'We're going to vote for you because your father kept us alive during the Depression.' My father had a breadline." Nancy B. Katz is shown looking through the display cases at Silber's Bakery in 1968. (Courtesy of the JMM, 2006.20.6.)

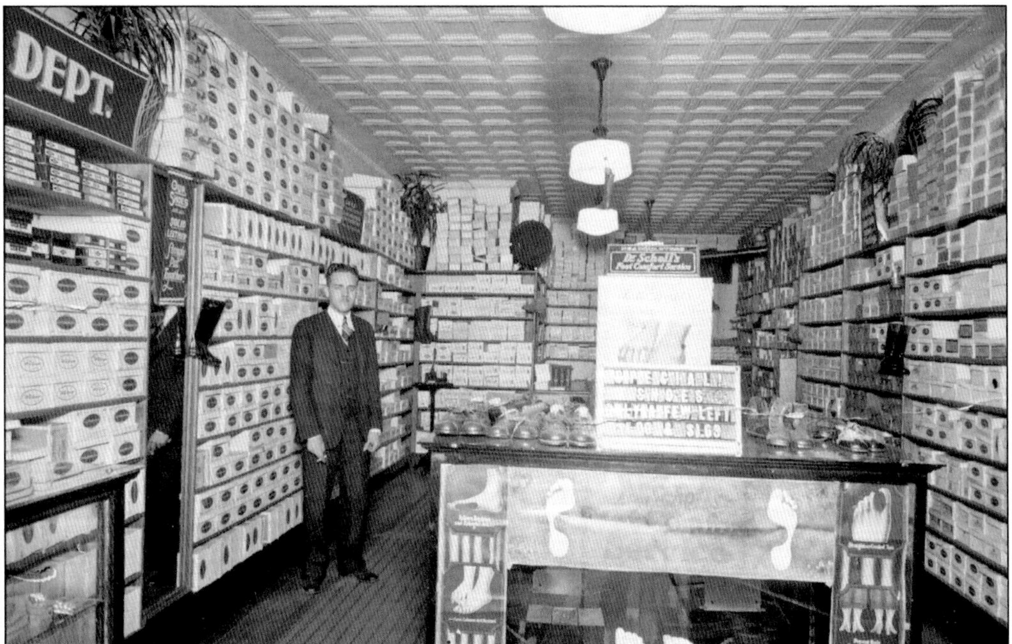

Not all early Jewish businesses were in East or West Baltimore. Joseph Strauss ran the shoe store owned by the Strauss family on Falls Road in Hampden in 1928. (Courtesy of the JMM, 1986.113.10.)

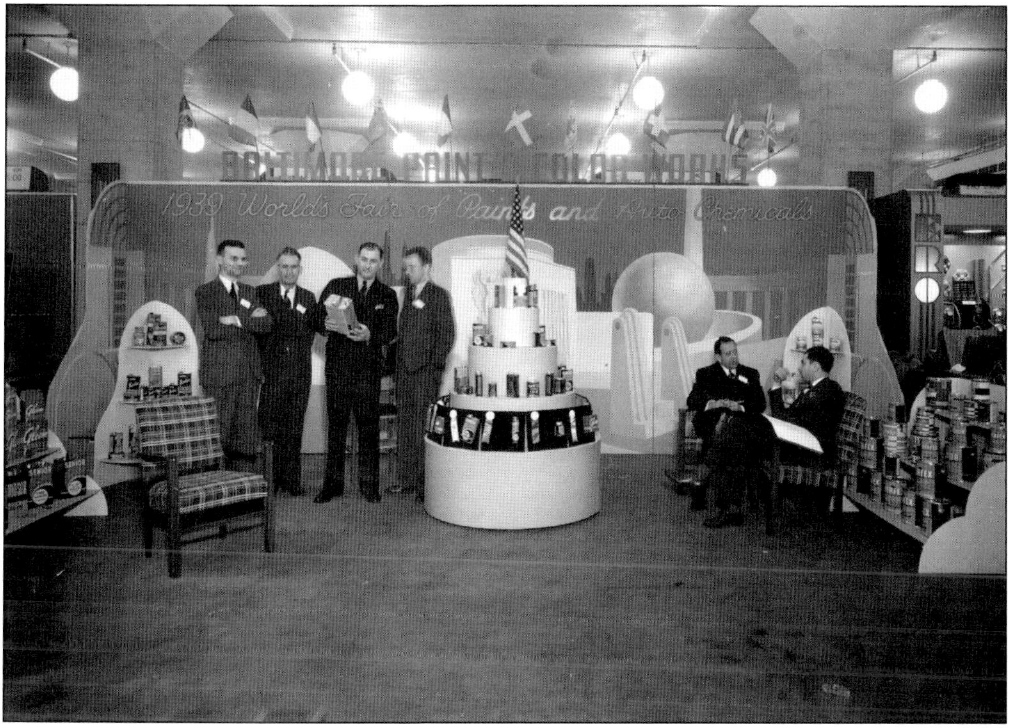

In this photograph by Seidman Photo Service, the Baltimore Paint and Color Works displays its products at the World's Fair of Paint and Auto Chemicals in 1939. (Courtesy of the JMM, 2005.51.2.)

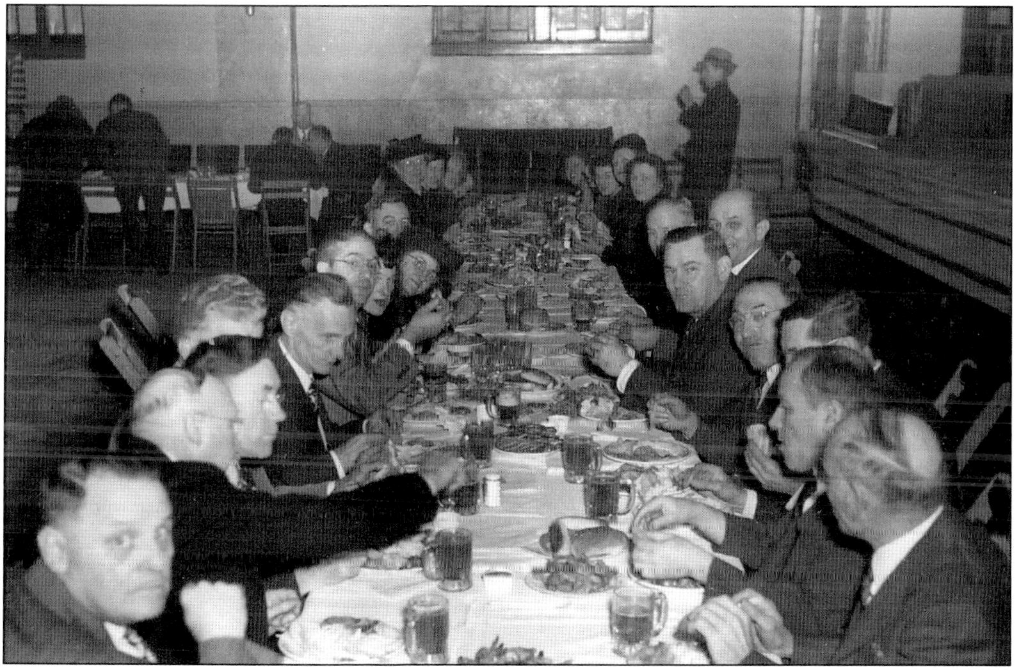

Schloss Brothers holds its annual employee holiday party at the Lithuanian Hall on December 12, 1945. (Courtesy of the JMM, 1991.36.9.)

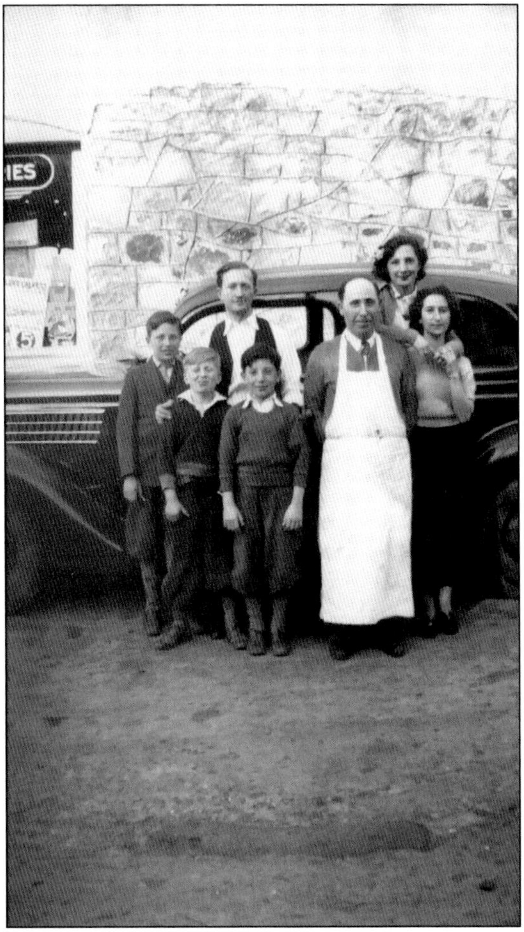

The Burke family stands outside their namesake grocery store in the 1940s. (Courtesy of the JMM, 1994.185.7.)

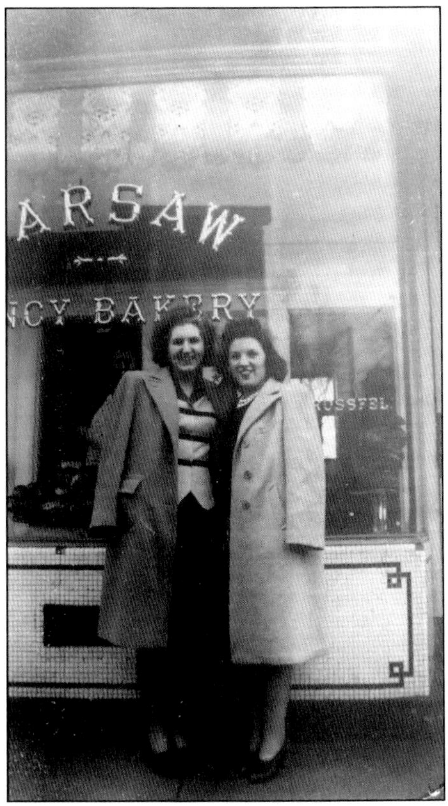

In 1943, Gertrude (Grossfeld) Katz and Nora Cross pose outside the Warsaw Fancy Bakery, which was owned by Katz's parents, Eva and Sol Grossfeld. (Courtesy of the JMM, 1992.12.1d.)

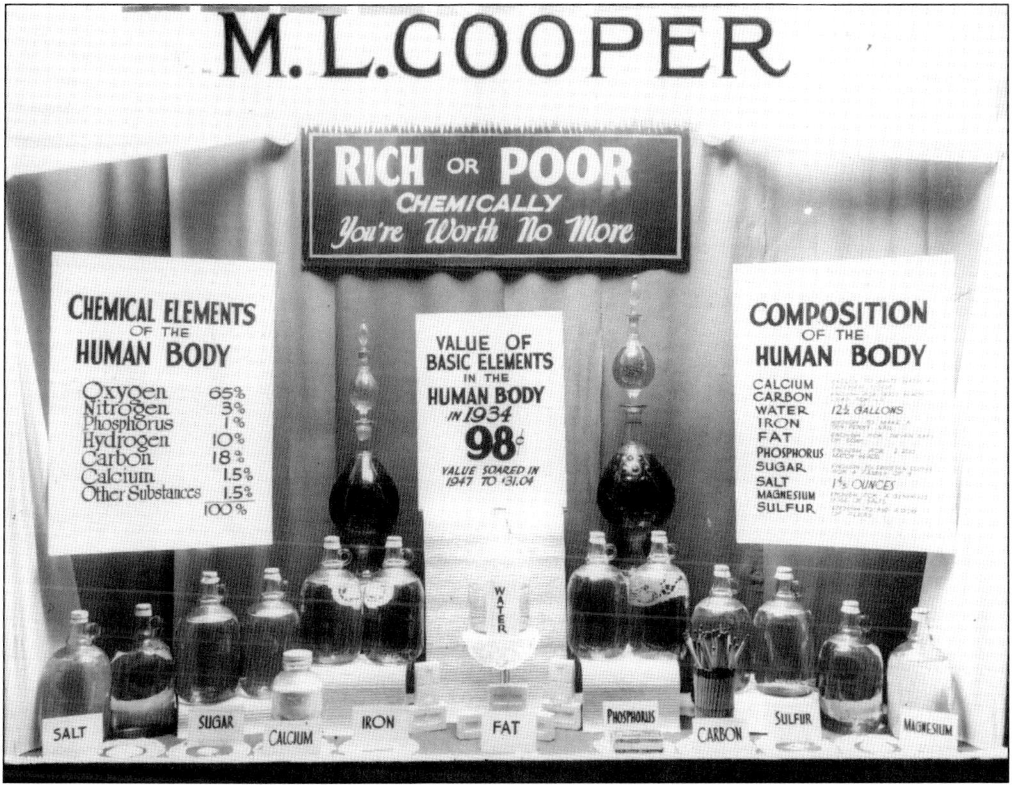

This whimsical M. L. Cooper Pharmacy store window display dates to 1947. It reads, "Rich or Poor—Chemically You're Worth No More." (Courtesy of the JMM, 1983.13.11.)

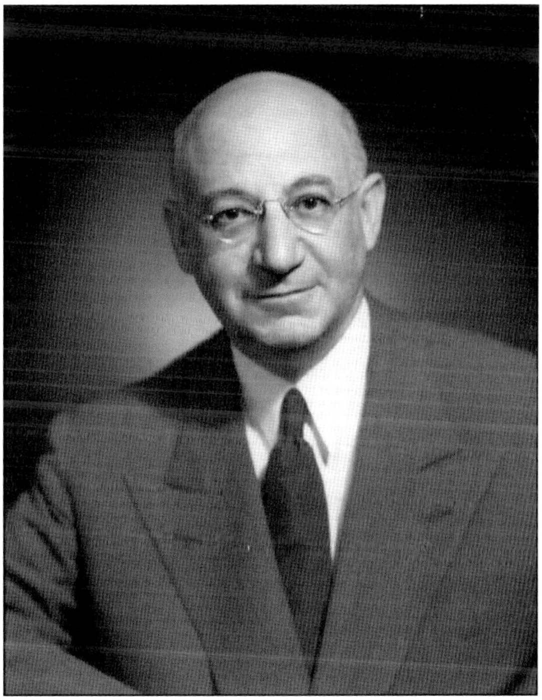

Jacob Blaustein (1892–1970) cofounded American Oil Company with his father, Louis. The company's anti-knock, high-octane fuel was highly successful for high-compression engines, and the company flourished. In addition to being a successful businessman, Blaustein was involved in national and international causes. In 1945, President Roosevelt appointed him to the United Nations (UN). Blaustein was successful in placing human rights provisions in the UN charter. (Courtesy of the JMM, 1988.209.21a.)

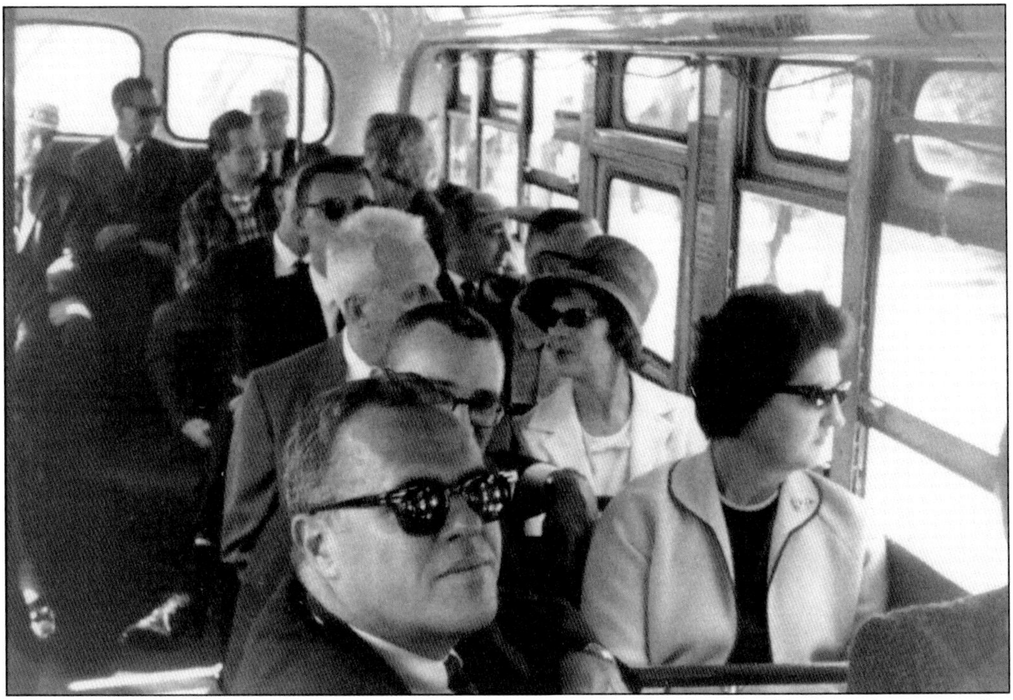

In this 1966 photograph, Eastern Products sponsors a trip to the World Series between the Baltimore Orioles and the Los Angeles Dodgers. (Courtesy of the JMM, 2005.51.42.)

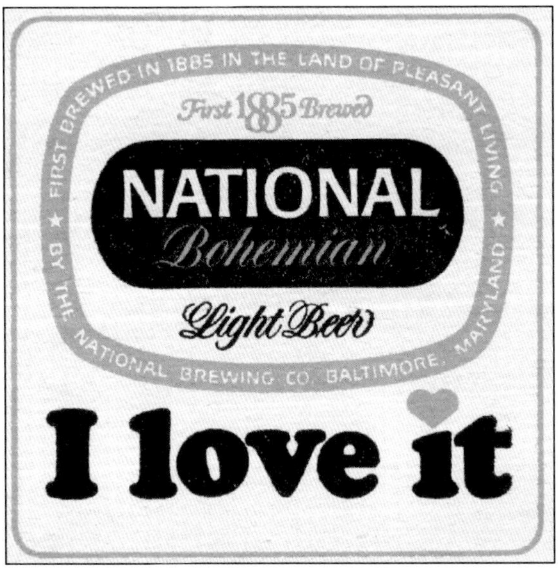

For several decades, Jerold C. Hoffberger (1919–1999) ran the National Brewing Company, which made National Bohemian Beer (or "Natty Boh," as it is known locally). Hoffberger also owned the Baltimore Orioles from 1965 to 1979, during which time the team won five American League pennants and two World Series titles. He was a major contributor to several universities and other organizations. (Courtesy of the JMM, 1998.8.42.)

The family of Calman "Buddy" Zamoiski (born 1928) achieved success in several businesses. In 1921, his father, Joseph, started Baltimore's first commercial radio station, WKC, in a room in his home and began Joseph M. Zamoiski Company, an electronics distributor. His family also started the Zamoiski Beverage Company, which developed Schlitz Beer. Buddy Zamoiski was president of the Associated Jewish Charities and Welfare Fund, as well as chairman of the Baltimore Symphony Orchestra for 15 years. (Courtesy of the JMM, 1987.65.21.)

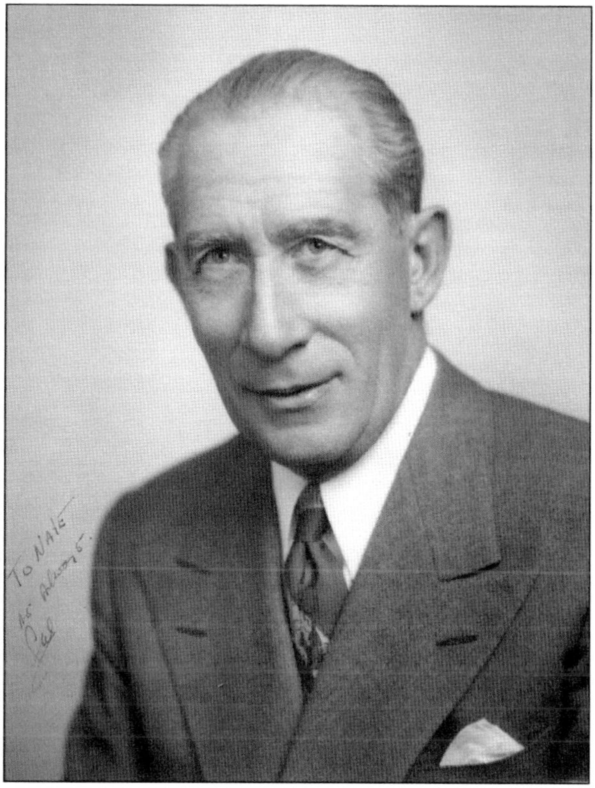

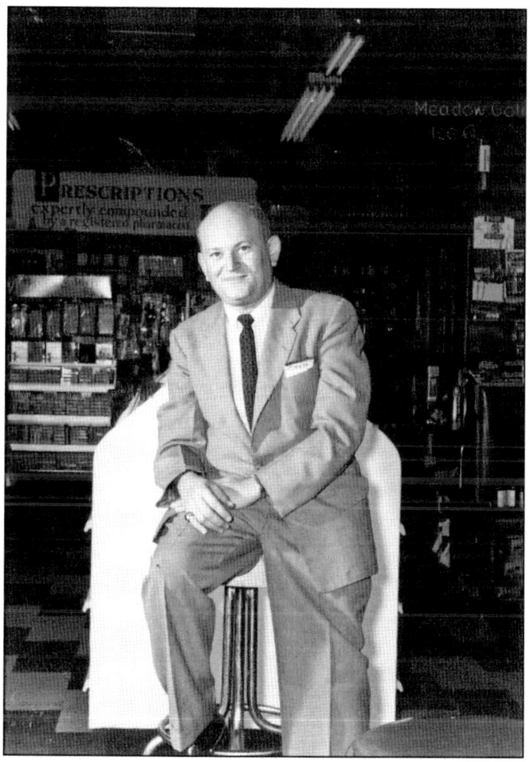

In this 1950s photograph, Morris R Walman poses in his drugstore, the Brookhill Pharmacy, on Park Heights Avenue. Walman served as president of Suburban Orthodox Synagogue. (Courtesy of the JMM, 1991.180.9.)

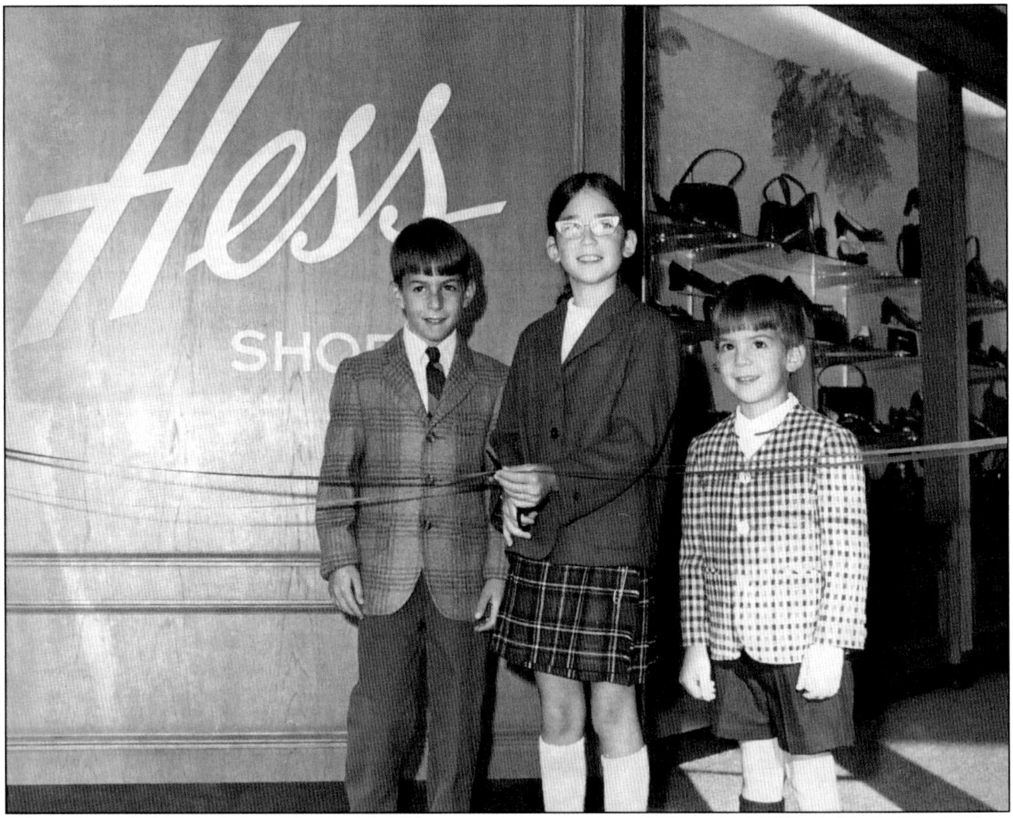

The Hess children participate in a ribbon-cutting ceremony for a new Hess Shoes store that opened in the 1960s. (Courtesy of the JMM, 1989.98.3a.)

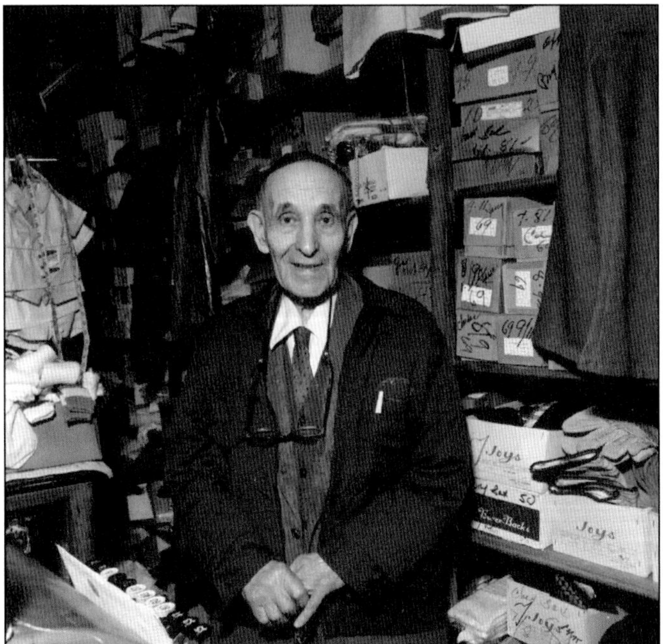

By the late 1970s, most Jewish businesses had moved away from East Baltimore. One of the few holdouts was Solomon Faiman and his used clothing store on Lombard Street, pictured here in 1984. (Photograph by Elinor B. Cahn; courtesy of the JMM, 1985.31.7.)

Six

Providing Relief

Baltimore's Jewish Civic Commitment

Since its inception, Baltimore's Jewish community has displayed a strong civic commitment. Both individuals and organizations have played key roles in providing social services to the community at large. From serving in the military to running for public office, Jews have long demonstrated loyalty and dedication to public society. Additionally, Baltimore's Jewish community is one of the best organized in the country, served by the Associated: Jewish Community Federation of Baltimore and an abundance of agencies and services ranging from the Comprehensive Housing Aid Initiative to the Baltimore Jewish Council.

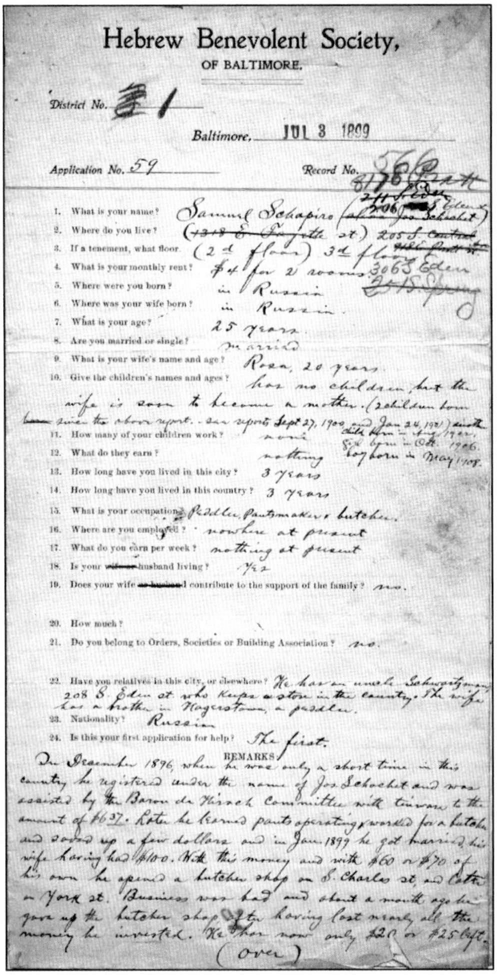
Hebrew Benevolent Society,
OF BALTIMORE.

District No. 1

Baltimore, JUL 3 1899

Application No. 59 Record No. 566

1. What is your name? Samuel Schapiro (alias Jos. Schachet)
2. Where do you live? (1318 E. Fayette st.) 205 S. Central
3. If a tenement, what floor. (2d floor) 3d floor
4. What is your monthly rent? $4 for 2 rooms. 3065 Eden
5. Where were you born? in Russia
6. Where was your wife born? in Russia.
7. What is your age? 25 years.
8. Are you married or single? married
9. What is your wife's name and age? Rosa, 20 years.
10. Give the children's names and ages? has no children, but the wife is soon to become a mother. (2 children born since the above report. - see reports Sept 27, 1900 and Jan 24, 1901) another child born in Aug. 1902, girl born in Oct. 1906. boy born in May 1908.
11. How many of your children work? none
12. What do they earn? nothing
13. How long have you lived in this city? 3 years
14. How long have you lived in this country? 3 years
15. What is your occupation? Peddler, pantsmaker & butcher.
16. Where are you employed? nowhere at present
17. What do you earn per week? nothing at present
18. Is your ~~wife or~~ husband living? Yes
19. Does your wife ~~or husband~~ contribute to the support of the family? no.
20. How much?
21. Do you belong to Orders, Societies or Building Association? no.
22. Have you relatives in this city, or elsewhere? He has an uncle Schwartzman 208 S. Eden st. who keeps a store in the country. The wife has a brother in Hagerstown, a peddler.
23. Nationality? Russian
24. Is this your first application for help? The first.

REMARKS.

In December 1896, when he was only a short time in this country he registered under the name of Jos. Schachet and was assisted by the Baron de Hirsch Committee with tinware to the amount of $6.37. Later he learned pants operating & worked for a butcher and saved up a few dollars and in Jan. 1899 he got married, his wife having had $100. With this money and with $60 or $70 of his own he opened a butcher shop on S. Charles st, and later on York st. Business was bad and about a month ago he gave up the butcher shop after having lost nearly all the money he invested. He has now only $20 or $25 left.

(Over)

The United Hebrew Benevolent Society (established 1834) was the community's first attempt at establishing a Jewish charity with the "purpose of providing relief for the destitute of their religion." (Courtesy of the JMM, 1975.13.6.)

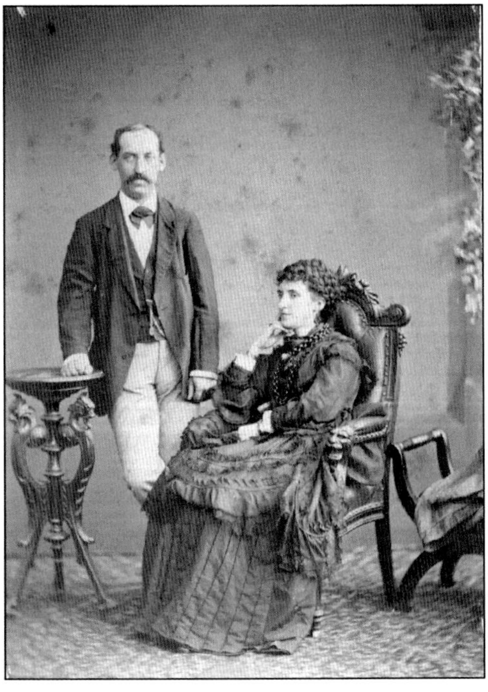

In the late 1800s, several Jewish women's societies were formed to provide social services, including the Frank Free Sabbath School, which was established in 1887 by Bertha Rayner Frank (shown here with her husband, Dr. Samuel Leon Frank). The school gave religious lessons to Russian Jewish children on Saturday afternoons. An 1889 report described how "the cry of the children reached this woman. . . . With what loving sympathy and wise tenderness she answered, can best be told in the future, when the good and useful lives of these children will be as an everlasting monument to her wisdom, generosity, and forethought." (Courtesy of the JMM, 1984.174.6.)

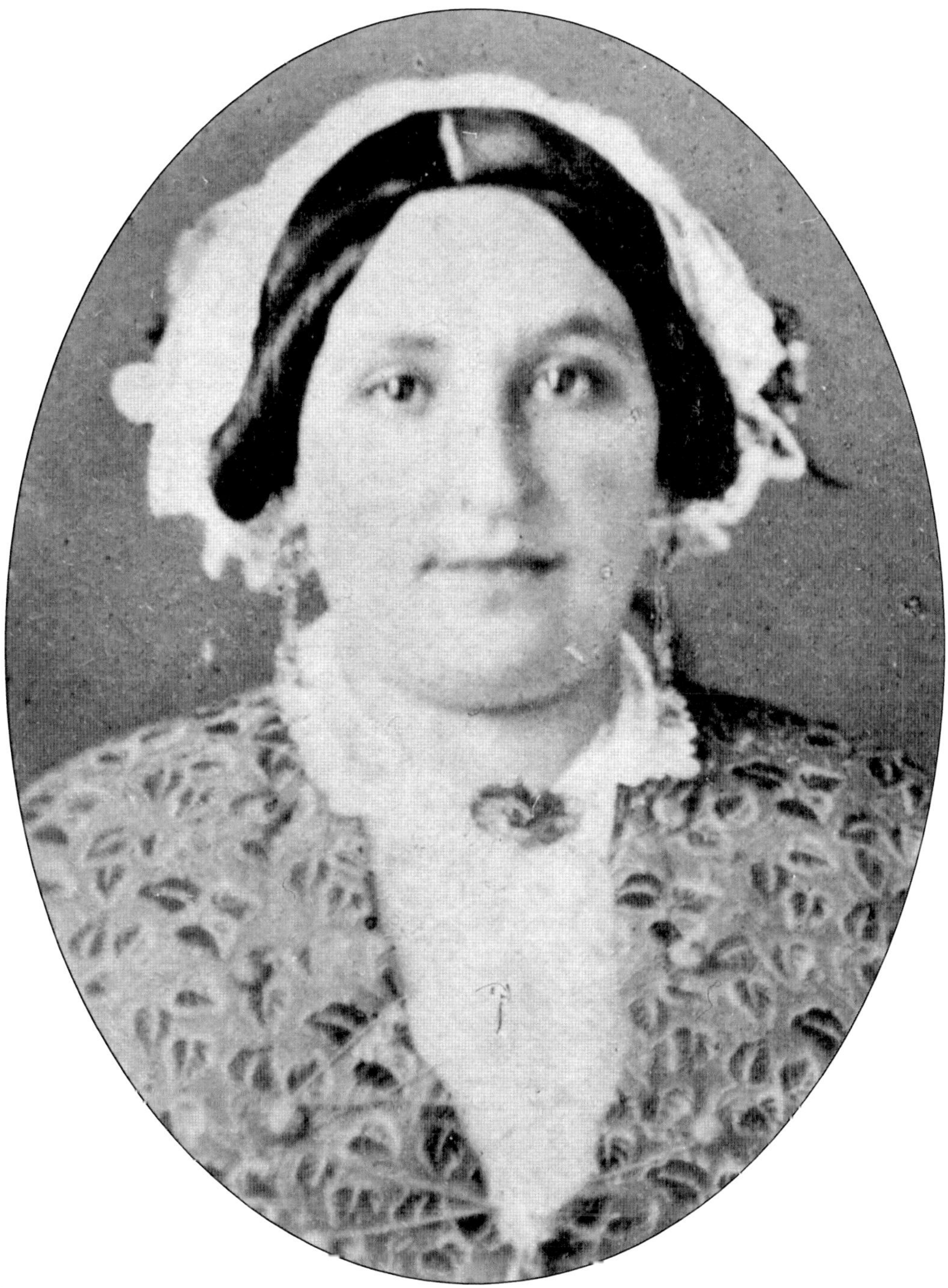

In 1893, Betsy Friedenwald Wiesenfeld wrote a report on the activities of the Hebrew Ladies' Sewing Society (established 1856), which had been created to distribute "wearing apparel among poor Jewish women and children." The society was the women's arm of the Hebrew Benevolent Society. The society also provided linens and clothing for the Hebrew Hospital and Asylum Association and the Hebrew Orphan Asylum. The society's members opened a sewing school for young women in 1879. (Courtesy of the JMM, 1990.2.13.)

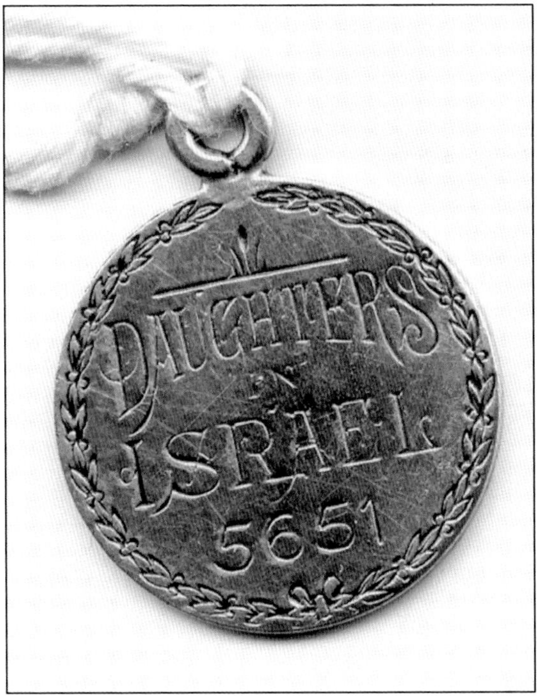

This medal, presented to Adelaide Rosenfeld Eiseman in 1890, bears the motto of the Daughters in Israel (established 1890), "Thou shalt love thy neighbor as thyself." The organization consisted of smaller groups of women who started different social services, including sewing schools, working-girls clubs, dressmaking clubs, and Mothers' Meetings. In 1893, Mrs. Eugene Jackson described how successful the Mothers' Meetings had become: "both a Chanukah and Purim entertainment were given, cakes, candy with toys for the children and more substantial gifts to the women." (Courtesy of the JMM, 1978.1.1.)

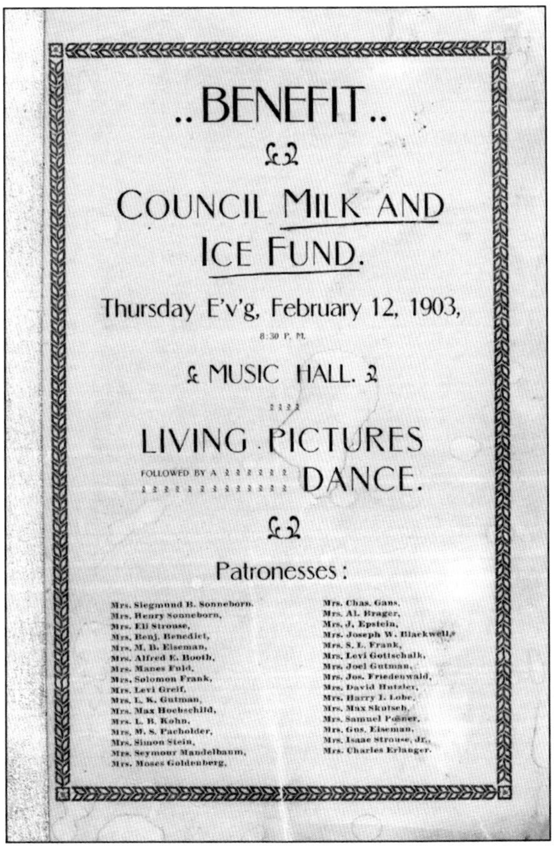

..BENEFIT..

COUNCIL MILK AND ICE FUND.

Thursday E'v'g, February 12, 1903,

8:30 P. M.

MUSIC HALL.

LIVING PICTURES

FOLLOWED BY A DANCE.

Patronesses:

Mrs. Siegmund B. Sonneborn.
Mrs. Henry Sonneborn,
Mrs. Eli Strouse,
Mrs. Benj. Benedict,
Mrs. M. B. Eiseman,
Mrs. Alfred E. Booth,
Mrs. Manes Fuld,
Mrs. Solomon Frank,
Mrs. Levi Greif,
Mrs. L. K. Gutman,
Mrs. Max Hochschild,
Mrs. L. B. Kohn,
Mrs. M. S. Pacholder,
Mrs. Simon Stein,
Mrs. Seymour Mandelbaum,
Mrs. Moses Goldenberg,
Mrs. Chas. Gans,
Mrs. Al. Brager,
Mrs. J. Epstein,
Mrs. Joseph W. Blackwell,
Mrs. S. L. Frank,
Mrs. Levi Gottschalk,
Mrs. Joel Gutman,
Mrs. Jos. Friedenwald,
Mrs. David Hutzler,
Mrs. Harry L. Lobe,
Mrs. Max Skutsch,
Mrs. Samuel Posner,
Mrs. Gus. Eiseman,
Mrs. Isaac Strouse, Jr.,
Mrs. Charles Erlanger.

In 1896, the Council of Jewish Women started the Milk and Ice Fund to meet the needs of undernourished and ill children, poverty-stricken elderly, and victims of tuberculosis. (Courtesy of the JMM, 1989.47.1.)

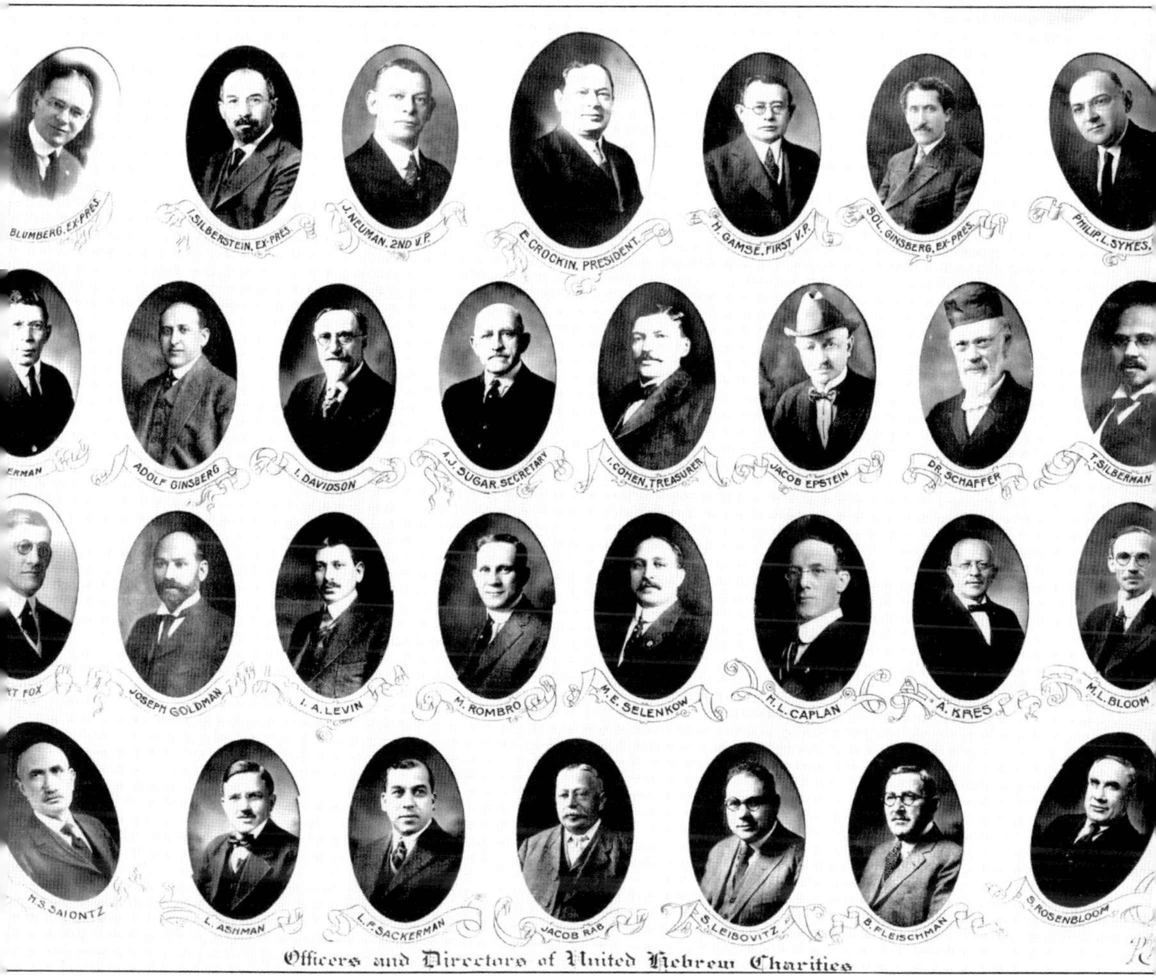

These portraits of the directors and officers of the United Hebrew Charities (established 1909) were all taken by N. Levinsohn. (Courtesy of the JMM, 1996.7.1.)

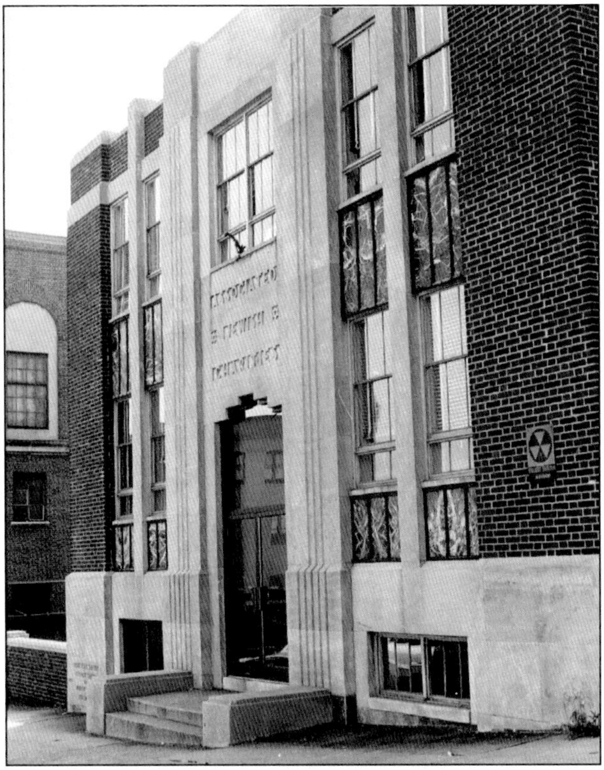

In 1920, the uptown German-Jewish Federated Jewish Charities (established 1906) and the downtown East-European United Hebrew Charities (established 1909) merged into the Associated Jewish Charities, which is the forerunner of today's the Associated: Jewish Community Federation of Baltimore. The Associated stood on Monument Street from 1930 to 1980. (Courtesy of the JMM, 1982.25.3.)

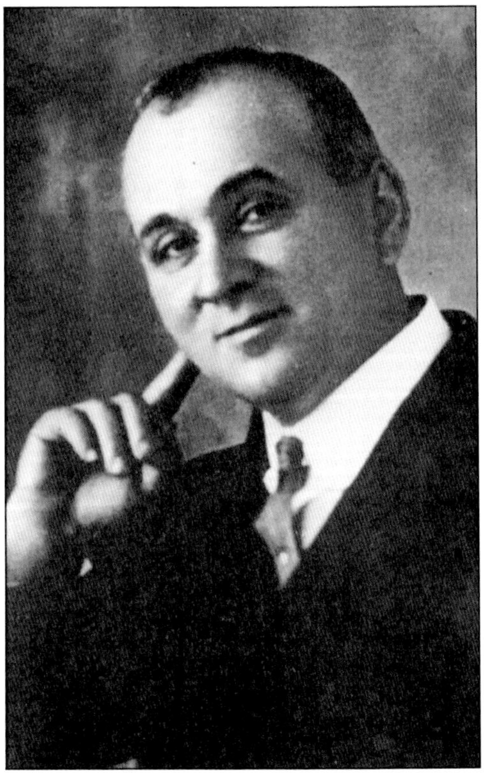

In 1901, Louis H. Levin (1866–1923) created the *Jewish Comment*, which he edited for 19 years. He was the first and only secretary of the Federated Jewish Charities. In 1915, he was sent abroad by the American Jewish Relief Committee to help feed war refugees in Europe and Palestine. He was the first director of the Associated Jewish Charities. The Levindale Hebrew Geriatric Center and Hospital is named for him. (Courtesy of the JMM, 1987.80.2.)

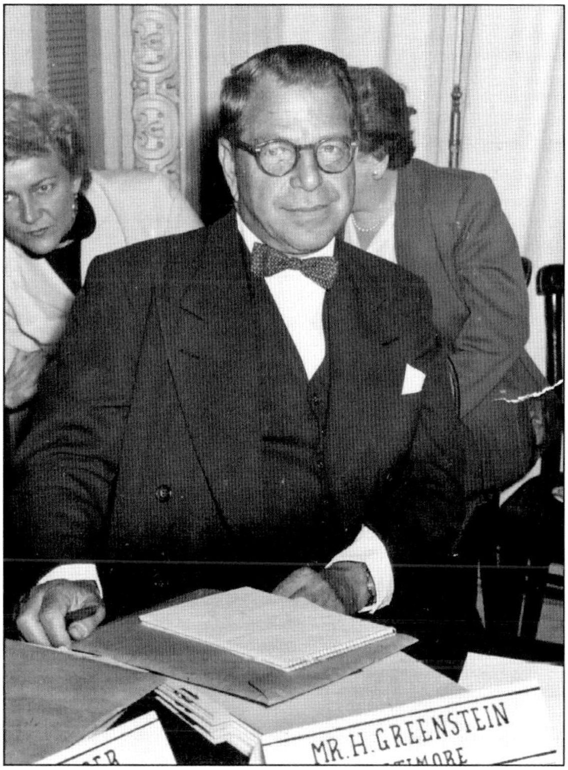

Harry Greenstein served as director of the Associated Jewish Charities from 1928 to 1965. Additionally, he organized Maryland's welfare program in the 1930s and was the first president of the Health and Welfare Council of the Greater Baltimore Area. Here he is shown as a delegate at the field directors' conference of the American Jewish Distribution Committee in 1953. (Photograph by Jerome Silberstein; courtesy of the JMM, 2002.79.327.)

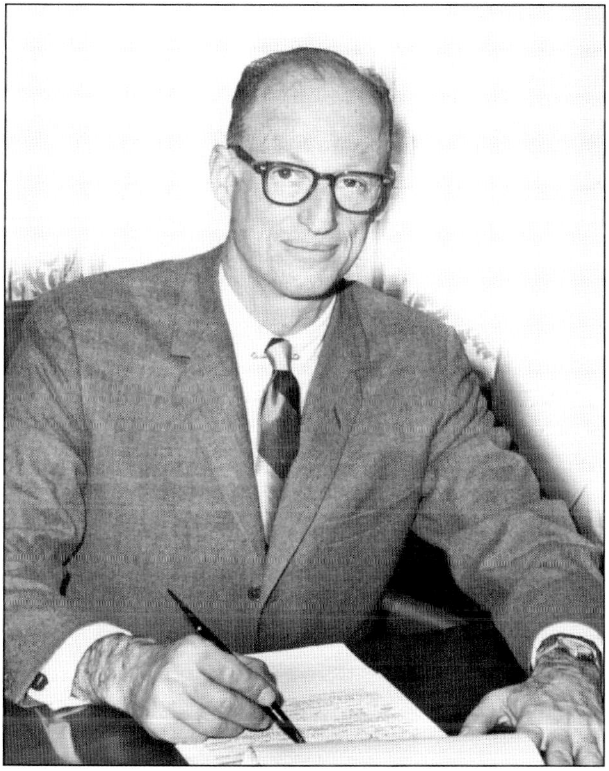

Sidney Lansburg Jr. was president of the Associated Jewish Charities and Welfare Fund when he arrived in Israel for a mission in 1973. The Associated Jewish Charities had merged with the Jewish Welfare Fund in 1950. They combined names in 1969. (Courtesy of the JMM, 1992.278.7a.)

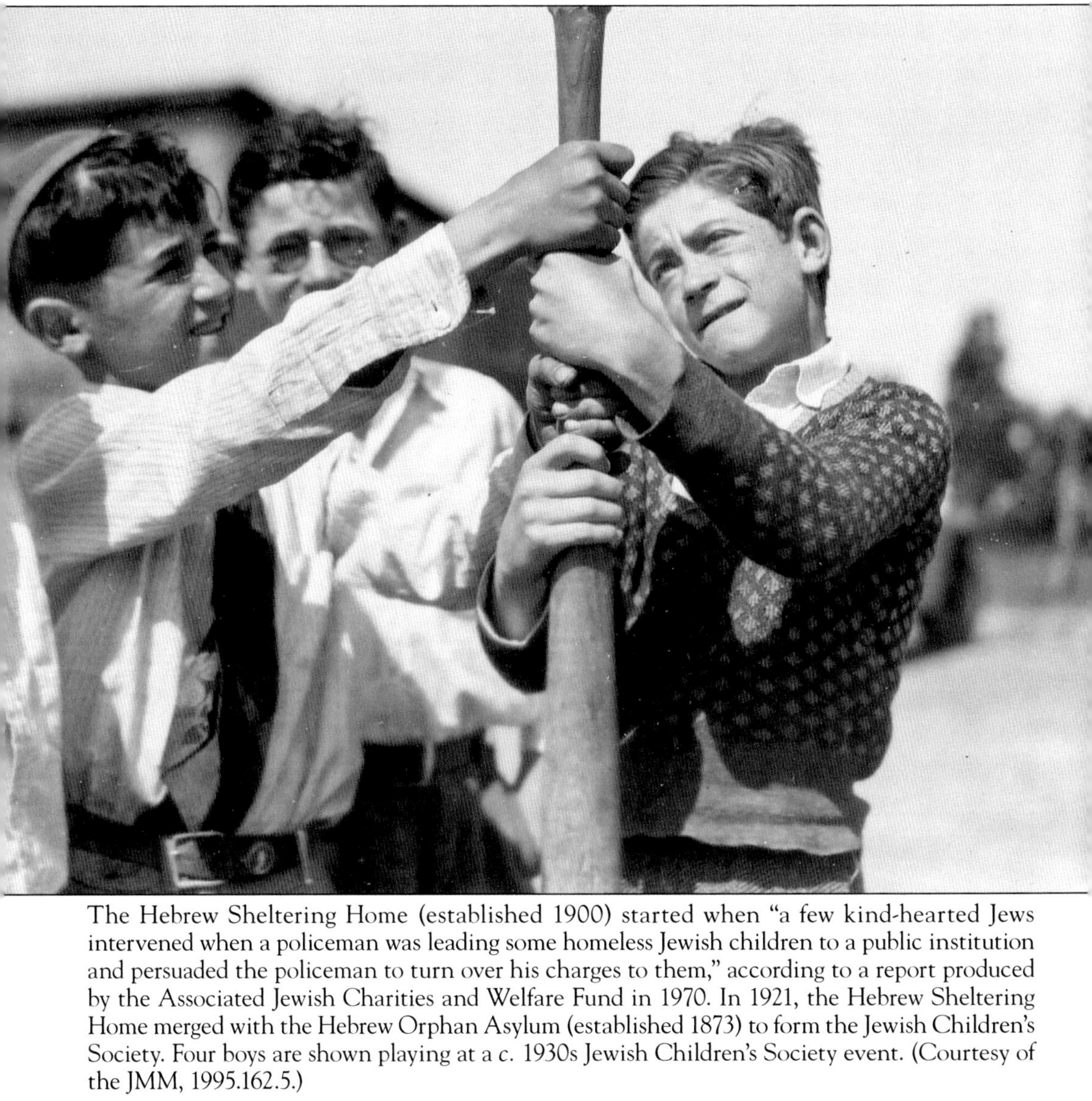

The Hebrew Sheltering Home (established 1900) started when "a few kind-hearted Jews intervened when a policeman was leading some homeless Jewish children to a public institution and persuaded the policeman to turn over his charges to them," according to a report produced by the Associated Jewish Charities and Welfare Fund in 1970. In 1921, the Hebrew Sheltering Home merged with the Hebrew Orphan Asylum (established 1873) to form the Jewish Children's Society. Four boys are shown playing at a c. 1930s Jewish Children's Society event. (Courtesy of the JMM, 1995.162.5.)

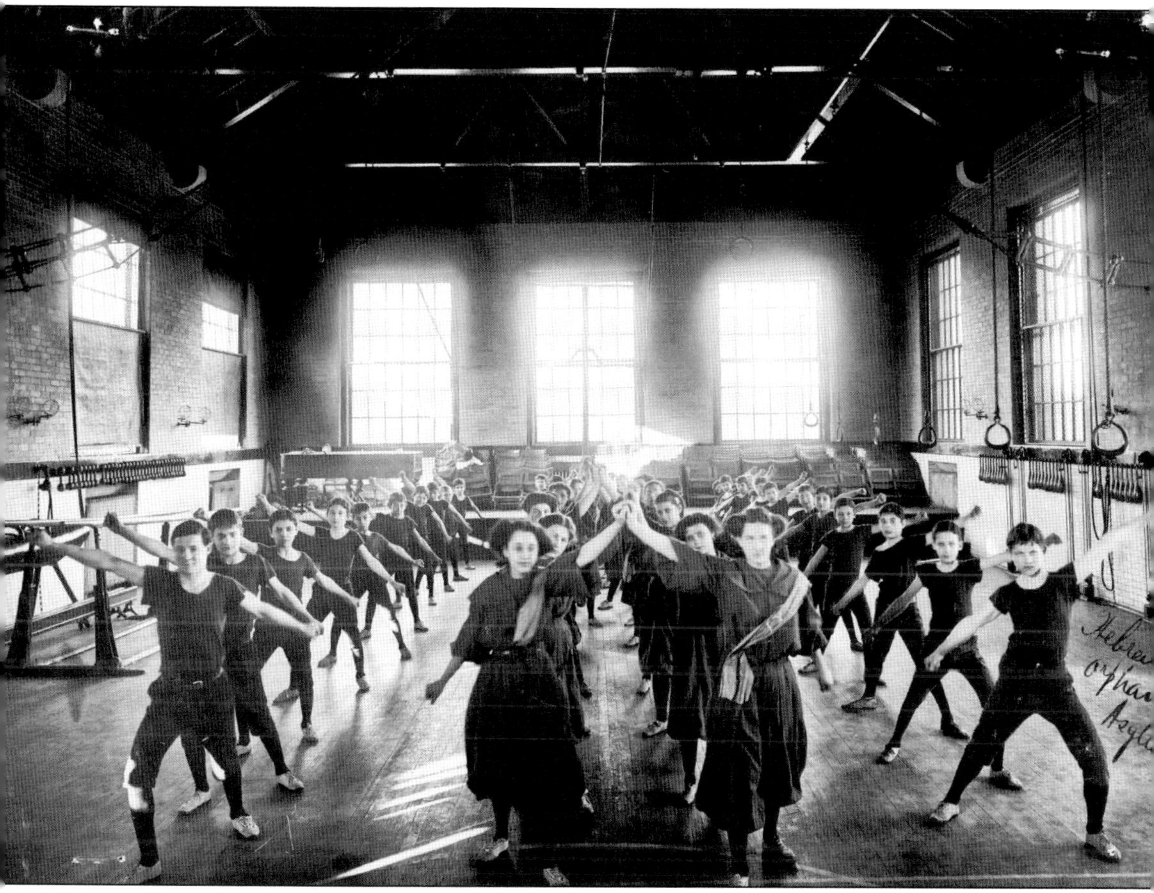

This photograph depicts the Hebrew Orphan Asylum around 1911. When the Hebrew Orphan Asylum (established 1873) and the Hebrew Sheltering Home merged in the early 1900s, they purchased land in the "country" (Belvedere and Greenspring Avenues) for a new building. However, the President Taft's administration and social organizations began recommending that orphans should be placed in foster families rather than institutions. This was seen as both morally superior and more cost effective since raising a child in a foster family cost only $400 per year as opposed to in an institution, where the cost was $1,500 per year. The newly finished building was sold to two geriatric organizations that became the Levindale Hebrew Geriatric Center and Hospital. (Courtesy of the JMM, 1990.179.1.)

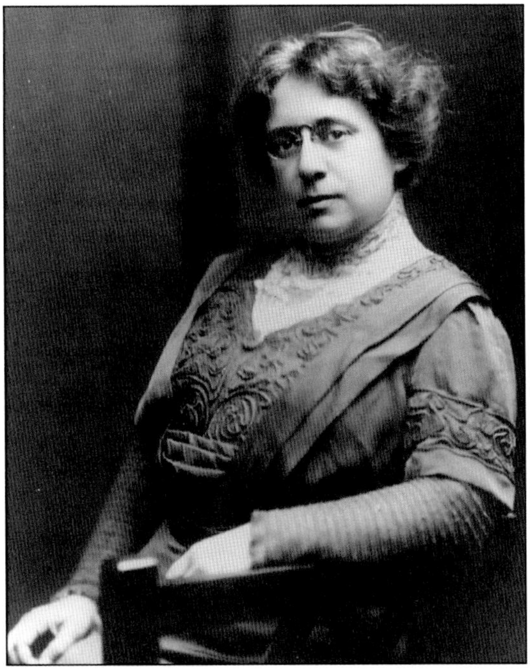

Henrietta Szold visited Palestine with her mother in 1909. They were shocked by the "misery, poverty, filth, [and] disease." After returning, she recommended to her study group, the Daughters of Zion, that they assist the cause. In 1913, the group sent nurses to Palestine to open a clinic. This formed the basis of Hadassah, the Women's Zionist Organization of America. Today this society boasts more than 300,000 members. They provide funding for medical facilities in Israel and support health, educational, and vocational training in both Israel and America. (Courtesy of the JMM, 1991.104.2.)

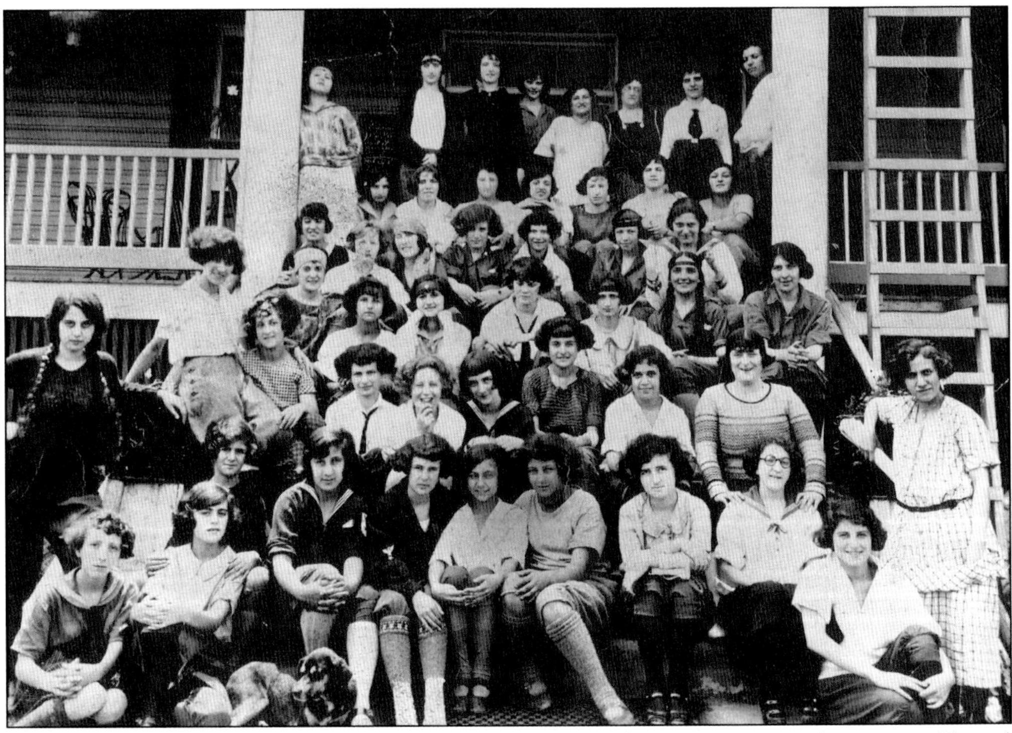

The Daughters in Israel created the Home for Working Girls in 1890 to provide room and board for young East European ladies without parents. In 1916, the organization purchased a "delightful summer cottage" in Maryland's Blue Ridge Mountains. This became Camp Louise in 1922, which is still active today as an all-girls camp, along with its brother camp, Camp Airy. (Courtesy of the JMM, 1998.153.2.)

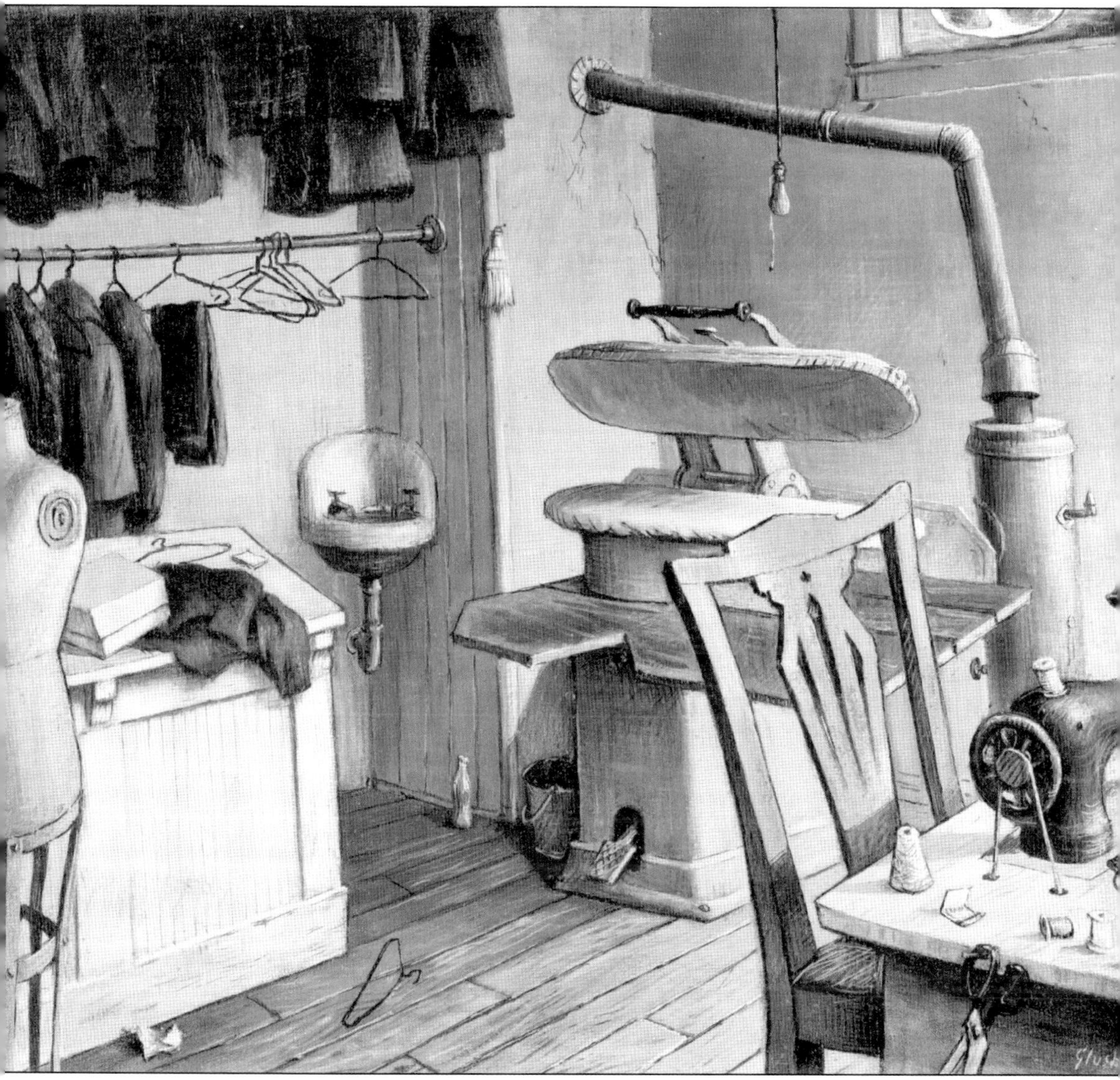

In 1909, the Daughters in Israel merged with the Macabbean House to form the Jewish Educational Alliance (JEA). The organization continued the social work of the two original societies. "I remember [Kate Fineman] showing my work to some of the [JEA] board members," recalled Jacob Glushakow, "and one woman bought a drawing for two bucks!" The board members helped Glushakow win a scholarship to the Art Students League of New York. His painting "Gold's Tailor Shop" (seen here) was created in the early 1970s, based on sketches from the Whitelock Street shop in the 1950s. (Courtesy of the JMM, 1992.156.1 and in memory of Emanuel ("Mannie") Hettleman by his family and friends.)

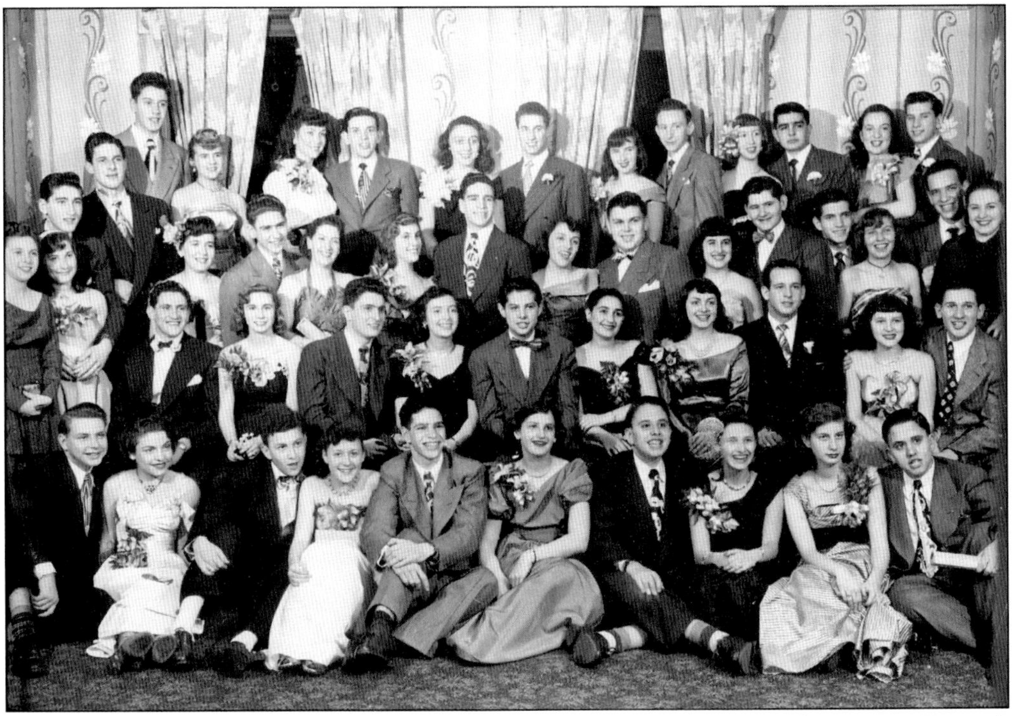

The Young Men's Hebrew Association (established 1920) merged with the Young Women's Hebrew Association (established 1918) in 1935. Together with the Jewish Educational Alliance (established 1909), these institutions formed the modern Jewish Community Center in 1950. In this 1948 photograph, youth group Aleph Zadik Aleph holds their annual anniversary dance at the YM&YWHA on Monument Street. (Courtesy of the JMM, 1998.79.1.)

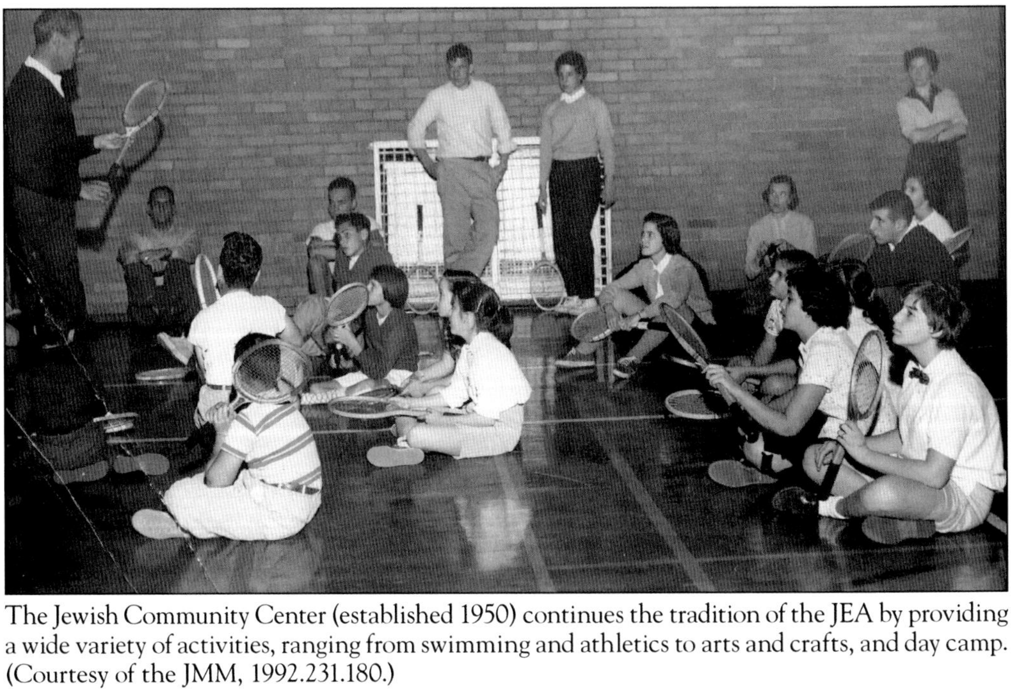

The Jewish Community Center (established 1950) continues the tradition of the JEA by providing a wide variety of activities, ranging from swimming and athletics to arts and crafts, and day camp. (Courtesy of the JMM, 1992.231.180.)

From synagogue religious schools to day schools, there is a cornucopia of Jewish educational resources within Baltimore. In 1852, the Hebrew Education Society was organized to provide access to the Jewish education programs for the community. It merged with Baltimore Talmud Torah (established 1890) in 1921, forming the Board of Jewish Education (BJE), which is now the Center for Jewish Education. In this 1979 photograph, two women promote the BJE at the Jewish Festival. (Courtesy of the JMM, 1992.108.59.)

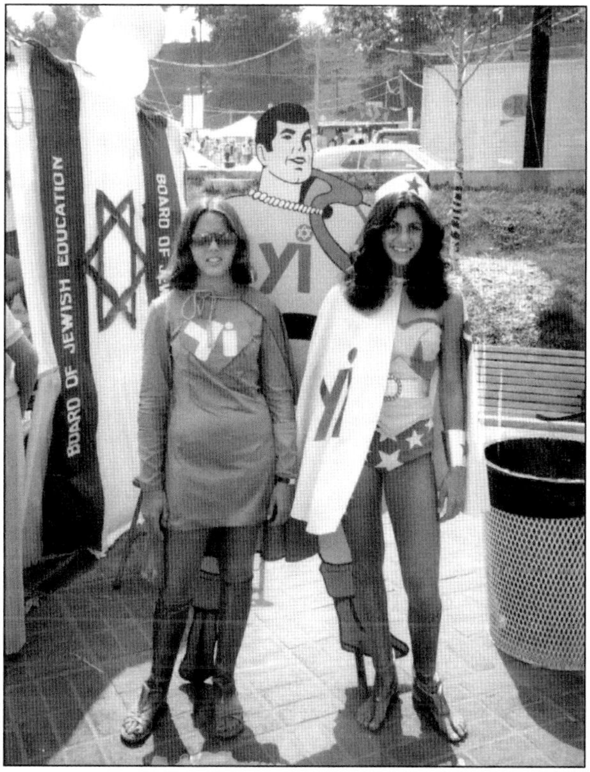

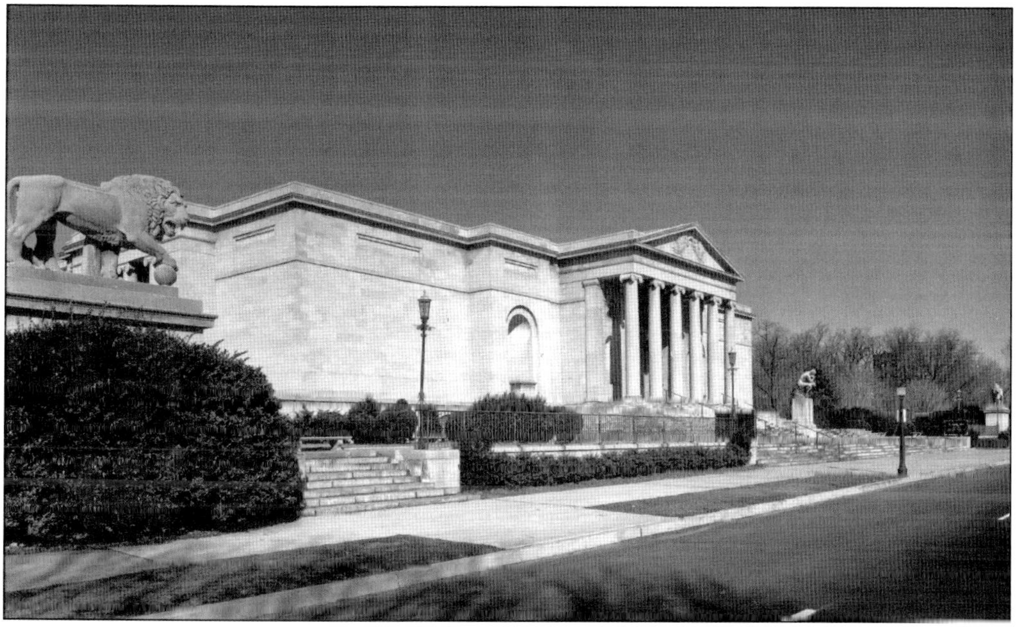

Dr. Claribel and Etta Cone's collection of paintings are a treasure of the Baltimore Museum of Art (BMA). Their collection of approximately 3,000 objects included works by Henri Matisse, Paul Cezanne, Paul Gauguin, Pablo Picasso, and Vincent van Gogh. Originally exhibited in their homes in the Marlborough Apartments on Eutaw Place, the artwork came to the BMA in 1949 following Etta's death. (Courtesy of the JMM, 2002.65.29.)

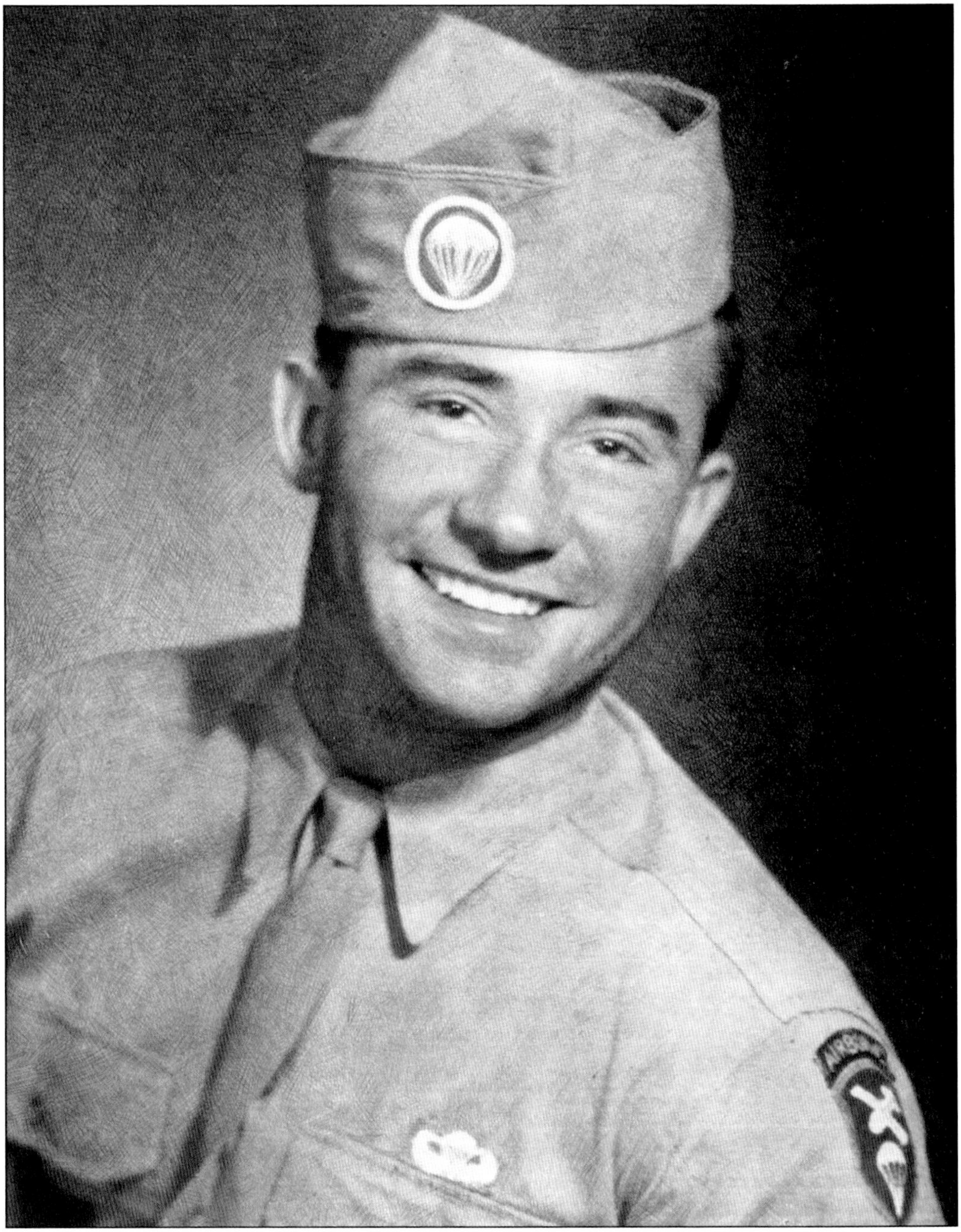

Sgt. Isadore Jachman (1922–1945) was one of only a few Jews to receive the Congressional Medal of Honor. During a battle at Flamierge, Belgium, in January 1945, Sergeant Jachman of Company B, 513th Parachute Infantry Regiment, advanced on enemy tanks with a bazooka. The official report from the White House explains, "Firing the weapon alone, he damaged one and forced both to retire. Sergeant Jachman's heroic action, in which he suffered fatal wounds, disrupted the entire enemy attack, reflecting the highest credit upon himself and the Parachute Infantry." (Courtesy of the JMM, 1996.112.1.)

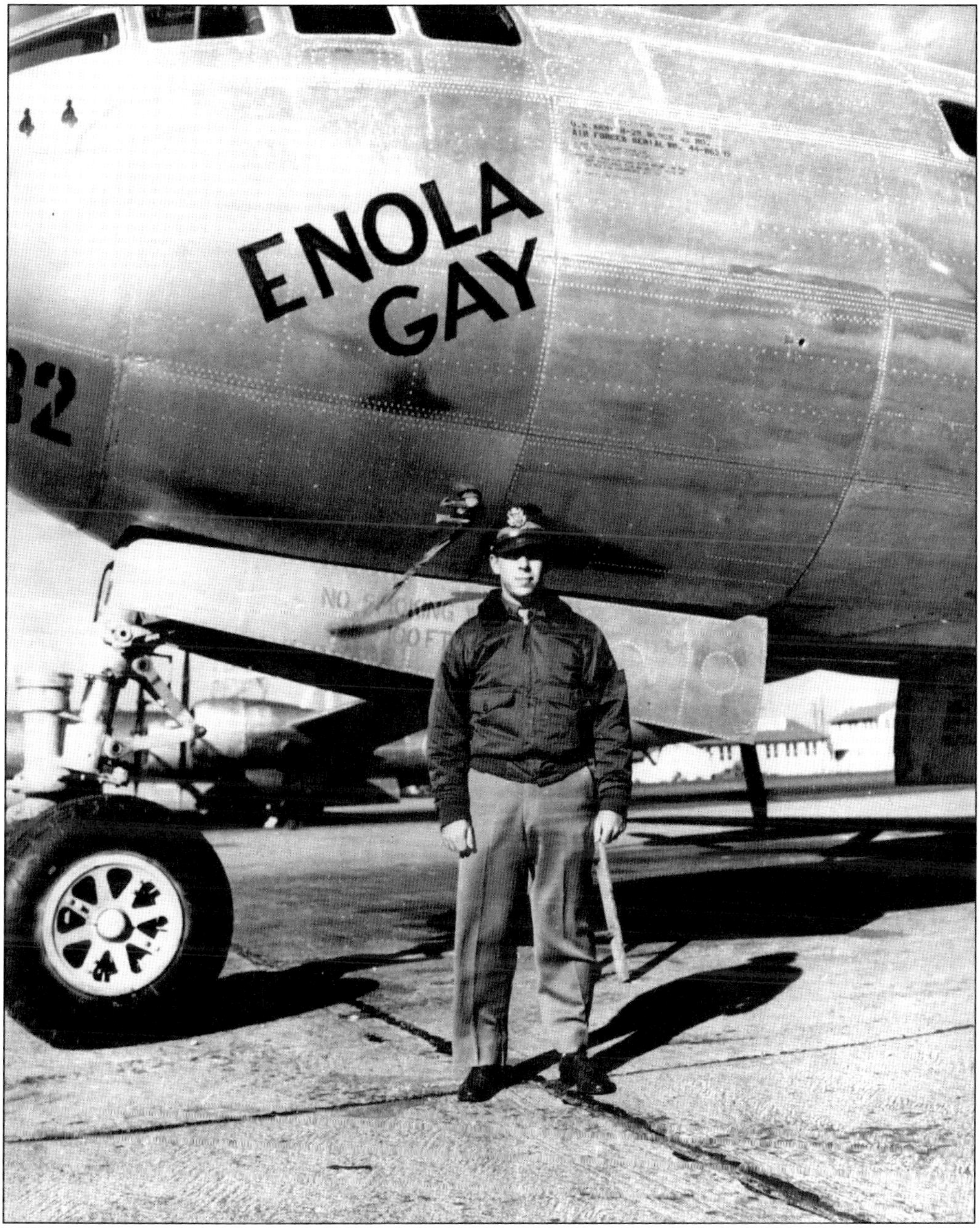

Lt. Jacob Beser (1921–1992) was the only person to serve on both airplanes that dropped atomic bombs in Japan. A radar specialist, Lieutenant Beser was in charge of setting and monitoring the fuses that detonated the bombs. On August 6, 1945, he was on the *Enola Gay* when it devastated Hiroshima and was on the *Bookcar* three days later when the bomb was dropped on Nagasaki. Five days later, Japan surrendered. Lieutenant Beser received the Silver Star and the Distinguished Flying Cross. After the war, he attended Johns Hopkins University, where he assisted in developing a heart-lung machine. (Courtesy of Eric Beser.)

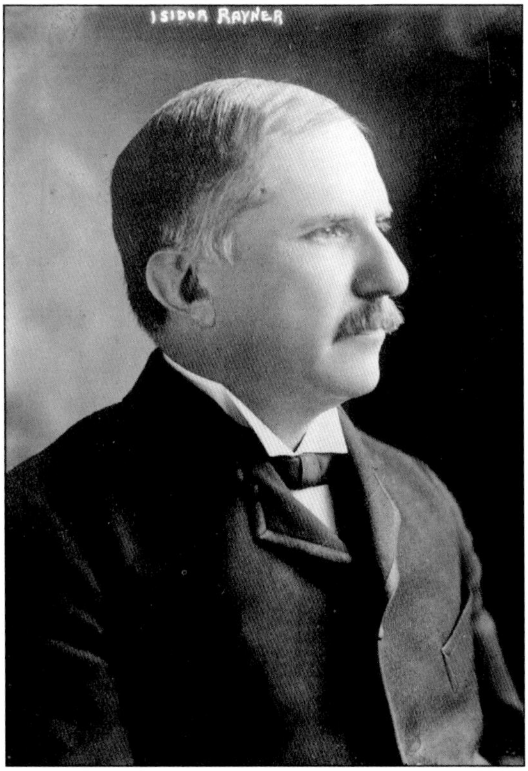

Sen. Isidor Raynor (1850–1912) was elected to the House of Delegates in 1874 and then the state senate in 1885. In 1887, the Democrat was elected to the U.S. House of Representatives. Though he was not initially reelected in 1888, he did serve again from 1891 to 1895 but declined renomination in 1894. He was the attorney general of Maryland from 1899 to 1903 and then was elected in 1905 to the Senate, where he served until his death in 1912. (Courtesy of the Library of Congress.)

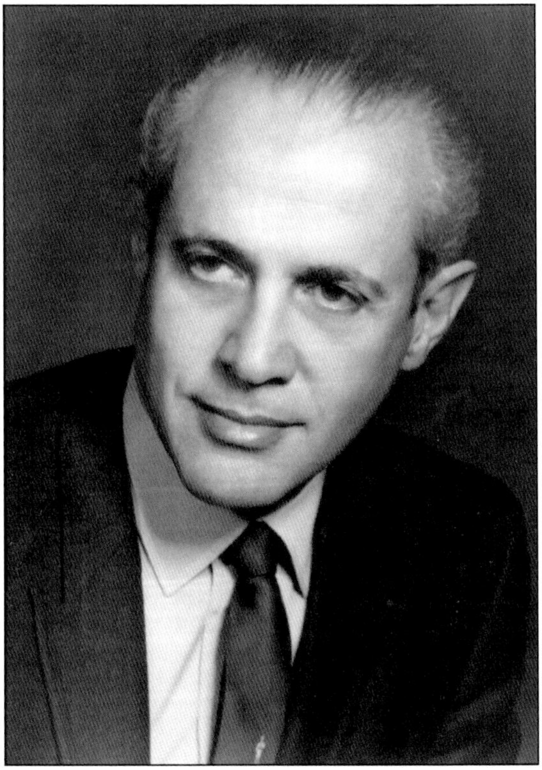

To date, Marvin Mandel (born 1920, pictured around 1960) has been Maryland's first and only Jewish governor, having served from 1969 to 1979. The Democrat sponsored and saw enacted strict handgun control, laws for the construction and renovation of Maryland public schools, and providing operating funds from the state for private colleges and universities. (Photograph by Stu Whelan; courtesy of the JMM, 1988.209.30.)

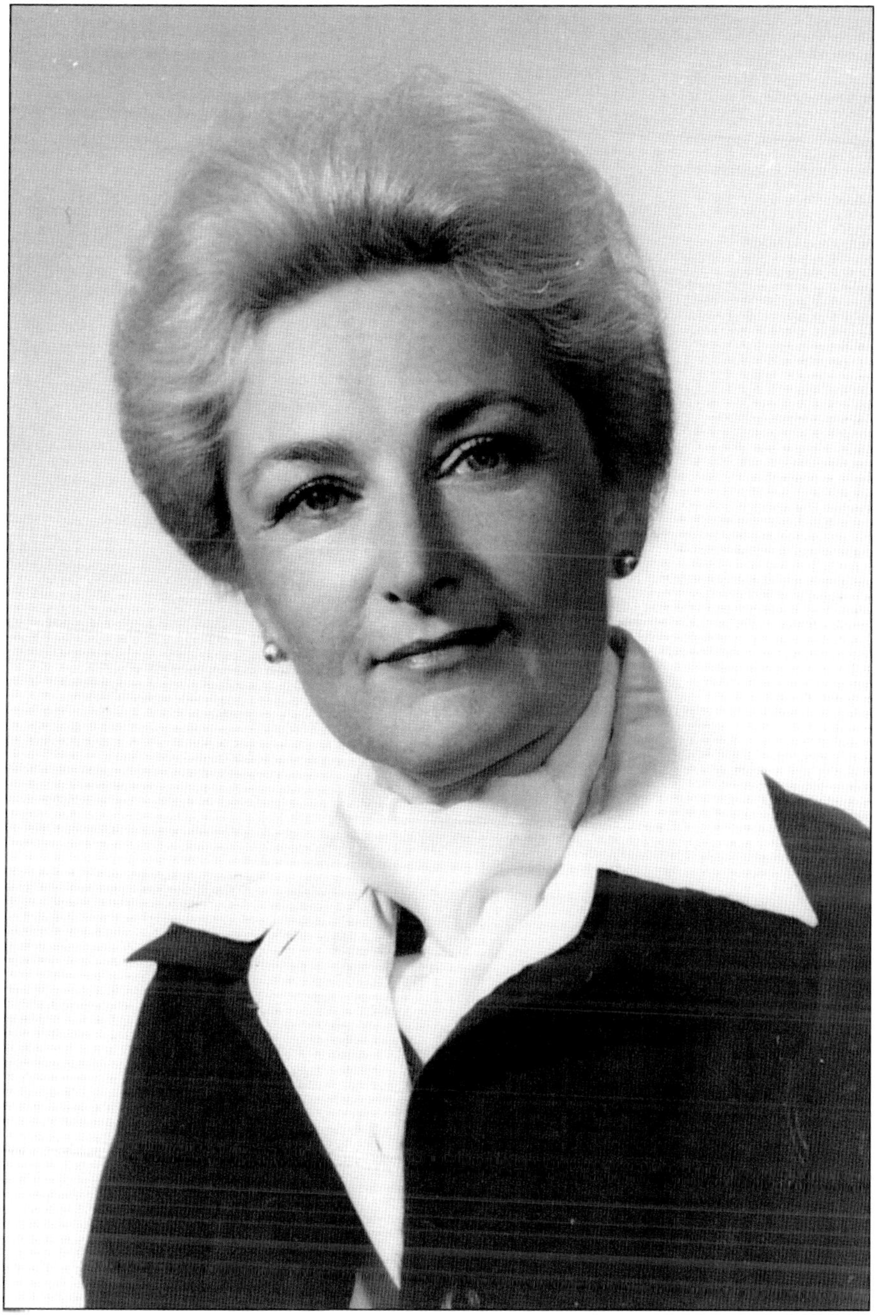

Shoshana Shoubin Cardin (born 1926) has headed many important Jewish organizations. She was the first female chairman of the board for the Associated: Jewish Community Federation of Baltimore from 1983 to 1985. Simultaneously, she was the first female president of the Council of Jewish Federations from 1984 to 1987. She was chairman of the National Conference on Soviet Jewry when the Soviet Union collapsed in 1991 and as Soviet Jewish immigrants surged into America. She became chairman of the Conference of Presidents of Major American Jewish Organizations from 1991 to 1992. Additionally, she founded the Shoshana S. Cardin Jewish Community High School of Greater Baltimore. (Courtesy of the JMM, 2003.47.25.)

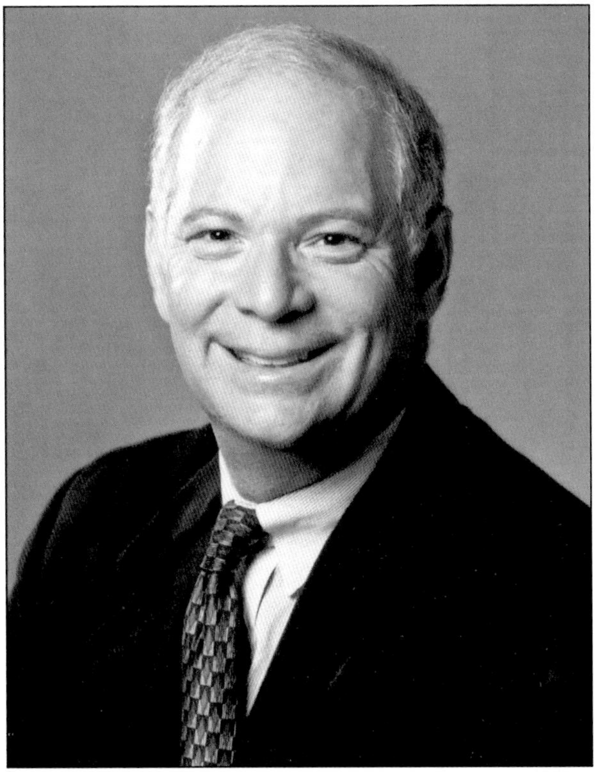

Civic responsibility runs in the family of U.S. senator Benjamin L. Cardin (born 1943). His father, Meyer Cardin, was a city judge for more than 40 years. His cousin by marriage is Shoshana Cardin. At the age of 23, Cardin was elected to the Maryland House of Delegates, capturing the spot vacated by his uncle Jack Cardin. In 1979, he was 35 when he became the youngest Speaker of the House. When elected to the U.S. House of Representatives, he won 82 percent of the vote in the third district. He was elected as a U.S. senator in 2007. (Courtesy of Sen. Ben Cardin.)

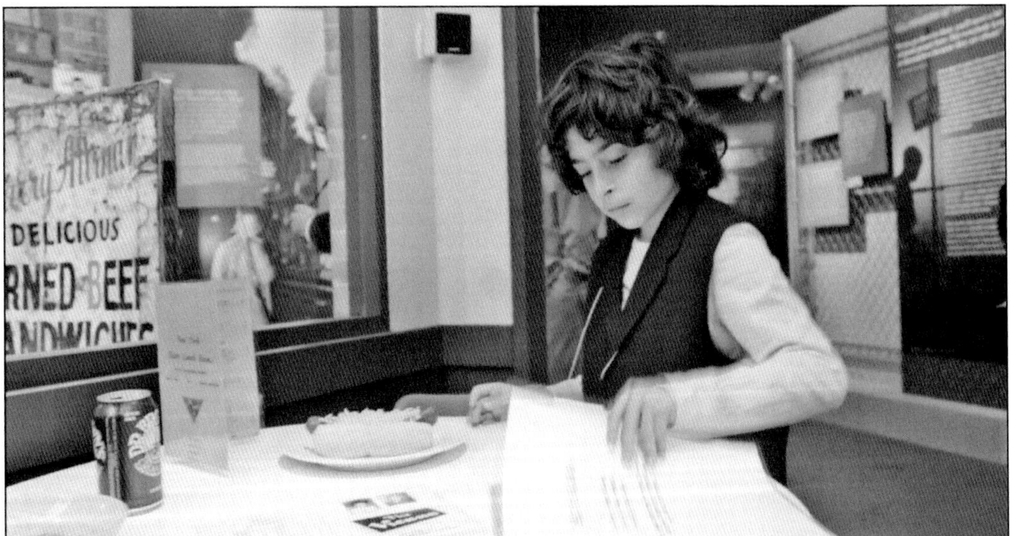

In October 2997, the Jewish Museum of Maryland (established 1960) opened an exhibition entitled Voices of Lombard Street: A Century of Change in East Baltimore. The exhibit brings to life the old immigrant Jewish neighborhood surrounding the museum. More than 600 people, including Rose Alon (pictured) attended the opening. Even as the story of Baltimore's Jewish community continues into the 21st century, the JMM preserves, studies, and interprets its history. The majority of the photographs for this book came from the JMM, which serves as a repository for the community's collective memory. (Courtesy of Will Kirk and the JMM.)

SELECTED BIBLIOGRAPHY

PRIMARY SOURCES

Baltimore Sun
Baltimore Jewish Times
Jewish Museum of Maryland, Manuscript and Oral History Collections and Vertical Files

SECONDARY SOURCES

Blum, Isidor. *The Jews of Baltimore: An Historical Summary of Their Progress and Status as Citizens of Baltimore From Early Days to the Year 1910*. Baltimore, MD: Historical Review Publishing Company, 1910.

Cahn, Louis F. *History of Oheb Shalom, 1853–1953*. Baltimore, MD: Oheb Shalom, 1953.

Decter, Avi Y., et al, eds. *Cornerstones of Community: The Historic Synagogues of Maryland, 1845–1945*. Baltimore, MD: Jewish Museum of Maryland, 1999.

Decter, Avi Y. and Karen Falk, eds. *Of Hats & Harmonies: The Recollections of Baltimore's Lester S. Levy*. Baltimore, MD: Jewish Museum of Maryland, 2005.

Enterprising Emporiums: The Jewish Department Stores of Downtown Baltimore. Baltimore, MD: Jewish Museum of Maryland, 2001.

Fee, Elizabeth, et al, eds. *The Baltimore Book: New Views of Local History*. Philadelphia, PA: Temple University Press, 1991.

Fein, Isaac. *The Making of an American Jewish Community: The History of Baltimore Jewry from 1773 to 1920*. Baltimore, MD: Jewish Publication Society of America, 1985.

Generations Magazine. Baltimore, MD: Jewish Museum of Maryland, 1978–2007

Goldstein, Eric. *Traders and Transports: The Jews of Colonial Maryland*. Baltimore, MD: Jewish Historical Society of Maryland, 1993.

Greenberg, Rose. *Chronicle of Baltimore Hebrew Congregation: 1830–1975*. Baltimore, MD: Baltimore Hebrew Congregation, 1976.

Kassof, Anita, et al, eds. *Lives Lost, Lives Found: Baltimore's German Jewish Refugees, 1933–1945*. Baltimore, MD: Jewish Museum of Maryland, 2004.

Kahn, Phillip. *Uncommon Threads: Threads that Wove the Fabric of Baltimore Jewish Life*. Baltimore, MD: PECAN Publishing, 1996.

Kessler, Barry, ed. *Daughter of Zion: Henrietta Szold and American Jewish Womanhood*. Baltimore, MD: Jewish Historical Society of Maryland, 1995.

Miller, Michael. *Memorial History*. Baltimore, MD: Beth Tfiloh Congregation, 1936.

Olson, Sherry. *Baltimore: The Building of an American City*. Baltimore, MD: Johns Hopkins University, 1997.

Pruce, Earl. *Synagogues, Temple and Congregations of Maryland: 1830–1990*. Baltimore, MD: Jewish Historical Society of Maryland, 1993.

Sandler, Gil. *Jewish Baltimore: A Family Album*. Baltimore, MD: Johns Hopkins University Press, 2000.

Schein, Jan Bernhardt. *On Three Pillars: The History of Chizuk Amuno Congregation, 1871–1996*. Baltimore, MD: Chizuk Amuno Congregation, 2000.

Shusterman, Abraham. *The Legacy of a Liberal*. Baltimore, MD: Har Sinai Congregation, 1967.

Weiner, Deborah R., et al, eds. *Voices of Lombard Street: A Century of Change in East Baltimore*. Baltimore, MD: Jewish Museum of Maryland, 2007.

Consistent with our mission to preserve history on a local level, this book was printed in South Carolina on American-made paper and manufactured entirely in the United States. Products carrying the accredited Forest Stewardship Council (FSC) label are printed on 100 percent FSC-certified paper.

MADE IN THE USA